Harvest of Enchantment

Harvest of Enchantment

Matthew Petchinsky

Harvest of Enchantment: 1,000 Spells of Gratitude, Love, and Fortune for Thanksgiving
By: Matthew Petchinsky

Introduction
The Spirit of Thanksgiving Magic

Thanksgiving is a season rich in symbolism and meaning, a time when we gather to give thanks for the abundance in our lives and celebrate the harvest. It is not just about the food we share, but the love, gratitude, and connections that are nurtured during this special time. Rooted in ancient traditions of harvest festivals, Thanksgiving carries with it the spirit of abundance—of gathering what we have sown throughout the year and sharing it with those around us. In this sense, Thanksgiving is deeply magical.

The very essence of Thanksgiving revolves around the themes of gratitude, love, and abundance. These are powerful energies in the practice of magic. By aligning with these energies during this season, we can tap into the natural rhythms of the Earth and the universe, enhancing our lives in ways both spiritual and material. This book serves as a guide for harnessing the magic of Thanksgiving, blending ancient practices with modern insights to help you create spells that resonate with the true spirit of the holiday.

The Symbolism of the Harvest

At its core, Thanksgiving is a celebration of the harvest, a time when the fruits of the Earth are gathered, and the hard work of planting and nurturing comes to fruition. In many cultures, this harvest is seen as not just a physical event but a spiritual one—a reminder of the cyclical nature of life, death, and rebirth. The harvest is a symbol of abundance and prosperity, a time to take stock of the blessings in our lives.

In the practice of magic, the harvest symbolizes both the physical and spiritual rewards of our efforts. It is a time for reflection, a time to acknowledge what we have worked for, and a time to show appreciation for all that we have received. Whether the harvest is a literal crop or the result of personal or professional growth, it serves as a powerful reminder that abundance is always within reach when we align ourselves with the natural flow of life.

Through the magic of Thanksgiving, we can amplify these symbols and direct them toward our intentions. Just as a farmer carefully tends their crops, so too can we use spells to nurture the seeds of our desires, ultimately bringing them to full fruition.

Enhancing Gratitude, Love, and Abundance with Magic

Thanksgiving is more than a single day of celebration; it is a state of mind that encourages us to focus on gratitude, love, and abundance. These qualities form the foundation of successful magic. By expressing gratitude, we acknowledge the energy we've received and open ourselves to receiving even more. Gratitude shifts our focus from lack to abundance, creating a vibrational match for prosperity in our lives. In this way, spells centered around gratitude can be transformative.

Love, too, is central to the spirit of Thanksgiving. It's the love we share with family and friends, the love we have for the Earth and all its bounties, and the love we cultivate for ourselves. Spells for love during this season aren't just for romantic relationships—they are for strengthening bonds of friendship, family, and self-love. They help foster connection and unity, both in our personal relationships and in our relationship with the universe.

Abundance is perhaps the most obvious theme of Thanksgiving. As the harvest season comes to a close, we celebrate the abundance of nature, food, and blessings. However, abundance in magic is not limited to material wealth—it encompasses spiritual, emotional, and relational wealth as well. Magic during Thanksgiving can help attract abundance in all its forms, from prosperity in finances to richness in personal relationships and inner fulfillment.

Using This Book

This book has been crafted as a comprehensive guide for channeling the magical energies of Thanksgiving. Each chapter focuses on a different aspect of Thanksgiving magic—gratitude, love, and abundance—with specific spells designed to enhance each of these areas in your life. Additionally, we explore practical rituals, affirmations, and meditations to help you integrate the spirit of Thanksgiving into your everyday life, not just during the holiday season but year-round.

The spells in this book are easy to follow, even for those new to magic, yet powerful enough for experienced practitioners to find value. Each spell includes a detailed list of ingredients, instructions, and tips on timing, making it accessible for anyone looking to work with Thanksgiving magic.

To use this book effectively, it's important to approach it with an open heart and a clear intention. Magic is most powerful when the caster's intentions are clear and aligned with their desires. Take time to reflect on what you wish to manifest during this Thanksgiving season and approach each spell with mindfulness and care.

Spell Safety

As with any magical practice, safety is of utmost importance. While the spells and rituals included in this book are designed to be safe, there are some key points to keep in mind:

1. **Work with Clear Intentions** – The clearer your intention, the more focused your spell will be. Vague or conflicted intentions can lead to unexpected or ineffective results.

2. **Respect Natural Cycles** – Thanksgiving magic aligns with the harvest, the seasons, and the cycles of the moon. Pay attention to these natural rhythms, and choose the right time for your spells to amplify their effectiveness.

3. **Protect Your Space** – Before casting any spell, create a safe and sacred space. This can be done by cleansing the area with sage, lighting protective candles, or using crystals. A well-prepared space keeps negative energies at bay and ensures a positive outcome.

4. **Grounding and Centering** – After spell work, always remember to ground yourself. This helps you return to the present moment and dissipates any excess energy that may have built up during the spell.

5. **Harm None** – Thanksgiving is a time for gratitude and love, and the spells in this book are designed to enhance those energies. Always approach spell work with a positive mindset, and never attempt to harm or manipulate others through your magic.

The Importance of Intention in Spellcasting

Perhaps the most crucial element of magic is intention. The power of a spell does not solely lie in the ingredients used or the timing of the ritual but in the intention behind it. Your thoughts, emotions, and beliefs all contribute to the success of your magic. For this reason, it's essential to approach each spell with clarity, focus, and a heart full of gratitude.

As you cast spells for gratitude, love, and abundance, allow yourself to fully embody these qualities. Feel the gratitude for what you already have, the love you wish to cultivate, and the abundance that is already present in your life. By focusing on these energies, you magnify their power and attract even more of the same.

Remember that magic is not just about the result; it's about the journey. As you work through the spells and rituals in this book, take time to reflect on the deeper meaning behind each one. What does gratitude mean to you? How can love bring you closer to your true self? In what ways can abundance show up in your life? By answering these questions and approaching magic with intention, you'll find that the power of Thanksgiving is magnified and enriched.

In conclusion, the spirit of Thanksgiving magic is about more than just casting spells—it's about aligning your heart and soul with the energies of gratitude, love, and abundance. This book will guide you through that process, helping you to bring the true essence of Thanksgiving into your magical practice. Whether you are seeking to deepen your relationships, attract prosperity, or simply cultivate a greater sense of thankfulness, the spells, rituals, and insights provided here will serve as a powerful foundation for your journey.

Chapter 1: Gratitude Charms

Gratitude is one of the most powerful forces in the universe, capable of transforming not just our internal state but also the external circumstances of our lives. It is the heart of the Thanksgiving season, and when we actively cultivate it through the practice of magic, we open the doors to abundance, love, and happiness. In this chapter, we will explore how gratitude can be channeled into charms, spells, and daily rituals that enhance our connection to the world around us, draw blessings into our lives, and elevate our magical practice.

Gratitude, when woven into spell work, serves as a magnet for positive energy. The spells and charms in this chapter are designed to help you cultivate a mindset of thankfulness, reminding you to focus on what you have rather than what you lack. As you cast these spells, you will find that they not only bring about immediate benefits but also help to create a long-lasting sense of fulfillment and contentment.

The Power of Gratitude in Magic

Before we dive into the spells, it's important to understand why gratitude is so powerful in magic. Gratitude aligns you with the energy of abundance. When you are grateful for what you already have, you send out a signal to the universe that you are ready to receive more. This creates a feedback loop where the more you appreciate what you have, the more you are given.

Gratitude is also a grounding force in magic. It helps you stay present, centered, and focused on what truly matters. When you approach your magical practice with gratitude, you work from a place of positivity and high vibration, which amplifies the effects of your spells.

Let's begin by exploring some simple yet effective gratitude charms that can be incorporated into your daily life. These charms are easy to create and require only a few ingredients, making them perfect for both beginners and seasoned practitioners.

Charm 1: The Thankful Heart Charm

This charm is designed to help you cultivate a sense of gratitude in your heart, allowing you to carry the energy of thankfulness with you wherever you go. It's a simple charm that can be worn as a necklace, kept in your pocket, or placed on your altar to remind you to give thanks every day.

Ingredients:

- A small heart-shaped locket or charm
- A piece of rose quartz (for love and gratitude)
- Lavender (for peace and calm)
- A small piece of paper
- A pen

Instructions:

1. Begin by cleansing your space with sage or incense to remove any negative energies.
2. Hold the rose quartz in your hand and take a few deep breaths. As you breathe, focus on the feeling of gratitude. Think about all the things in your life that you are thankful for, both big and small.
3. Once you feel that the energy of gratitude has filled your heart, place the rose quartz inside the heart-shaped locket or charm.
4. Next, take the small piece of paper and write down three things you are grateful for. Fold the paper and place it inside the locket or charm along with the lavender.
5. As you close the locket or seal the charm, say the following incantation:

"With this charm, I hold gratitude near,
For love and abundance, I need not fear.
With every heartbeat, I give thanks,
For life's many blessings and all its ranks."

1. Wear the charm or keep it with you, and whenever you feel disconnected from gratitude, hold it in your hand and repeat the incantation.

This charm will help you stay mindful of the blessings in your life and keep your energy aligned with gratitude.

Charm 2: The Gratitude Jar

The Gratitude Jar is a powerful ritual tool that can be used throughout the Thanksgiving season and beyond. It serves as a physical representation of the things you are thankful for, and each time you add to the jar, you reinforce the energy of gratitude in your life. Over time, this jar will become a beacon of positive energy that can be used to enhance your spells or simply as a reminder of your blessings.

Ingredients:

- A large glass jar
- Small pieces of paper or parchment
- A pen
- Dried herbs of your choice (optional, for added magical energy)
- A small candle (optional, for sealing intentions)

Instructions:

1. Cleanse your jar by wiping it down with salt water or smudging it with sage.
2. Each day, take a piece of paper and write down something you are grateful for. It can be as simple as "I am thankful for the sunshine today" or as significant as "I am grateful for the love of my family."
3. Fold the paper and place it inside the jar. If you wish, you can also add dried herbs like rosemary (for remembrance) or thyme (for strength) to enhance the jar's magical energy.

4. Continue this process daily or weekly, adding new notes of gratitude to the jar. As the jar fills, it will become a powerful vessel of gratitude energy.

5. Once a month, or at the end of the Thanksgiving season, you can read through the notes in the jar and reflect on all the blessings in your life. Light a small candle beside the jar and offer thanks to the universe for its abundance.

The Gratitude Jar can also be used as a magical tool. If you are working on a spell for abundance or love, you can draw energy from the jar by holding it during your spell work and focusing on the gratitude it contains.

Charm 3: The Abundant Harvest Spell

This spell is designed to draw abundance into your life by harnessing the energy of gratitude. It works particularly well during the Thanksgiving season but can be performed at any time when you need to attract prosperity and good fortune.

Ingredients:

- A small bowl
- Three coins (to represent prosperity)
- A green candle (for abundance)
- A bay leaf (for wishes and success)
- A small piece of bread or grain (to represent the harvest)
- A pen

Instructions:

1. Set up your altar or working space, ensuring it is clean and free of distractions. Place the small bowl in the center.
2. Light the green candle and take a moment to center yourself. Focus on the feeling of abundance and gratitude.
3. One by one, hold each coin in your hand and visualize what abundance means to you. It could be financial wealth, emotional richness, or spiritual fulfillment. As you hold each coin, say aloud:

*"I am grateful for the abundance that flows to me,
Prosperity in all forms, I clearly see."*

1. Place the coins in the bowl.
2. Next, write down a wish or intention on the bay leaf. This should be something you wish to manifest in your life, and it should be written from a place of gratitude (e.g., "I am thankful for the financial stability that is coming my way"). Place the bay leaf in the bowl.
3. Finally, add the small piece of bread or grain to the bowl, symbolizing the harvest and the abundance of the Earth.
4. Close your eyes and focus on the energy of gratitude. Feel it flowing through you and into the bowl, mixing with the coins, the bay leaf, and the bread. Visualize your life filled with abundance in all areas.
5. When you are ready, extinguish the candle and leave the bowl on your altar or in a safe place. Each day, hold the bowl in your hands and give thanks for the abundance that is coming into your life.

The Abundant Harvest Spell will help draw prosperity to you, whether in the form of money, opportunities, or blessings.

Daily Gratitude Ritual

In addition to charms and spells, daily gratitude rituals can have a profound impact on your magical practice. These rituals are simple yet effective ways to integrate gratitude into your everyday life, keeping your energy aligned with positivity and abundance.

Morning Gratitude Ritual

1. Upon waking, take a few deep breaths and place your hands over your heart.
2. Think of three things you are grateful for in that moment. They can be as simple as "I am grateful for this new day" or as profound as "I am grateful for the love and support of my family."
3. As you hold these thoughts in your heart, say aloud:

"I give thanks for the blessings in my life,
And I welcome even more with open arms."

1. Carry this feeling of gratitude with you throughout the day, allowing it to shape your interactions and experiences.

Evening Gratitude Ritual

1. Before bed, light a small candle or incense.
2. Reflect on your day and think of three things that happened for which you are grateful. These can be specific events, like a kind gesture from a friend, or general feelings, like the warmth of the sun.
3. As you reflect, say aloud:

"I am thankful for today's blessings,
And I rest in the knowledge that I am supported by the universe."

1. Allow the feeling of gratitude to fill you as you extinguish the candle and prepare for a restful night.

By incorporating these daily rituals, you will continuously nurture the energy of gratitude in your life, making it easier to manifest your desires and maintain a positive, high-vibration state.

In this chapter, we have explored the fundamental role of gratitude in magic and how it can be woven into everyday practice through charms, spells, and rituals. Gratitude is not just a fleeting emotion but a powerful force that can transform your life and your magical practice. As you work with the charms and spells in this chapter, remember to keep your heart open and your intentions pure. The more you give thanks, the more the universe will provide in return.

Chapter 2: Harvest Blessings

The harvest season has always been a time of celebration, gratitude, and reflection. It is the moment when we gather the fruits of our labor, whether in the form of crops from the land, personal achievements, or the rewards of our relationships and endeavors. In ancient cultures, the harvest was revered as a sacred event, marked by rituals and offerings to ensure that the abundance of the Earth would continue to provide. In this chapter, we will explore how to perform Harvest Blessing spells, designed to honor and bless the food we eat, the abundance in our lives, and the continued prosperity that the universe offers.

Harvest Blessing spells are a form of gratitude, but they also have a practical purpose. By blessing your harvest, whether it's physical food, your work, or the blessings in your life, you are imbuing it with positive energy, ensuring that it nourishes you in the best possible way. These blessings also act as offerings to the universe, showing your appreciation for its bounty and asking for continued abundance in the future.

The Importance of Blessing the Harvest

Harvest blessings are an ancient tradition. In many cultures, from the Celts to the Native Americans, harvest festivals were times to honor the gods and spirits of the land for providing sustenance. These blessings were not limited to just crops, but extended to all forms of abundance—whether in personal achievements, wealth, love, or health. Blessing your harvest is a way to show gratitude for what you have received while simultaneously asking for future prosperity.

In modern times, we can adapt these ancient practices to fit our own lives. Harvest Blessing spells can be performed to bless the food we eat, the money we earn, the love we experience, and the opportunities that come our way. By doing so, we honor the cyclical nature of life and acknowledge that all forms of abundance are interconnected.

When we perform Harvest Blessing spells, we invite positive energy into our lives and set the stage for continued growth and prosperity. Whether you are blessing a literal harvest of crops from your garden, your paycheck, or the fruits of your personal growth, these spells will help you solidify your connection to abundance.

Spell 1: The Blessing of the Harvest Feast

This spell is designed to be performed before a meal, particularly during the Thanksgiving season or other times when food is shared in abundance. It blesses the food, ensuring that it nourishes both the body and the spirit, while also expressing gratitude for the Earth's bounty.

Ingredients:

- A small bowl of salt (to purify and protect)
- A candle (white or green, to represent abundance and purity)
- A loaf of bread or a symbolic food item (to represent the harvest)
- A sprig of rosemary (for remembrance and protection)
- A small dish of water (to symbolize life and sustenance)

Instructions:

1. Set the table for your meal, placing the small bowl of salt, the candle, the bread, the rosemary, and the dish of water in the center.
2. Light the candle to symbolize the divine light and the warmth of the harvest.
3. Take a pinch of salt and sprinkle it over the loaf of bread, saying:

"Blessed be this bread, the fruit of the Earth.
May it nourish our bodies and spirits.
With this salt, I purify and protect the harvest,
Grateful for the Earth's bounty."

1. Hold the sprig of rosemary in your hand and pass it over the dish of water. As you do this, say:

"Blessed be this water, the source of all life.
May it cleanse and sustain us.

With this water, I bless the harvest,
Grateful for its abundance and grace."

1. Place the sprig of rosemary beside the bread and water. Close your eyes and take a moment to reflect on all the things you are thankful for. Feel the energy of the harvest—the hard work, the growth, the abundance—all around you.
2. Once you feel centered in your gratitude, say:

"I bless this food, this table, and all who gather here.
May we be nourished, may we be sustained,
And may the Earth continue to provide in abundance."

1. Take a piece of bread and dip it into the water, then eat it as a symbolic gesture of receiving the blessings of the Earth. Encourage those gathered with you to do the same.
2. Extinguish the candle and proceed with your meal, knowing that the food has been blessed with the energy of gratitude, nourishment, and abundance.

This simple yet powerful ritual can be performed before any meal, particularly during times of celebration or when you wish to show appreciation for the food you are about to eat.

Spell 2: The Bountiful Harvest Ritual

This spell is perfect for those who have a garden or work with the land and wish to bless their literal harvest of fruits, vegetables, or other crops. It honors the cycle of planting, growth, and reaping, ensuring that the abundance of the Earth is both recognized and respected. This spell can also be adapted for those who wish to bless their personal achievements, financial gains, or creative works.

Ingredients:

- A basket (to represent the harvest)
- Three different types of fruits or vegetables from your garden (or symbolic food items if you are not working with crops)
- A handful of soil from your garden or a nearby natural area
- A green or gold candle (for prosperity and abundance)
- A small bottle of spring water or rainwater
- A bay leaf (for success)
- A piece of string or ribbon (green or brown)

Instructions:

1. Begin by taking a moment to center yourself. Find a quiet place outdoors or in your garden where you feel connected to the Earth. Place the basket in front of you.
2. Light the green or gold candle and say:

"By the light of this candle, I honor the harvest,
The gifts of the Earth, and the abundance it brings."

1. Place the three fruits or vegetables into the basket one by one. As you place each item in the basket, say:

"Blessed be this harvest, the fruit of my labor.
May it nourish and sustain me,
And may the Earth continue to provide in abundance."

1. Take a handful of soil and sprinkle it over the fruits or vegetables in the basket, saying:

"I return to the Earth what she has given me,
Grateful for the cycle of life, death, and rebirth."

1. Hold the bay leaf in your hand and focus on your intention for continued abundance and success. As you do so, say:

"With this bay leaf, I ask for blessings upon the harvest.
May success and prosperity continue to flow,
Just as the Earth's bounty continues to grow."

1. Place the bay leaf into the basket and take the piece of string or ribbon. Tie it around the handle of the basket, symbolizing the completion of the harvest cycle and your gratitude for the Earth's gifts.
2. Sprinkle a few drops of spring water or rainwater over the fruits and soil, saying:

"With this water, I bless the harvest,
And I give thanks for the life it sustains."

1. Once the ritual is complete, leave the basket on your altar or a special place in your home for 24 hours to allow the blessings to take root. Afterward, enjoy the fruits of your harvest with gratitude, sharing them with family or friends if possible.

This ritual not only blesses the physical harvest but also ensures that the cycle of abundance continues in your life, bringing prosperity in all forms.

Spell 3: The Cornucopia of Abundance

The cornucopia, or horn of plenty, is a powerful symbol of abundance and prosperity. This spell invokes the spirit of the cornucopia to bless all forms of abundance in your life—whether it be financial, emotional, or spiritual. It is a perfect spell to perform during Thanksgiving or whenever you feel the need to attract more abundance into your life.

Ingredients:

- A cornucopia basket or a symbolic horn of plenty (this can be handmade if necessary)
- Various fruits, vegetables, or items that symbolize abundance (such as coins, crystals, or symbolic representations of what you wish to attract)
- A gold candle (for prosperity)
- A green candle (for growth)
- A small dish of honey (to attract sweetness and abundance)

Instructions:

1. Begin by setting up your altar or working space with the cornucopia basket in the center. Surround it with the fruits, vegetables, coins, crystals, or other items that symbolize abundance to you.
2. Light the gold candle, focusing on the energy of prosperity. Say:

"By the light of this gold flame,
I call upon the energy of abundance and prosperity.
May my life be filled with blessings,
Just as the cornucopia overflows with bounty."

1. Light the green candle and focus on growth and renewal. Say:

"By the light of this green flame,
I invite growth and renewal into my life.
May the seeds of my intentions grow strong,
And may abundance continue to flow."

1. Take the small dish of honey and place it inside the cornucopia, saying:

"With this honey, I sweeten my life with abundance.
May prosperity flow to me, like nectar from the Earth,
And may I share the sweetness of life with those around me."

1. One by one, place the fruits, vegetables, coins, crystals, or symbolic items into the cornucopia, visualizing your life being filled with the type of abundance you wish to attract—whether it be wealth, love, or personal growth.
2. Once you have filled the cornucopia, hold your hands over it and say:

"Great Cornucopia, symbol of the Earth's abundance,
I call upon your energy to bless my life.
May my heart overflow with gratitude,
And may the bounty of the universe be mine."

1. Leave the cornucopia on your altar or in a special place for as long as you feel necessary. Each time you see it, offer a word of thanks for the abundance in your life.

This spell taps into the ancient symbolism of the cornucopia, ensuring that you remain connected to the energy of abundance and prosperity.

Daily Harvest Blessing Ritual

In addition to the spells outlined above, incorporating a daily harvest blessing into your routine can help maintain a constant flow of gratitude and abundance in your life. This simple ritual can be performed in the morning or evening to give thanks for the blessings you have received and to ask for continued prosperity.

Ingredients:

- A small bowl of grain (rice, wheat, or any grain that symbolizes abundance to you)
- A green or white candle
- A small bell or chime

Instructions:

1. Begin by lighting the candle and placing the bowl of grain in front of you.
2. Close your eyes and take a few deep breaths, focusing on the feeling of gratitude. Reflect on the blessings you have received that day or throughout the week.
3. Pick up a handful of grain and let it sift through your fingers back into the bowl. As you do so, say:

"Just as the Earth provides grain,
May abundance continue to rain upon me.
I give thanks for the harvest,
And I welcome the blessings yet to come."

1. Ring the bell or chime to signal the end of the ritual, symbolizing the completion of the harvest cycle.
2. Extinguish the candle and leave the bowl of grain on your altar as a reminder of the abundance in your life.

By performing this daily ritual, you will maintain a close connection with the energy of abundance and gratitude, ensuring that prosperity continues to flow into your life.

In this chapter, we have explored the significance of blessing the harvest and the various ways in which we can honor the abundance in our lives. Whether you are blessing the food on your table, the fruits of your labor, or the prosperity that flows through your life, these spells and rituals will help you cultivate a deeper connection to the Earth's bounty. As you work with these blessings, remember that gratitude is the key to abundance. The more you give thanks, the more the universe will provide.

Chapter 3: Family Harmony

Family is at the heart of the Thanksgiving season. It's a time for loved ones to come together, share stories, meals, and moments of joy. However, as anyone who has hosted or attended a family gathering knows, these events can sometimes come with tension, disagreements, or past issues resurfacing. In this chapter, we will explore spells and charms specifically designed to foster love, peace, and understanding within family gatherings, ensuring that your home is filled with harmony and connection during this season of togetherness.

Family Harmony spells and charms can be used before, during, or after gatherings to smooth over difficult relationships, encourage open communication, and heal old wounds. By incorporating magic into your family dynamics, you can create an environment where everyone feels heard, respected, and valued, allowing for deeper bonds and a more joyful celebration.

The Importance of Family Harmony

Families are complex, and even in the most loving relationships, misunderstandings, differences of opinion, and old grievances can create tension. Thanksgiving is a time when these challenges can become particularly apparent, as family members who may not see each other often are brought together in close quarters. The energy of a gathering can shift quickly, sometimes going from laughter to discomfort in a matter of moments.

Family Harmony spells are not about manipulating or controlling the emotions of others, but rather about creating an environment that fosters positive energy, mutual respect, and understanding. These spells help to clear away negative energy, encourage open-hearted communication, and create a sense of unity among those gathered. Whether you are seeking to heal a rift, prevent arguments, or simply ensure that the day is filled with love and peace, the spells in this chapter will guide you.

Spell 1: The Circle of Peace Charm

The Circle of Peace Charm is designed to create a protective and calming energy around your home or the space where your family gathering will take place. It helps to ward off negativity, tension, and conflict, ensuring that only positive energy enters the space. This charm can be set up before guests arrive and is particularly effective for large family gatherings where different personalities may clash.

Ingredients:

- A white candle (for peace and purity)
- A bowl of salt (for protection)
- Lavender oil or dried lavender (for calm and relaxation)
- Four small crystals (amethyst for calm, rose quartz for love, citrine for happiness, and black tourmaline for protection)
- A small dish of water

Instructions:

1. Begin by setting up the white candle in the center of your space. Light it, focusing on the flame as a symbol of peace and calm energy filling the room.
2. Take the bowl of salt and walk clockwise around the room, sprinkling a little salt in each corner. As you do this, say:

"By the power of Earth, I create a circle of peace.
Let this space be filled with harmony,
And may all who enter feel love and tranquility."

1. Place a drop of lavender oil in each corner of the room, or sprinkle dried lavender if you prefer. As you do this, say:

"By the power of Air, I calm all tension.
Let the winds of peace blow through this space,
Bringing calmness and relaxation to all."

1. Place the four small crystals in the four corners of the room, each representing a different element:
    - Amethyst (North, Earth) – For calmness and grounding
    - Rose Quartz (East, Air) – For love and understanding
    - Citrine (South, Fire) – For happiness and joy
    - Black Tourmaline (West, Water) – For protection from negativity As you place each crystal, say:

"By the power of Fire, I bring warmth and joy.
By the power of Water, I wash away discord and disharmony.
May love, peace, and unity fill this space."

1. Lastly, take the small dish of water and sprinkle a few drops around the room, saying:

"By the power of Water, I cleanse this space,
Washing away all negativity and leaving only peace."

1. Allow the candle to burn for at least an hour before your family arrives, visualizing the room filling with peaceful energy and any potential conflict being dissolved. When you feel the room is sufficiently charged with harmony, extinguish the candle and leave the crystals in place throughout the gathering.

This charm creates a protective shield around the space, ensuring that family members are more likely to feel at ease, open-hearted, and cooperative during the gathering.

Spell 2: The Heart of Understanding Ritual

This ritual is designed to foster deeper understanding and empathy within your family. It helps dissolve misunderstandings, encourages compassionate communication, and promotes forgiveness and reconciliation where needed. This ritual is particularly useful if there have been recent arguments or if there are unresolved tensions between family members.

Ingredients:

- A pink candle (for love and understanding)
- A blue candle (for communication and truth)
- A white feather (for clarity and peace)
- A small piece of rose quartz (for healing and love)
- A piece of parchment and a pen

Instructions:

1. Begin by lighting the pink candle, focusing on its warm glow as a symbol of love, compassion, and understanding. Say:

"I call upon the energy of love and unity,
To fill this space and the hearts of those who gather.
May we speak from a place of kindness and understanding,
And may old wounds be healed with love."

1. Light the blue candle, focusing on its flame as a symbol of clear and open communication. Say:

"I call upon the energy of truth and clarity,
To guide our words and thoughts.
May we listen with open hearts,
And may understanding blossom between us."

1. Hold the white feather in your hand and gently wave it through the air as if brushing away tension and misunderstandings. Say:

"With this feather, I clear the air between us,
Dissolving all conflict and bringing peace.
May our words be kind, our hearts be open,
And our family united in love and harmony."

1. Place the rose quartz in the center of the room or table where the family will gather, setting the intention that it will radiate love and healing energy throughout the gathering.
2. On the piece of parchment, write down the names of the family members who will be attending. As you write each name, visualize that person surrounded by a soft pink light, feeling loved, heard, and understood. Once all names are written, say:

"I send love to each person gathered here,
May we come together in peace,
And may understanding fill our hearts."

1. Fold the parchment and place it beneath the rose quartz. Allow the candles to burn for the duration of the gathering, ensuring that their energies infuse the space with love, truth, and understanding.

This ritual is particularly effective in creating an atmosphere of open-hearted communication, making it easier for family members to connect on a deeper level and resolve any lingering issues.

Spell 3: The Knot of Unity Charm

The Knot of Unity is a simple yet powerful charm that can be used to tie together the energies of family members, promoting a sense of unity, cooperation, and mutual respect. This charm is particularly useful for families with differing opinions or where tensions run high, as it helps to bind the family together in love and harmony.

Ingredients:

- A length of red thread or yarn (to represent love and connection)
- A small pouch or bag (to hold the charm)
- A sprig of rosemary (for protection and remembrance)
- A piece of rose quartz or amethyst (for love and calmness)
- A small piece of paper and a pen

Instructions:

1. Begin by holding the red thread in your hands and focusing on your intention for family unity. Visualize the thread as a symbol of the love that connects your family members, even in difficult times.
2. Tie a knot in the center of the thread, saying:

"With this knot, I tie together the hearts of my family.
May we be bound in love and understanding,
And may peace flow between us."

1. Tie a second knot on one end of the thread, saying:

"With this knot, I secure our connection.
May we respect and honor one another."

1. Tie a third knot on the other end of the thread, saying:

"With this knot, I bless our family with harmony.
May our gatherings be filled with peace and joy."

1. Place the knotted thread inside the small pouch or bag, along with the sprig of rosemary and the piece of rose quartz or amethyst.
2. On the small piece of paper, write the words "Love, Peace, Unity" and fold it into the pouch as well.
3. Close the pouch and hold it in your hands, focusing on your intention for family harmony. Say:

"I bless this charm with love and unity,
May it bring peace to all who gather,
And may our family be bound by harmony and respect."

1. Keep the pouch in a special place during family gatherings, or place it on the table where everyone will sit. The charm will work to foster a sense of unity, ensuring that the bonds of love and respect remain strong even in challenging moments.

This simple charm can be used before any family gathering, or kept in the home as a constant reminder of the importance of love and unity within the family.

Daily Family Harmony Ritual

In addition to spells and charms, incorporating a daily or weekly ritual focused on family harmony can help maintain a peaceful and loving atmosphere in your home throughout the Thanksgiving season and beyond.

Ingredients:

- A small candle (pink or white for peace and love)
- A small bowl of water
- A family photo or a symbolic item that represents your family

Instructions:

1. Begin by lighting the candle and placing the family photo or symbolic item in front of it.
2. Hold the bowl of water in your hands and focus on your intention for family harmony. As you gaze into the water, say:

"I bless this water with the energy of peace,
Just as water flows smoothly and easily,
May peace flow through my family,
Washing away all tension and conflict."

1. Dip your fingers into the water and sprinkle a few drops over the family photo or symbolic item, saying:

"I bless my family with love and understanding,
May we come together in harmony,
And may our bonds be strengthened with each passing day."

1. Allow the candle to burn for a few minutes while you focus on the feeling of love and peace flowing through your home. When

you feel ready, extinguish the candle and carry the feeling of harmony with you throughout your day.

By performing this simple ritual regularly, you can maintain a positive and peaceful energy within your home, ensuring that family gatherings are filled with love and understanding.

In this chapter, we have explored various spells, charms, and rituals to foster family harmony during the Thanksgiving season. Whether you are seeking to create a peaceful environment, heal past wounds, or simply ensure that everyone feels loved and valued, these magical practices will help you cultivate a sense of unity and respect among your family members. Remember, the foundation of any family is love, and by working with these spells and charms, you can strengthen the bonds that bring you all together, creating lasting harmony in your home.

Chapter 4: Kitchen Witchery

Food has always been central to magic. In many traditions, food and cooking are seen as sacred acts, opportunities to infuse nourishment with intentions, love, and positive energy. Kitchen Witchery is the practice of using food and cooking as a form of magic, where ingredients are chosen not just for their flavor but for their magical properties. In this chapter, we will explore how to create recipes and cooking spells that infuse meals with love, luck, and positive energy, turning everyday dishes into magical feasts.

Whether you're preparing a Thanksgiving meal for your family, baking a treat for a loved one, or making a simple soup for yourself, the spells and recipes in this chapter will guide you in bringing magic into the heart of your kitchen. Kitchen Witchery is about more than just the ingredients you use—it's about the energy you put into the food and the intention behind every stir, every pinch of spice, and every bite.

The Magic of Food

Food is more than just fuel for the body—it is also nourishment for the soul. In many cultures, food has been used as an offering to gods, spirits, and ancestors, making it a powerful conduit for spiritual energy. When we cook, we have the opportunity to infuse the food with our intentions, whether they are for love, healing, protection, or prosperity. Just as a spell is cast with intention and focus, so too is food prepared with love and care, creating a magical bond between the cook, the ingredients, and those who eat the meal.

Each ingredient we use in cooking carries its own magical properties. Herbs, fruits, grains, and spices are all imbued with their own energies, and when combined in a recipe, these energies can be directed toward specific intentions. For example, cinnamon is known for attracting prosperity, while basil is associated with protection and love. By incorporating these ingredients into your cooking, you are creating a spell that can be consumed, bringing magic directly into the body.

The act of cooking itself is a magical ritual. The stirring of a pot, the kneading of dough, the sprinkling of salt—all these actions can be done with intention, transforming an ordinary meal into a magical feast. Kitchen Witchery is accessible to everyone, regardless of skill level, and can be practiced in any kitchen. All it takes is mindfulness, intention, and a desire to connect with the magic of food.

Recipe 1: Love-Infused Apple Pie

Apples are a symbol of love, healing, and prosperity, making them a perfect ingredient for a magical dessert that brings warmth and connection to family gatherings. This Love-Infused Apple Pie is more than just a delicious treat—it's a spell for fostering love and harmony among those who share it.

Magical Properties of Ingredients:

- **Apples:** Love, healing, and abundance
- **Cinnamon:** Prosperity, protection, and success
- **Nutmeg:** Luck and harmony
- **Honey:** Sweetness, love, and happiness
- **Butter:** Wealth and grounding
- **Sugar:** Attraction and love

Ingredients:

- 6 medium-sized apples (preferably red, for love and passion)
- 1 cup of sugar
- 1 tablespoon of cinnamon
- 1 teaspoon of nutmeg
- 2 tablespoons of honey
- 1/4 cup of butter
- 2 pie crusts (store-bought or homemade)
- A pinch of salt (to protect and purify)
- A splash of lemon juice (to cleanse and brighten)

Instructions:

1. Begin by creating a peaceful and loving atmosphere in your kitchen. Light a pink candle (for love) and focus on your inten-

tion to foster love and harmony through this dish. As you prepare the pie, keep your thoughts focused on love and connection.

2. Preheat your oven to 375°F (190°C).
3. Peel, core, and slice the apples, placing them in a large bowl. As you slice each apple, say aloud or in your mind:

*"With each slice, I fill this pie with love and warmth.
May it nourish the hearts of those who share it."*

1. Add the sugar, cinnamon, nutmeg, and a pinch of salt to the apples. Gently toss them together, saying:

*"Cinnamon for prosperity, sugar for sweetness,
Nutmeg for luck, and salt for protection.
With these spices, I bless this pie,
May it bring harmony and love to all."*

1. Drizzle the honey over the mixture, saying:

"As honey sweetens this pie, so too may love and joy sweeten the hearts of those who eat it."

1. Place one pie crust into a pie dish and pour the apple mixture into the crust. Dot the apples with small pieces of butter, saying:

*"Butter for wealth and grounding,
May this pie bring blessings to those who partake in it."*

1. Cover the apples with the second pie crust, crimping the edges to seal it. As you do this, visualize the love and warmth you are sealing inside the pie, ready to be released when it is shared.
2. Use a knife to cut small slits in the top crust for ventilation. As you cut each slit, say:

"With each cut, I open the way for love to flow,
Into the hearts of those who gather."

1. Bake the pie for 45-50 minutes, or until the crust is golden brown and the filling is bubbling. As the pie bakes, visualize the kitchen filling with the energy of love, peace, and warmth.
2. When the pie is finished baking, let it cool for a few minutes before serving. As you serve each slice, say:

"May this pie bring love, joy, and harmony,
To all who share it."

This Love-Infused Apple Pie is perfect for family gatherings or any occasion where you want to create a warm, loving atmosphere. The magical properties of the ingredients, combined with your intention, will help foster connection and harmony.

Recipe 2: Prosperity Cornbread

Cornbread is a traditional comfort food with deep connections to the harvest and prosperity. This Prosperity Cornbread recipe is designed to attract wealth, abundance, and good fortune to those who eat it, making it a wonderful addition to any Thanksgiving meal or family gathering.

Magical Properties of Ingredients:

- **Cornmeal:** Prosperity and abundance
- **Honey:** Sweetness, luck, and happiness
- **Butter:** Wealth and grounding
- **Eggs:** Fertility and new beginnings
- **Salt:** Protection and purification
- **Baking powder:** Growth and expansion

Ingredients:

- 1 cup of yellow cornmeal
- 1 cup of all-purpose flour
- 1 tablespoon of baking powder
- 1/4 teaspoon of salt
- 1/4 cup of honey
- 1/4 cup of melted butter
- 1 cup of milk
- 2 eggs

Instructions:

1. Begin by cleansing your kitchen space and focusing on your intention to attract prosperity. Light a green candle (for wealth and abundance) and set it on your kitchen counter.
2. Preheat your oven to 400°F (200°C) and grease a baking pan or cast-iron skillet.

3. In a large bowl, combine the cornmeal, flour, baking powder, and salt. As you mix the dry ingredients together, say:

"Cornmeal for abundance, flour for growth,
Salt for protection, and baking powder for expansion.
With these ingredients, I call forth prosperity."

1. In a separate bowl, whisk together the eggs, milk, melted butter, and honey. As you whisk, say:

"Honey for sweetness, butter for wealth,
Eggs for new beginnings, and milk for nourishment.
With these ingredients, I create a foundation for abundance."

1. Slowly pour the wet ingredients into the dry ingredients, stirring gently until combined. As you stir, visualize wealth and prosperity flowing into your life and the lives of those who will share this meal.
2. Pour the batter into the prepared baking pan or skillet. Before placing it in the oven, hold your hands over the pan and say:

"I bless this cornbread with abundance,
May it bring prosperity and joy to all who eat it."

1. Bake the cornbread for 20-25 minutes, or until the top is golden and a toothpick inserted into the center comes out clean.
2. As the cornbread bakes, visualize the kitchen filling with the energy of prosperity, and imagine that energy being absorbed into the cornbread.
3. Once the cornbread is baked, allow it to cool slightly before serving. As you serve each piece, say:

*"May this bread bring prosperity and good fortune,
To all who partake in it."*

This Prosperity Cornbread is a perfect side dish for Thanksgiving or any meal where you wish to invite abundance and good fortune into your home.

Recipe 3: Luck-Enhancing Herb Butter

This Luck-Enhancing Herb Butter is a simple yet powerful recipe that infuses your food with good fortune and positive energy. It can be used as a spread for bread, a topping for vegetables, or an ingredient in other dishes, bringing a touch of magic to any meal.

Magical Properties of Ingredients:

- **Butter:** Wealth and grounding
- **Parsley:** Luck and protection
- **Thyme:** Courage and strength
- **Rosemary:** Healing and clarity
- **Garlic:** Protection and purification

Ingredients:

- 1/2 cup of softened butter
- 1 tablespoon of finely chopped parsley
- 1 tablespoon of finely chopped thyme
- 1 tablespoon of finely chopped rosemary
- 1 clove of garlic, minced
- A pinch of salt

Instructions:

1. Begin by creating a peaceful atmosphere in your kitchen. Light a yellow candle (for luck) and focus on your intention to bring good fortune to those who will eat this herb butter.
2. In a small bowl, combine the softened butter, parsley, thyme, rosemary, garlic, and salt. As you mix the ingredients, say:

"Parsley for luck, thyme for courage,
Rosemary for healing, and garlic for protection.
With these herbs, I infuse this butter with good fortune."

1. As you stir, visualize golden light filling the butter, imbuing it with luck and positive energy.
2. Once the herbs are fully incorporated into the butter, hold the bowl in your hands and say:

"I bless this butter with luck and joy,
May it bring good fortune to all who taste it."

1. Transfer the herb butter to a small dish or container. You can use it immediately or store it in the refrigerator until ready to serve.
2. As you serve the herb butter, either as a spread or as a cooking ingredient, say:

"With each bite, may good fortune flow,
And may luck follow wherever we go."

This Luck-Enhancing Herb Butter is a versatile addition to your magical kitchen and can be used to bring a touch of luck to any meal.

Daily Kitchen Blessing Ritual

Incorporating a daily blessing into your cooking routine can help infuse every meal with love, luck, and positive energy. This simple kitchen blessing ritual can be performed each morning or before preparing any meal.

Ingredients:

- A small bowl of salt (for protection)
- A sprig of rosemary (for clarity and protection)
- A candle (any color that aligns with your intention—white for peace, green for abundance, etc.)

Instructions:

1. Begin by lighting the candle and placing the bowl of salt and the sprig of rosemary on your kitchen counter.
2. Hold the sprig of rosemary in your hands and say:

"I bless this kitchen with love and light,
May it be a place of warmth and delight.
May every meal prepared with care,
Be filled with magic, joy, and prayer."

1. Sprinkle a pinch of salt on the counter or in the sink, saying:

"Salt of the Earth, protect this space,
Keep it safe and free from harm's embrace."

1. As you prepare your meals, focus on your intention, whether it's to infuse the food with love, luck, or positive energy. Stir with care, chop with mindfulness, and always keep your thoughts aligned with your desired outcome.

By incorporating this simple blessing into your daily routine, you will create a kitchen filled with positive energy, ensuring that every meal is a magical experience.

In this chapter, we have explored the art of Kitchen Witchery and how to use recipes and cooking spells to infuse food with love, luck, and positive energy. Whether you are baking a pie, stirring a pot of soup, or simply seasoning your meal, every action in the kitchen can be turned into a magical act. By working with the magical properties of ingredients and focusing on your intentions, you can transform everyday meals into powerful spells that nourish the body, mind, and spirit. Remember, the most important ingredient in any dish is love, and when you cook with love, magic is always present.

Chapter 5: Love and Friendship

Love and friendship are the cornerstones of a fulfilling life. Whether it's the deep love shared with a partner or the steadfast loyalty of a close friend, these relationships offer us support, joy, and a sense of belonging. Strengthening these bonds is an important aspect of maintaining healthy and meaningful connections. In this chapter, we will explore spells designed to enhance love, nurture friendships, and create harmony in relationships. By using magic, we can foster deeper connections, encourage understanding, and heal any rifts that may have developed.

Love and Friendship spells focus on positive energy, mutual respect, and the deepening of emotional bonds. They are not about manipulation or forcing affection, but rather about enhancing the natural flow of love and connection between people. These spells can be used to strengthen romantic relationships, improve friendships, or even foster greater self-love, which is essential for healthy relationships with others.

The Power of Love and Friendship in Magic

Love and friendship are powerful forces that resonate deeply within the human spirit. They bring warmth, joy, and a sense of belonging, but they also require nurturing and attention to flourish. In magic, love is seen as a universal energy, a force that binds people together and enhances the flow of positive energy between them. Friendship, too, is a form of love, one that is built on trust, loyalty, and mutual respect.

The spells in this chapter are designed to work with these energies, amplifying the love and connection that already exists between you and your loved ones. They help remove any obstacles or negative influences that may be hindering your relationships and create an environment where love and friendship can thrive. Whether you are looking to strengthen a romantic relationship, heal a rift between friends, or simply enhance the love and harmony in your life, these spells will guide you in bringing more love and connection into your world.

Spell 1: The Loving Bond Charm

This charm is designed to strengthen the bond between you and a loved one, whether it's a romantic partner, a close friend, or a family member. It works by amplifying the love and positive energy between you, ensuring that your connection remains strong even through difficult times.

Ingredients:

- A pink candle (for love and affection)
- A piece of rose quartz (for love and harmony)
- Two pieces of string or ribbon (one pink, one red, to represent love and passion)
- A small pouch or charm bag
- Lavender oil (for calm and understanding)
- A small piece of paper and a pen

Instructions:

1. Begin by lighting the pink candle and focusing on your intention to strengthen the bond between you and your loved one. Visualize the love you share, the joy you bring to each other, and the ways in which your relationship can continue to grow.
2. Take the piece of rose quartz in your hand and hold it close to your heart. As you do, say aloud or in your mind:

"Rose quartz, stone of love so pure,
Strengthen the bond between us sure.
Let love flow, strong and bright,
Bringing us joy and healing light."

1. Place the rose quartz in the small pouch.

2. Next, take the two pieces of string or ribbon and tie them together in a knot, saying:

"With this knot, our bond I tie,
Stronger still as days go by.
Love and passion, friendship true,
May our connection always renew."

1. Place the tied strings into the pouch with the rose quartz.
2. On the small piece of paper, write both of your names and a short affirmation, such as "Our love is strong and enduring" or "Our friendship grows with each passing day." Fold the paper and place it in the pouch.
3. Finally, add a drop of lavender oil to the pouch, saying:

"Lavender for peace and calm,
May our bond be free from harm.
Understanding, love, and care,
May we find joy in all we share."

1. Seal the pouch and hold it in your hands, visualizing the love and connection between you and your loved one growing stronger. When you feel ready, say:

"This charm I make with love so true,
To strengthen the bond between us two.
May love and friendship never fade,
In light and joy, our bond is made."

1. Keep the pouch in a safe place, or give it to your loved one as a token of your affection. The charm will work to keep your bond strong and filled with positive energy.

Spell 2: The Friendship Candle Ritual

This ritual is designed to enhance and nurture the bonds of friendship. Whether you are seeking to deepen an existing friendship or heal a rift between you and a friend, this spell will help bring clarity, understanding, and harmony to your relationship. The Friendship Candle Ritual can also be performed as a group ritual with friends to celebrate your connection.

Ingredients:

- A blue candle (for loyalty and communication)
- A yellow candle (for joy and friendship)
- A piece of citrine or clear quartz (for happiness and clarity)
- A small dish of water (to cleanse and refresh the relationship)
- A sprig of rosemary (for protection and remembrance)
- A photo or token that represents your friendship

Instructions:

1. Begin by setting up your space with the blue and yellow candles, placing them side by side. The blue candle represents loyalty and trust, while the yellow candle represents joy and friendship.
2. Light the blue candle first, saying:

"Blue candle of loyalty,
Burn bright and true.
Strengthen the bonds of trust between us,
And let clear communication ensue."

1. Next, light the yellow candle, saying:

"Yellow candle of joy and light,
Burn with warmth and cheer.

Bring laughter and happiness to our friendship,
And may it grow stronger year by year."

1. Hold the piece of citrine or clear quartz in your hand and focus on your intention to nurture and grow your friendship. Visualize the moments of joy you have shared, the support you have given each other, and the happiness you bring into each other's lives. Say:

"With this stone, I call forth joy,
Happiness shared without end.
May our friendship flourish,
And our hearts always mend."

1. Place the stone between the two candles.
2. Take the small dish of water and the sprig of rosemary. Dip the rosemary in the water and sprinkle a few drops around the candles, saying:

"Water of life, cleanse and renew,
Let our friendship be fresh and true.
May any rift be healed with care,
And understanding always be there."

1. Place the photo or token that represents your friendship beside the candles. As you do this, focus on the love, trust, and connection that exists between you. Say:

"This friendship I cherish, pure and bright,
May it be blessed by day and night.
Through laughter, tears, and all we share,
May we always know how much we care."

1. Allow the candles to burn for at least 30 minutes, focusing on the positive energy and love flowing between you and your friend. When you feel ready, extinguish the candles, but leave the citrine or quartz in a special place as a reminder of the joy and strength of your friendship.

This ritual can be performed whenever you feel the need to nurture your friendship, or as a way to celebrate your bond with your friends during special occasions.

Spell 3: The Heart Healing Spell

The Heart Healing Spell is designed to mend and heal any rifts or misunderstandings that may have occurred between you and a loved one. Whether it's a romantic partner, a close friend, or a family member, this spell helps to clear away negative emotions, encourage forgiveness, and restore harmony to your relationship.

Ingredients:

- A pink or green candle (for love and healing)
- A piece of rose quartz (for emotional healing and love)
- A small dish of salt (for purification)
- A piece of parchment and a pen
- A small piece of cloth or a pouch
- A lavender sprig or essential oil (for calm and peace)

Instructions:

1. Begin by lighting the pink or green candle and focusing on your intention to heal the relationship. Visualize the negative emotions or misunderstandings being gently cleared away, leaving space for love, forgiveness, and understanding.

2. Hold the rose quartz in your hand and close your eyes. As you hold the stone, focus on the love and positive energy you feel for the person you wish to heal the relationship with. Imagine that love radiating from your heart, surrounding both of you in a warm, healing light. Say:

"Rose quartz, stone of love and care,
Heal the bond that we both share.

Let forgiveness flow like a gentle stream,
And restore our love in this healing dream."

1. Place the rose quartz in front of the candle.
2. Take the piece of parchment and write down your feelings about the situation. This can include any hurts, misunderstandings, or emotions that need to be released. As you write, focus on releasing these feelings in a way that promotes healing. Once you have written everything down, say:

"With these words, I release the pain,
Let love and healing flow again.
May our bond be strong and true,
And all wounds be healed anew."

1. Fold the parchment and place it in the small dish of salt. As you do this, visualize the salt purifying and cleansing the negative energy. Say:

"Salt of the Earth, purify and cleanse,
Let all discord come to an end.
May love and harmony replace the strife,
And bring peace to our shared life."

1. Once you feel the energy has shifted, remove the parchment from the salt and place it in the small pouch or piece of cloth, along with the rose quartz and lavender. Tie the pouch closed and hold it in your hands, focusing on the love and healing energy you are sending to the relationship.
2. Say:

"This spell I cast with love and light,
To heal the wounds and make things right.

Let understanding and peace now grow,
And let our hearts again bestow
Love, forgiveness, and joy once more,
Restoring the bond we had before."

1. Keep the pouch in a safe place, or if possible, give it to the person you are healing the relationship with as a token of your intention to mend the bond.

This Heart Healing Spell is perfect for situations where misunderstandings or conflicts have arisen, helping to clear away negative energy and bring love and understanding back into the relationship.

Daily Love and Friendship Affirmation Ritual

In addition to the spells outlined above, incorporating a daily affirmation ritual focused on love and friendship can help maintain a positive and harmonious energy in your relationships. This simple ritual can be done each morning or evening to strengthen the bonds of love and friendship in your life.

Ingredients:

- A small candle (pink or white for love and harmony)
- A small piece of rose quartz or amethyst
- A photo or token that represents your loved ones or friends

Instructions:

1. Begin by lighting the candle and placing the photo or token in front of you.
2. Hold the rose quartz or amethyst in your hand and close your eyes. Take a few deep breaths and focus on the love and positive energy you wish to send to your loved ones or friends.
3. As you hold the stone, say the following affirmation:

"I send love and light to those I hold dear,
May our bonds be strong, and our hearts be clear.
Through love and friendship, we are blessed,
And in each other, we find rest."

1. Visualize the love and positive energy flowing between you and your loved ones, strengthening your connection and bringing harmony into your relationships.
2. When you feel ready, extinguish the candle and carry the feeling of love and connection with you throughout the day.

By performing this daily affirmation ritual, you can continuously nurture the love and friendship in your life, ensuring that your relationships remain strong and filled with positive energy.

In this chapter, we have explored various spells and rituals designed to enhance love and friendship in your life. Whether you are seeking to deepen your bond with a romantic partner, strengthen a friendship, or heal a rift, these spells will guide you in bringing more love, understanding, and harmony into your relationships. Remember, love and friendship are living energies that require nurturing and care. By working with the magic of love and friendship, you can create lasting connections that bring joy, support, and fulfillment to your life.

Chapter 6: Fortune and Prosperity

The holiday season is a time of giving, receiving, and celebrating abundance. Whether it's the physical abundance of food and gifts or the intangible richness of love and community, this time of year offers an opportunity to reflect on the blessings in our lives and to attract even more good fortune and prosperity. In this chapter, we will explore rituals designed to attract abundance, financial blessings, and good fortune into your life, helping to set the stage for prosperity during the holiday season and beyond.

Fortune and prosperity rituals work with the natural flow of energy to invite abundance into your life. Whether you are seeking financial stability, new opportunities, or simply the peace that comes from knowing you have enough, these rituals will guide you in focusing your intentions and manifesting prosperity. By aligning your energy with the frequency of abundance, you open yourself up to receiving the wealth and blessings that the universe has to offer.

The Power of Prosperity Rituals

Prosperity is more than just financial wealth. It includes abundance in all aspects of life—health, relationships, personal growth, and opportunities. Prosperity rituals focus on attracting and maintaining this abundance, ensuring that your needs are met and that you have more than enough to share with others. When we approach prosperity with a mindset of gratitude and openness, we create a cycle of abundance that continues to grow.

The rituals in this chapter are designed to enhance your ability to manifest wealth and good fortune. They work by aligning your intentions with the energies of abundance, helping to clear away any blocks or negative beliefs about money and prosperity. Whether you're looking to improve your financial situation, attract new opportunities, or simply feel more abundant in your life, these rituals will help you cultivate a prosperous mindset and attract the blessings you seek.

Ritual 1: The Prosperity Bowl

The Prosperity Bowl is a simple yet powerful ritual designed to attract financial abundance and good fortune. By creating a physical representation of prosperity in your home, you invite the energy of wealth and success to flow into your life. This ritual is perfect for setting intentions around financial growth and stability, especially during the holiday season when expenses may increase.

Ingredients:

- A small bowl (gold, green, or white to symbolize wealth and prosperity)
- Coins (any denomination, but gold or silver coins are preferred)
- A handful of dried herbs (basil for abundance, cinnamon for prosperity, and bay leaves for success)
- A small piece of citrine or pyrite (for wealth and abundance)
- A green candle (for growth and prosperity)
- A pinch of salt (for protection)
- A few drops of essential oil (patchouli or bergamot, which are associated with wealth)

Instructions:

1. Begin by cleansing your space with sage or incense to clear away any negative energy. Set up your Prosperity Bowl in a quiet area where it will remain undisturbed.
2. Light the green candle and place it next to the bowl. Focus on the flame, visualizing it as a symbol of the wealth and abundance you are calling into your life. Say aloud or in your mind:

"I call upon the energy of abundance,
To fill my life with prosperity and success.
May the wealth I seek flow to me with ease,
And may I always have more than enough to share."

1. Take the coins and place them into the bowl one by one, saying:

"With each coin, I invite prosperity,
May my financial blessings grow and multiply."

1. Next, add the dried herbs (basil, cinnamon, and bay leaves) to the bowl. As you sprinkle the herbs, say:

"Herbs of wealth, success, and gain,
Bring fortune to me again and again."

1. Add the piece of citrine or pyrite to the bowl, saying:

"Citrine (or pyrite) of golden light,
Attract abundance, wealth, and all that's bright.
Let prosperity flow to me with grace,
Filling my life and my sacred space."

1. Sprinkle a pinch of salt into the bowl for protection, ensuring that your wealth is safeguarded. Then add a few drops of essential oil to the bowl to enhance the energy of wealth.

2. Hold your hands over the bowl and focus on your intention for financial abundance. Visualize your bank account growing, your debts dissolving, and opportunities for wealth flowing effortlessly into your life. Say:

"This bowl I fill with wealth and light,
To attract prosperity day and night.
May fortune bless me in all I do,
And may my blessings multiply too."

1. Allow the candle to burn for at least 15 minutes, then extinguish it. Keep the Prosperity Bowl in a special place, and add to it over

time by placing additional coins or symbolic items that represent wealth and abundance.

This ritual creates a powerful energy of financial growth and good fortune, helping to attract money and prosperity into your life. You can perform it at the start of each month, during the new moon, or anytime you feel the need to boost your financial situation.

Ritual 2: The Abundance Bath

This ritual uses the cleansing and energizing power of water to wash away financial blocks and attract wealth and success. By bathing in ingredients that symbolize abundance, you can immerse yourself in the energy of prosperity and set a strong intention for financial growth. The Abundance Bath is perfect for preparing yourself to receive blessings and wealth during the holiday season.

Ingredients:

- A handful of dried herbs (mint for prosperity, basil for abundance, and chamomile for luck)
- A tablespoon of honey (for sweetness and attraction)
- A small piece of citrine or clear quartz (for wealth and clarity)
- A pinch of sea salt (for protection and cleansing)
- A few drops of essential oil (patchouli, bergamot, or orange)
- A green or gold candle (for prosperity)

Instructions:

1. Begin by preparing your bath. Fill the tub with warm water and light the green or gold candle to represent prosperity and abundance.
2. Add the dried herbs to the bathwater, saying:

"Herbs of wealth and good fortune flow,
With your power, abundance I'll know.
Prosperity and blessings come my way,
With every step I take today."

1. Add the honey to the water, saying:

"Honey sweet, bring wealth to me,
Let abundance flow like a golden sea.
May my life be rich with love and light,
And may fortune bless me day and night."

1. Place the citrine or clear quartz in the bathwater, saying:

"Stone of wealth and clarity bright,
Fill my life with prosperous light.
Let success and fortune be mine,
As abundance flows like a steady line."

1. Sprinkle the sea salt into the water to cleanse and protect your energy. Add a few drops of essential oil to enhance the atmosphere of wealth and abundance.
2. Step into the bath and immerse yourself in the water. As you soak, close your eyes and visualize yourself surrounded by golden light. Imagine money, opportunities, and blessings flowing toward you effortlessly. Feel the energy of abundance soaking into your skin, filling every part of your being.
3. Say the following affirmation as you bathe:

"I am open to receiving abundance,
Wealth flows to me with ease and grace.
I am deserving of financial blessings,
And my prosperity grows in this sacred space."

1. Soak in the bath for at least 20 minutes, allowing the energy of abundance to fully integrate into your body and spirit.
2. Once you feel ready, step out of the bath and allow yourself to air dry, if possible, to keep the energy of the bath with you. Extinguish the candle and thank the universe for the blessings you are about to receive.

This Abundance Bath is a powerful way to cleanse yourself of any financial worries or blocks and open yourself up to receiving prosperity. It's especially effective when performed before important financial decisions, job interviews, or during times when you need a boost in wealth.

Ritual 3: The Golden Coin Spell

The Golden Coin Spell is a ritual that uses the symbolic power of coins and candles to attract financial success and good fortune. This spell is ideal for those looking to increase their income, find new financial opportunities, or enhance their overall wealth during the holiday season.

Ingredients:

- A gold or green candle (for wealth and abundance)
- A gold coin (or any coin painted gold)
- A small pouch or bag
- Cinnamon powder (for prosperity and success)
- A bay leaf (for wishes and success)
- A pinch of sugar (for sweetness and attraction)
- A pen and small piece of paper

Instructions:

1. Begin by lighting the gold or green candle. As the flame burns, focus on your desire for financial abundance and good fortune. Visualize money flowing into your life, new opportunities arising, and your financial situation improving.
2. Take the gold coin in your hand and hold it over the candle's flame (without touching the flame), saying:

"Golden coin, symbol of wealth,
Bring me fortune and financial health.
As you shine, so shall my wealth,
Bringing abundance and financial stealth."

1. Sprinkle a small amount of cinnamon powder over the coin, saying:

"Cinnamon of success and gain,
Let my wealth grow like golden rain.
With your power, I call forth fortune,
May my financial blessings soon be certain."

1. Place the coin in the small pouch or bag. Write your financial goal or desire on the small piece of paper, such as "I attract wealth easily" or "I find financial success in my endeavors." Fold the paper and place it in the pouch.
2. Add the bay leaf to the pouch, saying:

"Bay leaf of wishes and success,
Bring me wealth, bring me the best.
With your power, I attract good fortune,
And my financial life becomes a sweet tune."

1. Sprinkle a pinch of sugar into the pouch, saying:

"Sugar for sweetness and attraction,
Bring wealth and joy in every transaction.
May my finances grow and bloom,
Filling my life with golden room."

1. Seal the pouch and hold it in your hands. Focus on your intention for financial abundance and good fortune. Visualize your life filled with wealth, security, and opportunity. Say:

"This spell I cast with fortune's grace,
To bring abundance in every space.

May wealth and luck flow to me fast,
And financial blessings ever last."

1. Keep the pouch with you, in your wallet, or near your financial documents as a charm to attract wealth and good fortune. You can also place it under your pillow at night to invite prosperity while you sleep.

This Golden Coin Spell is an effective way to draw financial success into your life, especially during times of increased expenses or when seeking new opportunities for income. It can be performed at the start of the new year, during the full moon, or any time you wish to increase your wealth.

Daily Prosperity Affirmation Ritual

In addition to the rituals outlined above, incorporating a daily affirmation ritual focused on prosperity can help maintain a positive and abundant mindset. This simple ritual can be done each morning or evening to attract financial blessings and good fortune into your life.

Ingredients:

- A small green or gold candle (for prosperity and abundance)
- A piece of citrine or pyrite
- A gold coin or a symbolic token that represents wealth to you

Instructions:

1. Begin by lighting the green or gold candle and placing the citrine or pyrite in front of you.
2. Hold the coin or symbolic token in your hand and close your eyes. Take a few deep breaths and focus on your desire for prosperity and abundance. Visualize your bank account growing, opportunities coming your way, and wealth flowing effortlessly into your life.
3. As you hold the token, say the following affirmation:

"I am open to receiving abundance and wealth,
Prosperity flows to me with ease and grace.
I am deserving of financial blessings,
And I welcome wealth in every space."

1. Visualize golden light surrounding you, filling your aura with the energy of prosperity. Imagine this light attracting wealth, opportunities, and financial blessings into your life.

2. When you feel ready, extinguish the candle and carry the feeling of abundance with you throughout your day.

By performing this daily affirmation ritual, you will continuously align your energy with the frequency of prosperity, helping to attract financial blessings and good fortune into your life.

In this chapter, we have explored a variety of rituals and spells designed to attract fortune, prosperity, and financial blessings during the holiday season. Whether you are looking to increase your income, attract new opportunities, or simply feel more abundant in your life, these rituals will help you focus your intentions and align your energy with the frequency of wealth. Remember, prosperity is not just about financial gain—it's about feeling abundant in all areas of your life. By working with these rituals, you can cultivate a prosperous mindset and invite more blessings and abundance into your world.

Chapter 7: Moon Phases and Thanksgiving

The moon has long been revered as a powerful force in magic and spiritual practices. Its phases, from new to full, wax and wane in a cyclical rhythm that mirrors the cycles of life, death, and rebirth. During the Thanksgiving period, we are called to reflect on abundance, gratitude, and the blessings we've received throughout the year. By aligning our magical workings with the phases of the moon, we can enhance the power of our intentions and deepen the connection between the energies of the cosmos and the Thanksgiving season.

In this chapter, we will explore spells that are specifically timed to the phases of the moon, amplifying the energy of gratitude, prosperity, and renewal. Each phase of the moon offers unique energies that can be harnessed to create powerful spells. By working in harmony with these phases, you can align your magical intentions with the natural rhythms of the universe, making your spells even more potent.

The Power of the Moon in Magic

The moon's phases are a reflection of the natural cycles of life, growth, and change. From the new moon, which symbolizes beginnings and potential, to the full moon, which represents culmination and abundance, each phase offers specific energies that can enhance your magical practice. Understanding these phases and how they align with your intentions is key to successful moon magic.

During the Thanksgiving season, the moon's energy can be particularly helpful for spells focused on gratitude, abundance, prosperity, and emotional renewal. Whether you are looking to set new intentions for personal growth, attract wealth and blessings, or release old patterns that no longer serve you, working with the moon's phases will amplify your intentions and bring you closer to your goals.

Let's explore how each phase of the moon can be harnessed for specific types of Thanksgiving magic and the spells you can perform during each phase to align with these energies.

New Moon: Setting Intentions for Abundance

The new moon is the phase of beginnings, a time for setting intentions, planting seeds, and creating the foundation for future growth. This is the perfect time to focus on what you want to manifest during the holiday season, whether it's increased financial prosperity, a deeper connection with family and loved ones, or personal growth.

The energy of the new moon is subtle but powerful—it's the dark phase of the moon when potential is at its peak. By focusing on your desires and setting clear intentions during this phase, you can plant the seeds of abundance that will grow and flourish as the moon waxes.

Spell 1: New Moon Thanksgiving Intention Setting Ritual
This ritual is designed to help you set powerful intentions for abundance, gratitude, and prosperity during the Thanksgiving season. It works by harnessing the energy of the new moon to plant the seeds of your desires, which will grow and manifest as the moon waxes toward fullness.

Ingredients:

- A black or white candle (for new beginnings and potential)
- A small piece of paper and a pen
- A bowl of earth or a small plant pot with soil (to symbolize growth)
- A seed (any kind of seed that symbolizes what you wish to grow)
- A green crystal (such as aventurine or citrine for abundance)

Instructions:

1. Begin by lighting the black or white candle, focusing on the flame as a symbol of new beginnings. As the candle burns, take a moment to reflect on what you wish to manifest during this new moon cycle, especially in relation to abundance, gratitude, and the blessings of Thanksgiving.
2. On the small piece of paper, write down your intentions. Be specific about what you wish to attract. For example, "I intend to welcome financial prosperity into my life," or "I intend to deepen my relationships with my family and express my gratitude openly."
3. Fold the paper and place it in the bowl of earth or soil. As you do this, plant the seed in the soil, saying:

"As I plant this seed, so too I plant my intentions.
May they grow strong and full, nourished by the energy of the moon.
With each day, I welcome abundance and blessings into my life."

1. Place the green crystal in the soil beside the seed, symbolizing the abundance you wish to attract. Hold your hands over the soil and visualize your intentions growing, just as the seed will sprout and flourish.
2. Extinguish the candle and place the bowl of soil or plant pot in a sunny spot. Water it regularly, caring for it as you would care for your intentions.

As the moon begins to wax, your intentions will grow stronger, and you will begin to see signs of manifestation in your life. This ritual can be repeated each new moon to set new intentions or reinforce existing ones.

Waxing Moon: Growth and Attraction

The waxing moon is the phase between the new moon and the full moon. During this time, the energy of the moon is increasing, making it an ideal time for spells focused on growth, attraction, and bringing new opportunities into your life. It's a time of action, where the seeds planted during the new moon begin to take root and grow.

During the Thanksgiving season, the waxing moon can be used to attract abundance, financial blessings, and prosperity. It's also a time to nurture relationships and encourage growth in areas of your life that you want to expand.

Spell 2: Waxing Moon Prosperity Charm

This charm is designed to attract financial blessings and prosperity during the waxing moon phase. It works by harnessing the growing energy of the moon to bring abundance into your life, whether in the form of money, opportunities, or material wealth.

Ingredients:

- A green candle (for growth and prosperity)
- A small pouch or charm bag
- A gold coin (or any coin symbolizing wealth)
- A sprig of basil (for abundance)
- A piece of citrine or pyrite (for financial success)
- A pinch of cinnamon (for prosperity)
- A few drops of patchouli oil (for wealth attraction)

Instructions:

1. Begin by lighting the green candle, focusing on your intention to attract prosperity and financial blessings during the waxing moon. As the candle burns, visualize yourself surrounded by wealth and abundance.
2. Take the gold coin and hold it in your hands, saying:

"Golden coin, symbol of wealth,
Bring me fortune, joy, and health.
As the moon grows, so too shall my wealth,
Filling my life with abundance and stealth."

1. Place the coin in the small pouch.
2. Add the sprig of basil, saying:

"Basil of abundance, bring me success,
Let wealth and fortune find me, nonetheless."

1. Add the piece of citrine or pyrite, saying:

"Citrine (or pyrite) of gold and light,
Attract prosperity, shining bright.
Let success come to me with ease,
And may my finances grow like trees."

1. Sprinkle a pinch of cinnamon into the pouch, saying:

"Cinnamon for prosperity and gain,
Let abundance flow like gentle rain."

1. Add a few drops of patchouli oil to the pouch, saying:

"Patchouli, bring wealth and joy to me,
With your power, I call prosperity."

1. Hold the pouch in your hands and focus on your intention to attract financial blessings during the waxing moon. Visualize wealth flowing into your life and opportunities coming your way.
2. Seal the pouch and carry it with you during the waxing moon phase to attract prosperity. You can also place it near your financial documents or keep it in your home to enhance the flow of wealth.

This charm will work to attract financial blessings and opportunities as the moon waxes toward fullness, helping to manifest abundance in your life.

Full Moon: Abundance and Celebration

The full moon is the most powerful phase of the moon, symbolizing abundance, completion, and manifestation. It is a time when the intentions set during the new moon come to fruition, and the energy of the moon is at its peak. During Thanksgiving, the full moon is the perfect time to celebrate the abundance in your life, express gratitude, and manifest the blessings you desire.

The full moon is also a time for releasing anything that no longer serves you, making space for new opportunities and experiences. It is a time to reflect on what you have achieved and to honor the abundance that surrounds you.

Spell 3: Full Moon Gratitude and Abundance Ritual

This ritual is designed to celebrate the abundance in your life and express gratitude during the full moon. It works by harnessing the powerful energy of the full moon to manifest your desires and acknowledge the blessings you have already received.

Ingredients:

- A silver or white candle (for the full moon's energy)
- A bowl of water (to represent the moon's reflection)
- A small mirror (to reflect the light of the moon)
- A handful of dried herbs (rosemary for remembrance, basil for abundance, and mint for prosperity)
- A piece of moonstone or selenite (for full moon energy)
- A small piece of paper and a pen

Instructions:

1. Begin by lighting the silver or white candle, focusing on the energy of the full moon. If possible, perform this ritual outdoors under the light of the moon, or by a window where you can see the moonlight.
2. Place the bowl of water in front of the candle, allowing the light to reflect in the water. This represents the reflection of the moon's energy and its connection to the Earth.
3. Hold the small mirror in your hands, reflecting the light of the candle or the moon, and say:

"Full moon bright, I call your light,
Bring abundance to me this night.

As I reflect upon your glow,
Let my blessings continue to grow."

1. Sprinkle the dried herbs into the bowl of water, saying:

"Herbs of abundance, wealth, and grace,
Fill my life with blessings in every space.
May prosperity flow, and gratitude grow,
Under the full moon's shining glow."

1. Take the small piece of paper and write down the things you are grateful for in your life. This could include financial blessings, loving relationships, personal achievements, or anything else that brings you joy and fulfillment.
2. Fold the paper and place it under the bowl of water. Hold the moonstone or selenite in your hands and say:

"Moonstone bright, selenite clear,
I welcome abundance far and near.
With gratitude and love, I honor this night,
And invite more blessings in full moon's light."

1. Close your eyes and take a few deep breaths, focusing on the feeling of gratitude. Visualize the blessings in your life multiplying and new opportunities for abundance flowing toward you.
2. When you feel ready, extinguish the candle and leave the bowl of water under the moonlight for a few hours or overnight if possible. In the morning, pour the water into the earth as an offering of gratitude.

This ritual helps you connect with the energy of the full moon to celebrate the abundance in your life and express gratitude for the blessings you've received. It also sets the stage for continued prosperity and success.

Waning Moon: Releasing and Letting Go

The waning moon is the phase after the full moon, during which the moon's light begins to diminish. This is a time for releasing, letting go, and clearing away any energy or situations that no longer serve you. During the Thanksgiving season, the waning moon can be used to release financial worries, negative thought patterns, or emotional blockages that may be preventing you from fully embracing abundance and gratitude.

Spell 4: Waning Moon Releasing Ritual

This ritual is designed to help you release any blocks or negative energy that may be preventing you from fully receiving abundance and blessings. It works by harnessing the energy of the waning moon to clear away obstacles and create space for new opportunities.

Ingredients:

- A black candle (for banishing and release)
- A small piece of paper and a pen
- A bowl of salt (for cleansing)
- A small piece of obsidian or black tourmaline (for protection and grounding)
- A sprig of sage or incense for purification

Instructions:

1. Begin by lighting the black candle and setting your intention to release anything that is blocking your ability to receive abundance and blessings.
2. On the small piece of paper, write down anything you wish to release. This could include financial worries, limiting beliefs about money, or emotional blockages that are preventing you from feeling grateful or abundant.
3. Hold the paper in your hands and say:

"Under the waning moon, I release,
All that blocks my joy and peace.
Worries, doubts, and fears take flight,
As I step into the moon's soft light."

1. Place the paper in the bowl of salt and sprinkle a bit of salt over it to purify and cleanse the energy. Hold the obsidian or black tour-

maline in your hands and focus on grounding and protection, saying:

"Obsidian (or black tourmaline), ground me true,
Protect me in all that I do.
As I release, I stand in light,
Free from fear and full of might."

1. Pass the sprig of sage or incense over the bowl to further cleanse the energy, saying:

"With this smoke, I cleanse and clear,
All that no longer serves me here.
I release, I let go, I am free,
To welcome abundance and prosperity."

1. Allow the candle to burn down completely, symbolizing the release of the blocks and negative energy. Once the candle has burned out, bury the paper and salt in the earth, returning the energy to the ground to be transformed.

This Waning Moon Releasing Ritual is a powerful way to clear away anything that may be preventing you from fully embracing abundance and gratitude. By letting go, you create space for new opportunities and blessings to flow into your life.

In this chapter, we have explored how to work with the phases of the moon to enhance your Thanksgiving spells and rituals. Each phase of the moon offers unique energies that can be harnessed to set intentions, attract abundance, celebrate blessings, and release what no longer serves you. By aligning your magic with the moon's cycles, you can amplify the power of your intentions and create a deeper connection with the natural rhythms of the universe.

Whether you are planting new seeds of intention during the new moon, celebrating abundance during the full moon, or letting go of what no longer serves you during the waning moon, working with the moon's phases will help you manifest your desires and embrace the blessings of the Thanksgiving season.

Chapter 8: Herbal Gratitude

Herbs and plants have long been used in magical practices to harness the natural energies of the earth, bringing specific intentions to life through their unique properties. In this chapter, we will explore the use of herbs and plants associated with gratitude, love, and prosperity in spellwork. These natural allies enhance our ability to manifest our desires, heal emotional wounds, and cultivate abundance, making them particularly powerful when incorporated into rituals and spells.

During the Thanksgiving season, when gratitude and abundance are central themes, working with herbs can help amplify the energy of thankfulness and invite more blessings into your life. Each herb carries its own magical properties, whether it's basil for prosperity, lavender for peace, or rosemary for protection and remembrance. By using these plants in your spellwork, you can deepen your connection to the earth, align with the energies of the universe, and create more powerful magical outcomes.

The Power of Herbs in Magic

Herbs have been used for thousands of years for their healing properties and magical qualities. They carry the life force of the earth, and when harvested and used with intention, they can help transform energy, manifest desires, and heal emotional or spiritual wounds. Each herb has its own unique energy, associated with specific intentions such as love, gratitude, prosperity, protection, or healing.

By incorporating herbs into your spellwork, you are working directly with the energies of nature. Herbs can be used in a variety of ways: burned as incense, brewed as tea, carried in sachets or charms, or sprinkled around your home. When combined with your intentions, herbs serve as potent magical tools, enhancing the power of your spells and rituals.

Herbs Associated with Gratitude

Gratitude is one of the most powerful emotions for manifesting abundance and attracting blessings into your life. The following herbs are particularly associated with gratitude and can be used in spells and rituals to express thankfulness, invite blessings, and deepen your sense of appreciation for the abundance you already have.

1. Rosemary (Rosmarinus officinalis)

Magical Properties: Memory, gratitude, protection, and clarity

Uses in Spellwork: Rosemary is a powerful herb for remembering blessings and expressing gratitude. It helps to clear the mind, bringing clarity and focus to what you are grateful for, while also offering protection. Rosemary is often used in spells to honor ancestors or loved ones and to express thankfulness for the guidance and support you receive from them.

Spell: Rosemary Gratitude Incense

This simple yet powerful spell involves making your own rosemary incense to burn during rituals or meditation, helping you to focus on gratitude and invite more blessings into your life.

Ingredients:

- Dried rosemary
- A few drops of frankincense essential oil (for protection and spiritual clarity)
- A charcoal disc (for burning the incense)
- A fireproof bowl or incense burner

Instructions:

1. Begin by grinding the dried rosemary in a mortar and pestle or with your hands, focusing on your intention to express gratitude for the blessings in your life.
2. As you grind the herb, say:

"Rosemary, herb of memory and grace,
I honor the blessings I now embrace.
With each breath, I give thanks today,
For all the love and joy that comes my way."

1. Add a few drops of frankincense essential oil to the rosemary, enhancing the energy of protection and clarity. Mix the two together.
2. Light the charcoal disc and place it in your fireproof bowl or incense burner. Once the disc is glowing, sprinkle a small amount of the rosemary mixture onto the charcoal.
3. As the incense burns, close your eyes and take several deep breaths, focusing on the feelings of gratitude in your heart. Visualize the blessings you have received—both big and small—surrounding you like a warm, protective light.
4. Say aloud or in your mind:

"I give thanks for all that I have received,
For love, abundance, and dreams achieved.
With gratitude, I honor this day,
And welcome more blessings to come my way."

1. Allow the incense to burn out naturally, using this time to meditate on the things you are grateful for. You can repeat this ritual whenever you need to refocus on gratitude or during Thanksgiving as a way to honor the abundance in your life.

2. Basil (Ocimum basilicum)

Magical Properties: Prosperity, protection, love, and harmony

Uses in Spellwork: Basil is known as an herb of abundance, prosperity, and love. It is often used in spells to attract financial blessings, improve relationships, and enhance the flow of positive energy. In the context of gratitude, basil helps to attract more of what you are thankful for, whether it's love, wealth, or personal growth.

Spell: Basil Prosperity Sachet

This spell creates a sachet filled with basil and other prosperity herbs, designed to attract financial blessings and abundance into your life. It can be kept in your wallet, purse, or placed in your home to encourage the flow of prosperity.

Ingredients:

- A small cloth pouch or charm bag (green or gold, for prosperity)
- A handful of dried basil leaves (for prosperity)
- A pinch of cinnamon (for success and abundance)
- A few dried bay leaves (for wishes and success)
- A small piece of citrine (for wealth and abundance)
- A green ribbon or string (to tie the pouch)

Instructions:

1. Begin by cleansing your space and materials with sage or incense to remove any negative energy.
2. Place the dried basil leaves into the pouch, saying:

"Basil for abundance, wealth, and gain,
Bring me prosperity without strain.
With gratitude, I welcome the flow,
Of blessings and fortune as they grow."

1. Add a pinch of cinnamon to the pouch, saying:

"Cinnamon of success and golden light,
Let my wealth grow ever bright.
With each day, abundance will rise,
As I give thanks to the earth and skies."

1. Add the dried bay leaves to the pouch, saying:

"Bay leaves for wishes and dreams come true,
Bring success in all that I do.
With gratitude, I now call forth,
The blessings of abundance and infinite worth."

1. Place the piece of citrine into the pouch, visualizing it as a magnet for wealth and prosperity. Say:

"Citrine of gold and radiant fire,
Bring wealth and blessings that I desire.
With gratitude, I open the door,
To prosperity and so much more."

1. Tie the pouch with the green ribbon or string, sealing the energy of the spell. Hold the sachet in your hands and focus on your intention to attract abundance and prosperity into your life.
2. Carry the sachet with you, place it in your home, or keep it near your financial documents. Each time you see or touch the sachet, take a moment to express gratitude for the abundance that is flowing into your life.

This basil sachet will help you attract financial blessings and create an atmosphere of prosperity in your home.

3. Lavender (Lavandula angustifolia)

Magical Properties: Peace, love, protection, and healing

Uses in Spellwork: Lavender is a calming herb associated with love, peace, and harmony. It is often used in spells to soothe emotional wounds, bring clarity to relationships, and create an environment of calm and balance. In the context of gratitude, lavender helps to foster peace of mind and emotional healing, making it easier to focus on the blessings in your life.

Spell: Lavender Peace and Gratitude Candle Ritual

This ritual uses the calming energy of lavender to create a peaceful and harmonious atmosphere, making it easier to reflect on the blessings in your life and express gratitude for all that you have.

Ingredients:

- A lavender-scented candle (or a white candle dressed with lavender oil)
- Dried lavender flowers or lavender essential oil
- A small dish of salt (for protection and purification)
- A piece of rose quartz (for love and gratitude)

Instructions:

1. Begin by setting up your space with the lavender candle in the center. Place the dish of salt and the piece of rose quartz nearby.
2. Light the lavender candle and take a few deep breaths, allowing the calming scent to fill the room. As you breathe, focus on releasing any stress or tension and opening your heart to the energy of gratitude.
3. Hold the piece of rose quartz in your hands and close your eyes. Visualize the love and blessings in your life surrounding you like a warm, protective light. Say:

"Lavender of peace and love so true,
Bring harmony to all that I do.
With gratitude, I welcome the light,
Of love and blessings pure and bright."

1. Sprinkle a small pinch of salt around the candle, saying:

"Salt of the earth, protect this space,
Let gratitude and peace take their place.
With a heart that's open and free,
I give thanks for all that's given to me."

1. Spend a few moments in quiet reflection, focusing on the feelings of gratitude and peace in your heart. As the candle burns, imagine these feelings growing stronger, filling your home and your life with love and abundance.
2. When you feel ready, extinguish the candle and thank the universe for the blessings you have received. Keep the piece of rose quartz near your bed or in your home as a reminder of the love and peace that gratitude brings.

This Lavender Peace and Gratitude Candle Ritual is perfect for creating a peaceful atmosphere during the Thanksgiving season and for focusing on the love and blessings in your life.

Herbs Associated with Prosperity

Prosperity is about more than just financial wealth—it includes abundance in all aspects of life, from relationships and personal growth to health and happiness. The following herbs are associated with attracting prosperity, wealth, and success, and can be used in spells and rituals to invite more abundance into your life.

4. Mint (Mentha spp.)

Magical Properties: Prosperity, protection, and healing

Uses in Spellwork: Mint is a powerful herb for attracting financial success and good fortune. It is often used in prosperity spells to boost the flow of wealth and opportunity, as well as to protect existing financial resources. Mint can also be used to refresh and renew your energy, clearing away blockages that may be preventing abundance from flowing into your life.

Spell: Mint and Bay Prosperity Tea

This prosperity tea is designed to attract wealth and abundance while also offering protection for your finances. Drinking this tea regularly will help you align with the energy of prosperity and invite financial blessings into your life.

Ingredients:

- Fresh or dried mint leaves (for prosperity and financial growth)
- A few dried bay leaves (for success and protection)
- A cinnamon stick (for abundance)
- Honey (for sweetness and attraction)
- A small green candle (optional, to enhance the spell)

Instructions:

1. Begin by boiling water and setting up your space with the small green candle. Light the candle to symbolize your intention for prosperity and abundance.

2. Place the mint leaves, bay leaves, and cinnamon stick in a teapot or mug. As you pour the hot water over the herbs, say:

"Mint for wealth, bay for success,
Cinnamon for abundance, let it bless.
With each sip, prosperity grows,
And blessings flow in endless flows."

1. Let the tea steep for a few minutes, focusing on your intention to attract prosperity and protect your financial resources. Visualize your wealth growing and opportunities flowing to you effortlessly.
2. Add honey to taste, saying:

"Honey for sweetness, attract and flow,
Prosperity follows wherever I go."

1. Drink the tea slowly, savoring each sip as you reflect on the abundance in your life and the blessings you are inviting. As you drink, repeat the following affirmation:

"I welcome abundance into my life,
Prosperity flows without struggle or strife.
I am deserving of wealth and success,
And I give thanks for all that I possess."

1. When you have finished your tea, extinguish the candle and carry the energy of prosperity with you throughout the day.

This Mint and Bay Prosperity Tea is a simple yet effective way to align with the energy of wealth and abundance, helping to attract financial blessings into your life.

Herbs for Love and Emotional Healing

Love and emotional healing are essential aspects of gratitude and prosperity. Without a strong foundation of self-love and emotional balance, it can be difficult to fully receive the blessings that life offers. The following herbs are associated with love, emotional healing, and harmony, and can be used in spells and rituals to foster deeper connections with yourself and others.

5. Rose (Rosa spp.)

Magical Properties: Love, beauty, and emotional healing

Uses in Spellwork: Roses are one of the most powerful herbs for love and emotional healing. They are often used in spells to attract love, deepen relationships, and heal emotional wounds. Roses carry a high vibrational energy that opens the heart, allowing for greater self-love and compassion for others.

Spell: Rose Love and Gratitude Bath

This ritual bath is designed to promote self-love, emotional healing, and gratitude. By bathing in rose petals and other love-enhancing herbs, you open your heart to the energy of love and gratitude, making it easier to attract positive relationships and blessings into your life.

Ingredients:

- A handful of fresh or dried rose petals (for love and emotional healing)
- A few drops of rose essential oil (for self-love and beauty)
- A handful of dried lavender flowers (for peace and harmony)
- A small piece of rose quartz (for love and compassion)
- A pink or white candle (optional, for love and healing)

Instructions:

1. Begin by lighting the pink or white candle and setting up your bath space. Fill the tub with warm water and scatter the rose petals and lavender flowers into the water.
2. Add a few drops of rose essential oil to the bath, saying:

"Rose of love, beauty, and grace,
Open my heart to love's embrace.
With gratitude, I bathe in light,
Healing my heart, making it bright."

1. Hold the rose quartz in your hands and close your eyes. Focus on your intention to heal emotionally, open your heart, and welcome love and gratitude into your life. Say:

"Rose quartz of love, soft and kind,
Heal my heart, clear my mind.
With every breath, I welcome grace,
And give thanks for love's sweet embrace."

1. Place the rose quartz near the bath and step into the water. As you soak, visualize the warm water and rose petals infusing you with love and gratitude. Imagine any emotional wounds or blockages dissolving in the water, leaving you feeling open, loved, and at peace.
2. Spend at least 20 minutes in the bath, reflecting on the love and blessings in your life. When you feel ready, step out of the bath and allow yourself to air dry, if possible, to keep the energy of the ritual with you.
3. Extinguish the candle and keep the rose quartz near your bed or in a special place as a reminder of the love and gratitude you have cultivated.

This Rose Love and Gratitude Bath is perfect for moments when you need to reconnect with yourself, heal emotionally, and open your heart to love and gratitude.

In this chapter, we have explored the magical properties of herbs associated with gratitude, love, and prosperity, and how to incorporate them into spellwork. By working with these powerful plants, you can deepen your connection to the earth's natural energies and enhance your ability to manifest blessings, attract abundance, and heal emotionally. Whether you are creating a sachet for prosperity, a candle ritual for gratitude, or a bath for self-love, herbs provide a potent and beautiful way to work with magic during the Thanksgiving season and beyond.

Chapter 9: Candle Magic for Thanksgiving

Candle magic is one of the oldest and simplest forms of magic, harnessing the power of fire to focus and amplify intentions. Candles serve as a direct link between our intentions and the universe, transforming energy through the symbolism of light. By working with candles, we can channel our desires for gratitude, love, and success into the flame, allowing our intentions to manifest through the energy of fire. During Thanksgiving, candle magic becomes particularly powerful as it helps to enhance the energies of gratitude, abundance, and connection with loved ones.

In this chapter, we will explore the use of candles in spellwork, focusing on how to use them to foster gratitude, attract love, and invoke success. Whether you are performing a simple ritual of thanks or calling forth abundance and prosperity for the coming year, candle magic offers a focused and potent way to align your desires with the energy of the universe.

The Power of Candle Magic

Candles have long been used in rituals and ceremonies as a way to communicate with the divine, draw in specific energies, and symbolize transformation. The flame of a candle represents the element of fire, associated with change, purification, and the manifestation of will. When a candle burns, it releases energy into the universe, carrying your intention with it. The color, scent, and timing of a candle spell can be tailored to your specific goals, making candle magic a highly customizable practice.

In the context of Thanksgiving, candle magic can be used to express gratitude for the blessings in your life, attract love and harmony to your family and relationships, or call forth prosperity and success for the year ahead. Each candle's flame acts as a beacon of your desires, guiding them into manifestation.

Choosing the Right Candle for Your Spell

Selecting the right candle for your spell is an important step in candle magic. Each color corresponds to specific magical properties, and choosing the right color enhances the effectiveness of your spell. For Thanksgiving magic, colors like green (for abundance), gold (for success), pink (for love and harmony), and white (for gratitude and purity) are particularly powerful.

Here is a brief guide to candle colors and their meanings:

- **White:** Purity, gratitude, spiritual protection, cleansing
- **Green:** Abundance, growth, prosperity, healing
- **Gold:** Success, wealth, achievement, personal power
- **Pink:** Love, harmony, emotional healing, friendship
- **Red:** Passion, energy, courage, strength
- **Blue:** Peace, communication, emotional healing, clarity
- **Yellow:** Joy, creativity, mental clarity, confidence
- **Purple:** Spiritual insight, wisdom, psychic ability, power

In addition to color, you can also dress your candles with oils and herbs to enhance their magical properties. For example, rubbing cinnamon oil on a green candle can amplify its prosperity-attracting energy, while dressing a pink candle with rose oil enhances its love and harmony properties. Adding herbs such as basil, rosemary, or lavender can further strengthen the spell's focus and intention.

Preparing Your Candle for Magic

Before performing a candle spell, it's important to prepare or "dress" your candle. This process infuses the candle with your specific intention and sets the stage for the energy it will release. Here's how to dress a candle for spellwork:

1. **Cleansing the Candle:**

   Before you begin, cleanse the candle to remove any residual energy it may have picked up. You can do this by passing the candle through the smoke of sage or incense, or by wiping it down with a cloth dipped in saltwater.

2. **Anointing the Candle:**

   Choose an oil that corresponds to your intention (such as lavender oil for peace or cinnamon oil for prosperity) and rub it onto the candle. If you are attracting something (love, money, success), rub the oil from the base of the candle to the wick. If you are banishing or releasing something, rub the oil from the wick to the base.

3. **Inscribing the Candle:**

   You may choose to inscribe symbols, words, or names into the candle. Use a sharp object (like a pin or a small knife) to carve your desires directly into the wax. For example, inscribe "Abundance" or "Love" onto the candle, or draw a sigil that represents your intention.

4. **Charging the Candle:**

   Hold the candle in your hands and focus on your intention. Visualize the outcome you desire and imagine the energy of that outcome flowing into the candle. Feel the power of your intention being absorbed by the wax and wick.

Once your candle is prepared, it is ready to be used in a spell or ritual.

Spell 1: Thanksgiving Gratitude Candle Ritual

This simple yet powerful candle ritual is designed to express gratitude for the blessings in your life, while also inviting more abundance and joy into your future. The energy of the white candle symbolizes purity and gratitude, making it a perfect tool for this spell.

Ingredients:

- A white candle (for gratitude and purity)
- A small dish of salt (for cleansing and protection)
- A handful of rosemary (for remembrance and blessings)
- A piece of paper and a pen
- A small bowl of water (to symbolize life and blessings)

Instructions:

1. Begin by cleansing your space with sage or incense, clearing away any stagnant or negative energy.
2. Light the white candle, focusing on the flame as a symbol of purity and gratitude. As the candle burns, take a moment to reflect on the blessings in your life. Visualize the things you are grateful for, from the people you love to the abundance you've received.
3. On the piece of paper, write down three things you are deeply grateful for. These can be material blessings, relationships, personal achievements, or anything else that brings you joy.
4. Sprinkle a pinch of salt around the candle to purify the space, saying:

"Salt of the earth, cleanse this place,
Bring protection and blessings with grace.
As I give thanks for all I've been given,
I open my heart to more abundance in living."

1. Add the rosemary to the water, saying:

"Rosemary for blessings, love, and light,
I give thanks for the gifts in my sight.
With each breath, I welcome more,
As I open the door to what life has in store."

1. Hold the piece of paper in your hands and focus on the feelings of gratitude for the things you've written down. Visualize your heart filling with warmth and light as you acknowledge these blessings.
2. Place the paper under the candle, saying:

"I give thanks for the love, the joy, and the peace,
For the blessings that never cease.
With this candle's flame, I honor today,
And welcome more blessings along my way."

1. Let the candle burn for at least 15-20 minutes, meditating on the energy of gratitude and abundance. When you feel ready, extinguish the candle and keep the paper in a special place as a reminder of the blessings you have received.

This Thanksgiving Gratitude Candle Ritual helps you connect with the energy of thankfulness, allowing you to appreciate the abundance in your life and invite even more blessings in the future.

Spell 2: Love and Harmony Candle Spell

This spell is designed to foster love and harmony within your home, particularly during family gatherings or times of emotional connection. The pink candle represents love, emotional healing, and harmony, making it an ideal tool for spells centered around relationships.

Ingredients:

- A pink candle (for love and harmony)
- A few drops of rose oil (for love and emotional healing)
- Dried lavender or lavender essential oil (for peace and calm)
- A rose quartz crystal (for love and compassion)
- A small piece of paper and a pen

Instructions:

1. Begin by dressing the pink candle with rose oil, rubbing the oil from the base of the candle to the wick while focusing on your intention to bring love and harmony into your relationships.
2. Light the candle and take a moment to focus on the flame, visualizing the warmth and love that you wish to bring into your relationships. As the candle burns, say:

"Pink candle of love and light,
Bring harmony into my sight.
Let peace and love grow strong,
In my home, where we belong."

1. Hold the rose quartz in your hands and close your eyes. Focus on the feeling of love radiating from your heart and extending to those around you. Visualize your home being filled with warm, loving energy, where peace and understanding flow freely.

2. Sprinkle the dried lavender around the candle or add a few drops of lavender oil to enhance the energy of calm and peace. Say:

"Lavender for peace and calm,
Bring healing like a soothing balm.
Let love flow freely, pure and bright,
Bringing harmony into the light."

1. On the piece of paper, write down your intention for love and harmony in your home. This could be something like "I welcome love, peace, and understanding into my family" or "Our home is filled with joy and harmony."
2. Place the paper under the candle and let it burn for at least 15 minutes. As it burns, visualize your home being filled with love and harmony, and see any conflicts or misunderstandings dissolving into peace.
3. When you feel ready, extinguish the candle and keep the rose quartz in a central location in your home to continue fostering the energy of love and harmony.

This Love and Harmony Candle Spell is perfect for Thanksgiving gatherings or any time you wish to bring more peace and love into your relationships.

Spell 3: Prosperity and Success Candle Ritual

This candle ritual is designed to attract prosperity and success into your life, making it particularly useful during the holiday season when you may be focusing on financial abundance and future goals. The gold candle represents wealth, success, and personal power, while the green candle symbolizes growth and prosperity.

Ingredients:

- A gold or green candle (for prosperity and success)
- A pinch of cinnamon (for abundance and success)
- A pinch of basil (for financial prosperity)
- A small coin or piece of pyrite (for wealth)
- A few drops of patchouli oil (for wealth attraction)
- A small piece of paper and a pen

Instructions:

1. Begin by dressing the gold or green candle with patchouli oil, rubbing the oil from the base of the candle to the wick. Focus on your intention to attract prosperity and success into your life.
2. Light the candle and sprinkle a pinch of cinnamon around it, saying:

"Cinnamon of success and gain,
Let prosperity flow like gentle rain.
Bring abundance in all I do,
And let my blessings multiply too."

1. Sprinkle the basil around the candle, saying:

"Basil for wealth and fortune's grace,
Bring prosperity into this place.

Let my finances grow and thrive,
As abundance flows into my life."

1. Hold the coin or piece of pyrite in your hands and visualize your financial situation improving, new opportunities coming your way, and wealth flowing into your life. Say:

"Golden coin, symbol of wealth,
Bring me fortune, joy, and health.
As I give thanks for what I've received,
Let more abundance be achieved."

1. On the piece of paper, write down your financial or career goals. Be specific about what you want to achieve, such as "I welcome financial stability" or "I succeed in my business endeavors."
2. Place the paper under the candle and let it burn for at least 20 minutes. As the candle burns, visualize your goals manifesting and see yourself achieving success and prosperity.
3. When you feel ready, extinguish the candle and keep the coin or pyrite in your wallet or near your financial documents to continue attracting wealth and success.

This Prosperity and Success Candle Ritual is perfect for calling forth financial blessings and achieving your career goals, helping you align with the energy of abundance.

Daily Candle Magic Ritual for Gratitude and Success

In addition to specific spells, incorporating daily candle magic into your routine can help maintain a positive flow of energy, ensuring that gratitude, love, and success remain constant themes in your life. This simple daily ritual can be done each morning or evening to enhance your sense of thankfulness and attract blessings throughout the day.

Ingredients:

- A small white or gold candle (for gratitude and success)
- A piece of clear quartz (for clarity and manifestation)
- A small dish of salt (for cleansing and protection)

Instructions:

1. Begin by lighting the white or gold candle, focusing on your intention to cultivate gratitude and attract success.
2. Hold the clear quartz in your hands and close your eyes. Take a few deep breaths and focus on the things you are grateful for in your life. Visualize the energy of success and abundance flowing toward you.
3. Say the following affirmation:

"I am open to receiving abundance and blessings,
Gratitude flows freely from my heart.
I welcome success, joy, and prosperity,
As I give thanks for all I've been given."

1. Sprinkle a small pinch of salt around the candle to cleanse and protect the energy.
2. Let the candle burn for a few minutes while you meditate on your goals and express gratitude for the blessings in your life. When

you feel ready, extinguish the candle and carry the positive energy with you throughout the day.

By performing this daily candle magic ritual, you can maintain a positive and abundant mindset, attracting blessings and success while expressing gratitude for the abundance already present in your life.

In this chapter, we have explored various candle magic spells and rituals designed to enhance gratitude, attract love, and manifest success during the Thanksgiving season. Candle magic offers a simple yet powerful way to channel your intentions and focus your energy on the things you wish to cultivate in your life. Whether you are expressing gratitude, fostering love and harmony in your home, or calling forth prosperity, working with candles allows you to connect with the element of fire and the transformative power of intention. By incorporating these spells into your Thanksgiving celebrations, you can amplify your connection to the energies of gratitude, abundance, and success.

Chapter 10: Crystal Enchantment

Crystals are powerful tools in magic, revered for their ability to store, amplify, and focus energy. Each crystal carries a unique vibration that can be harnessed to align with specific intentions, such as love, abundance, healing, or protection. When used in combination with spells, rituals, or intention-setting, crystals act as conduits, magnifying the energy you put forth. During the Thanksgiving season, crystals can help you deepen your practice of gratitude, attract abundance, and strengthen bonds with loved ones.

In this chapter, we will explore how to use crystals to amplify your Thanksgiving spells. We'll dive into the creation of gratitude grids, gemstone charms, and other ways to incorporate the magic of crystals into your rituals. Crystals such as citrine, rose quartz, and green aventurine are particularly effective for spells involving gratitude, prosperity, and emotional healing, making them ideal tools for Thanksgiving magic.

The Power of Crystals in Magic

Crystals are formed over thousands of years through natural geological processes, making them powerful representations of the Earth's energy. Each type of crystal resonates with specific frequencies, making them ideal for channeling different intentions. For example, rose quartz is associated with love and emotional healing, while citrine is known for attracting prosperity and success.

When you use crystals in spellwork, you are working with the natural energy of the Earth to amplify your intentions. Crystals can store energy, enhance the focus of your spells, and act as anchors for the energy you wish to manifest. They are highly versatile and can be used in a variety of ways, including grids, charms, meditation, and ritual work.

Choosing the Right Crystals for Thanksgiving Spells

For Thanksgiving, crystals that resonate with gratitude, abundance, love, and emotional healing are particularly powerful. Here are some key crystals that can be used to amplify your Thanksgiving spells:

- **Citrine:** Known as the "Merchant's Stone," citrine is a powerful crystal for attracting abundance, success, and prosperity. It also promotes joy and optimism, making it ideal for gratitude spells.

- **Rose Quartz:** The stone of unconditional love, rose quartz helps to heal emotional wounds, foster self-love, and strengthen bonds with loved ones. It is perfect for spells centered around gratitude for relationships and emotional healing.

- **Green Aventurine:** This stone is associated with luck, abundance, and new opportunities. It's ideal for attracting prosperity and fostering a sense of gratitude for the blessings you have received.

- **Amethyst:** A stone of spiritual protection and clarity, amethyst helps to calm the mind and foster a sense of peace and gratitude. It's excellent for meditation and enhancing spiritual awareness during Thanksgiving rituals.

- **Clear Quartz:** Known as the "Master Healer," clear quartz amplifies the energy of other crystals and your intentions. It is highly versatile and can be used in any spellwork to enhance focus, clarity, and manifestation.

- **Pyrite:** Pyrite is often associated with wealth, abundance, and protection. It helps to attract financial success and can be used in spells that focus on prosperity during Thanksgiving.

Now that we've covered some key crystals, let's explore how to use them in Thanksgiving-specific spells and rituals.

Crystal Gratitude Grids

A crystal grid is a powerful tool for focusing energy in a specific direction or for a particular intention. It consists of a pattern of crystals laid out in a geometric formation, with each stone amplifying and directing energy toward a specific goal. Gratitude grids are designed to attract blessings, abundance, and joy by aligning your intentions with the energies of the crystals.

Gratitude grids can be used to enhance your feelings of thankfulness, bring more blessings into your life, and cultivate an abundant mindset. The combination of crystals and sacred geometry creates a strong energetic field that supports your intentions.

Spell 1: Gratitude Crystal Grid

This spell involves creating a crystal grid to amplify feelings of gratitude and attract more abundance into your life. It can be set up on your altar or in a special place in your home during the Thanksgiving season.

Ingredients:

- A large piece of citrine (for abundance and joy) – this will be the central stone
- Four rose quartz crystals (for love and emotional healing)
- Four green aventurine crystals (for abundance and gratitude)
- A clear quartz point (to amplify the energy of the grid)
- A piece of paper and a pen
- A grid template (optional, or you can simply create a symmetrical pattern)

Instructions:

1. Begin by cleansing your crystals with sage, incense, or sound to remove any residual energy. This will ensure that the crystals are clear and ready to amplify your intentions.

2. On the piece of paper, write down the things you are grateful for. These can include specific people, experiences, or blessings you've received. Fold the paper and place it in the center of your grid.

3. Place the large citrine crystal on top of the folded paper. This stone represents abundance and joy, acting as the central energy of your grid.

4. Arrange the four rose quartz crystals around the citrine in a square or circular formation. As you place each stone, say:

"Rose quartz of love and healing,
I give thanks for the love that fills my life.
May my heart be open, my spirit be kind,
As I reflect on the blessings I find."

1. Next, place the four green aventurine crystals in a pattern around the rose quartz. As you place each stone, say:

"Aventurine of gratitude and grace,
I honor the abundance in this sacred space.
May my blessings grow, my joy expand,
As I give thanks with an open hand."

1. Finally, place the clear quartz point at the top of the grid to amplify the energy. Point the quartz toward the center of the grid to direct the energy inward.

2. Hold your hands over the grid and focus on the feeling of gratitude. Visualize the energy of the crystals surrounding you, filling you with joy, love, and abundance. Say:

"I give thanks for the blessings I've known,
For the love, the joy, the seeds I've sown.
With this grid, I magnify,
The gratitude that I amplify."

1. Leave the grid in place for as long as you feel necessary, returning to it daily to reflect on gratitude. You can recharge the grid during each full moon or when you feel the need to amplify your connection to abundance.

This Gratitude Crystal Grid serves as a constant reminder of the blessings in your life and helps to attract even more abundance through the power of intention and crystal energy.

Gemstone Charms for Thanksgiving

Gemstone charms are another powerful way to incorporate crystal magic into your Thanksgiving spells. By creating small, portable charms, you can carry the energy of gratitude, love, and prosperity with you throughout the day. These charms can be worn, carried in your pocket, or placed around your home to continuously emit positive energy.

Spell 2: Prosperity and Gratitude Gemstone Charm

This spell involves creating a charm using crystals that attract prosperity and foster gratitude. It's ideal for those who wish to carry the energy of Thanksgiving with them beyond the holiday, continuously attracting abundance and maintaining a thankful mindset.

Ingredients:

- A small cloth pouch or charm bag (green or gold for prosperity)
- A piece of citrine (for abundance)
- A piece of pyrite (for wealth and protection)
- A small piece of rose quartz (for gratitude and love)
- A few basil leaves (for prosperity and success)
- A pinch of cinnamon (for abundance)
- A green ribbon or string

Instructions:

1. Begin by cleansing your crystals and materials with sage, incense, or a cleansing spray.
2. Hold the citrine in your hands and focus on your intention to attract abundance and prosperity into your life. Visualize yourself surrounded by wealth, success, and gratitude. Say:

"Citrine of light, abundance and gold,
Bring me prosperity, wealth untold.
With gratitude, I welcome thee,
Into my life, abundantly."

1. Place the citrine into the charm bag.
2. Next, hold the pyrite and focus on protection and financial stability. Visualize your financial situation improving and your resources growing. Say:

"Pyrite of gold, protection and gain,
Let my wealth grow without strain.
I give thanks for all I possess,
As I welcome more and release stress."

1. Place the pyrite into the charm bag.
2. Hold the rose quartz in your hands and focus on gratitude. Reflect on the love, relationships, and emotional blessings you've received. Say:

"Rose quartz of love, gentle and pure,
I give thanks for the love that is sure.
With this charm, I carry grace,
And open my heart to love's embrace."

1. Place the rose quartz into the charm bag, along with the basil leaves and cinnamon.
2. Tie the charm bag closed with the green ribbon or string, sealing your intentions inside. Hold the bag in your hands and visualize it glowing with the energy of prosperity, gratitude, and love. Say:

"With this charm, I welcome in,
Prosperity, love, and joy within.

I give thanks for all I've received,
And open my heart to be further relieved."

1. Carry the charm with you in your pocket, wallet, or bag to continuously attract abundance and gratitude into your life. You can also place it in your home, near your financial documents, or on your altar to amplify its energy.

This Prosperity and Gratitude Gemstone Charm is a powerful tool for attracting financial success and cultivating a mindset of thankfulness.

Crystal Meditation for Thanksgiving Gratitude

Crystals can also be used in meditation to deepen your connection to gratitude and abundance. Meditating with crystals helps you align your energy with the frequencies of the stones, amplifying the feelings of thankfulness and joy. This meditation is designed to help you reflect on the blessings in your life and foster a sense of peace and gratitude.

Spell 3: Thanksgiving Gratitude Meditation with Crystals

This meditation focuses on using rose quartz and citrine to enhance feelings of gratitude, love, and abundance. It's a simple yet powerful way to connect with the energy of Thanksgiving and reflect on the blessings in your life.

Ingredients:

- A piece of rose quartz (for love and emotional healing)
- A piece of citrine (for abundance and gratitude)
- A comfortable, quiet space for meditation
- A white or pink candle (optional, for focus and clarity)

Instructions:

1. Begin by creating a peaceful environment for your meditation. If you wish, light a white or pink candle to symbolize love, peace, and clarity.
2. Sit in a comfortable position and hold the rose quartz in your left hand and the citrine in your right hand.
3. Close your eyes and take a few deep breaths, allowing your body to relax and your mind to quiet.
4. Focus on the energy of the rose quartz in your left hand. Visualize a soft pink light surrounding you, filling your heart with love, compassion, and gratitude. As the pink light grows stronger, feel any emotional wounds or blockages gently dissolve. Say silently or aloud:

"I open my heart to love and gratitude.
I give thanks for the relationships in my life,
And for the love that surrounds me every day."

1. Shift your focus to the citrine in your right hand. Visualize a warm golden light radiating from the citrine, filling your body with joy, abundance, and gratitude. Feel the golden light attracting blessings, prosperity, and success into your life. Say silently or aloud:

"I open my life to abundance and joy.
I give thanks for the prosperity I've received,
And for the blessings that continue to flow into my life."

1. Continue to hold both crystals as you meditate on the blessings in your life. Reflect on the people, experiences, and opportunities that have brought you joy, growth, and fulfillment. Allow the feelings of gratitude to expand, filling your heart and mind with peace and contentment.
2. When you feel ready, slowly open your eyes and extinguish the candle (if used). Keep the rose quartz and citrine near you as a reminder of the love and abundance you carry with you every day.

This Thanksgiving Gratitude Meditation is a powerful way to align your energy with the frequencies of love and abundance, helping you reflect on your blessings and cultivate a grateful heart.

Daily Crystal Gratitude Ritual

Incorporating crystals into your daily routine is a wonderful way to maintain a consistent connection to gratitude, abundance, and love. This simple daily crystal gratitude ritual can be performed each morning or evening to center your energy and focus on the blessings in your life.

Spell 4: Daily Crystal Gratitude Ritual

This daily ritual uses a clear quartz crystal and a gratitude affirmation to align your energy with gratitude and abundance. It's a quick and easy way to start or end your day with a thankful heart.

Ingredients:

- A small piece of clear quartz (for clarity and amplification)
- A quiet space for reflection
- A gratitude journal or piece of paper (optional)

Instructions:

1. Begin by holding the clear quartz crystal in your hands. Take a few deep breaths, focusing on the energy of the crystal and allowing your mind to clear.
2. Close your eyes and think about one thing you are grateful for. This could be something small or significant, such as a kind gesture, a recent success, or simply the fact that you have food and shelter.
3. As you focus on this feeling of gratitude, visualize the energy of the clear quartz amplifying it, sending it out into the universe. Say aloud or silently:

"I give thanks for the blessings in my life.
May my heart always be open to receive,
And may gratitude guide my path."

1. If you wish, write down what you are grateful for in a journal or on a piece of paper. This helps to solidify the feeling of thankfulness and creates a record of your blessings.
2. Keep the clear quartz with you throughout the day, or place it by your bed to carry the energy of gratitude with you.

By incorporating this simple ritual into your daily routine, you can maintain a strong connection to gratitude, helping you attract more blessings into your life.

In this chapter, we have explored how to use crystals to amplify Thanksgiving spells and rituals. Whether you are creating gratitude grids, gemstone charms, or meditating with crystals, these powerful tools help to magnify your intentions and align your energy with the frequencies of love, abundance, and gratitude. By working with crystals during the Thanksgiving season, you can deepen your connection to the Earth's energy, cultivate a thankful heart, and attract more blessings into your life.

Chapter 11: Nature Offerings

Nature offers a bounty of magical elements that can be used to create powerful and meaningful spells, especially during the Thanksgiving season when the natural world is transitioning into autumn. By incorporating elements from nature such as leaves, pine cones, autumnal flowers, and even acorns, you can connect more deeply with the cycles of the Earth, express gratitude for the harvest, and channel the energies of abundance, love, and prosperity.

In this chapter, we will explore how to create and cast spells using elements from nature. These spells can be performed indoors or outdoors, making use of materials that are readily available in your environment. Whether you're creating nature offerings to give thanks, attract abundance, or strengthen your connection with the earth, working with natural materials allows you to harness the inherent energies of the season and align your intentions with the rhythms of nature.

The Magic of Nature Offerings

Nature offerings are a way to honor the natural world while drawing upon its energy for spellwork. They can be created from seasonal materials such as fallen leaves, acorns, pine cones, berries, flowers, and branches, all of which carry specific meanings and magical properties. By working with nature, you deepen your connection to the Earth's cycles, attuning your spells to the energies of growth, harvest, and transformation.

Using nature in your spells allows you to ground your intentions and work in harmony with the natural world. Each element you choose represents a facet of the earth's magic, from the grounding stability of a pine cone to the vibrant energy of autumn flowers. These materials are not only abundant but also imbued with the power of the land they come from.

Choosing the Right Natural Elements for Spells

Just as crystals and herbs have specific magical properties, so do natural elements like leaves, pine cones, and flowers. The energy of these materials is shaped by their connection to the earth and the time of year in which they are harvested. For Thanksgiving spells, we will focus on elements associated with gratitude, abundance, renewal, and love.

Here are some natural materials commonly used in autumnal spells and their magical properties:

- **Leaves (especially oak, maple, and birch):** Renewal, transformation, release of old energy, grounding
- **Pine Cones:** Fertility, abundance, protection, stability
- **Acorns:** New beginnings, potential, prosperity, luck
- **Autumnal Flowers (such as mums, sunflowers, and marigolds):** Happiness, abundance, blessings, joy
- **Berries (such as holly, rowan, or hawthorn berries):** Protection, love, abundance
- **Nuts (such as walnuts and hazelnuts):** Wisdom, protection, prosperity
- **Twigs and Branches:** Growth, stability, connection to the divine
- **Autumn Fruits (such as apples and pumpkins):** Abundance, gratitude, fertility, harvest energy

These elements are abundant during the autumn season and are rich with symbolism, making them ideal for spells focused on gratitude, abundance, and thanksgiving.

Spell 1: Leaf Offering for Gratitude and Renewal

This spell focuses on using fallen leaves to express gratitude for the blessings in your life while releasing old energy that no longer serves you. The act of offering leaves back to nature symbolizes renewal, allowing you to make space for new growth and opportunities.

Ingredients:

- Several fallen leaves (oak, maple, or birch are ideal)
- A piece of paper and a pen
- A small bowl of water (for cleansing and renewal)
- A candle (green or white for gratitude and renewal)
- A safe outdoor space (optional)

Instructions:

1. Begin by collecting several fallen leaves from your surroundings. As you gather each leaf, take a moment to reflect on the blessings in your life, as well as anything you wish to release or let go of.
2. Set up your space by lighting the green or white candle to symbolize gratitude and renewal. If you are performing this spell outdoors, you can place the candle on a safe surface where it won't be disturbed.
3. On the piece of paper, write down the things you are grateful for on one side and, on the other side, write the things you wish to release from your life. This could be old habits, negative thoughts, or stagnant energy.
4. Hold each leaf in your hands and focus on one blessing from your list. As you do, visualize the leaf absorbing your gratitude. Say aloud or silently:

"With this leaf, I give thanks for the blessing of [name the blessing]. May it be honored and cherished in my life."

1. After focusing on each blessing, place the leaves in a small pile near your candle.
2. Now, take a moment to focus on what you wish to release. Hold the paper with the things you want to let go of and reflect on how these things have affected your life. When you feel ready, tear the paper into small pieces and place them in the bowl of water, saying:

"As these words dissolve, I release the energy they hold.
May I be cleansed and renewed, making space for what is to come."

1. Take the leaves outside (or to a natural space if you are already outdoors) and offer them back to the earth by scattering them around. As you release each leaf, say:

"As these leaves return to the earth,
May my gratitude grow, and my burdens fall away.
I honor the cycles of life and renewal,
And I welcome the blessings of the future."

1. When you are finished, extinguish the candle and leave the bowl of water out for the earth to absorb. This completes the cycle of release and renewal, creating space for new energy to flow into your life.

This Leaf Offering spell is perfect for the Thanksgiving season, allowing you to express your gratitude while letting go of old energy that no longer serves you.

Spell 2: Pine Cone Abundance Charm

Pine cones are symbols of fertility, abundance, and protection. They are often associated with the seeds of new growth and the promise of future prosperity. In this spell, we will use a pine cone to create a charm for attracting abundance and success, which can be placed in your home or carried with you to continually invite prosperity into your life.

Ingredients:

- A large pine cone (symbolizing abundance and potential)
- A gold or green ribbon (for prosperity)
- A few cinnamon sticks (for abundance and success)
- A small piece of citrine or pyrite (for wealth)
- A few basil leaves (for prosperity)
- A green or gold candle (for abundance)
- A small pouch or charm bag

Instructions:

1. Begin by cleansing the pine cone and other materials with sage or incense to clear away any unwanted energy.
2. Hold the pine cone in your hands and focus on your intention to attract abundance and success. Visualize the pine cone as a symbol of growth, with seeds of prosperity waiting to unfold in your life. Say:

"Pine cone of abundance, growth, and wealth,
Bring me success and vibrant health.
With each seed, I plant my desire,
To manifest abundance and raise it higher."

1. Tie the gold or green ribbon around the pine cone, symbolizing the flow of prosperity into your life.

2. Add the cinnamon sticks to the small pouch or charm bag, saying:

"Cinnamon for success and gain,
Let abundance flow without strain."

1. Place the piece of citrine or pyrite into the pouch, saying:

"Citrine (or pyrite) of golden light,
Bring me wealth, shining bright."

1. Add the basil leaves to the pouch, saying:

"Basil of prosperity and grace,
Fill my life with abundant space."

1. Place the pouch near the pine cone and light the green or gold candle. Focus on the energy of abundance and success flowing into your life as you say:

"With this charm, I welcome in,
Prosperity, wealth, and blessings within.
I give thanks for what's yet to come,
And for all that I've already won."

1. Allow the candle to burn for at least 15 minutes, focusing on the feeling of abundance in your life. When you are ready, extinguish the candle and place the pine cone and pouch in a prominent place in your home (such as your altar, near your financial documents, or in your living room) to attract continuous prosperity.

This Pine Cone Abundance Charm helps to manifest wealth and success, and it can be refreshed by repeating the ritual during each new moon or whenever you wish to amplify your prosperity.

Spell 3: Autumnal Flower Blessing Ritual

Autumn flowers such as sunflowers, mums, and marigolds are associated with joy, abundance, and blessings. This spell uses the vibrant energy of these flowers to bless your home and bring happiness and positivity into your life during the Thanksgiving season.

Ingredients:

- A bouquet of autumnal flowers (such as sunflowers, marigolds, or chrysanthemums)
- A white or yellow candle (for blessings and positivity)
- A few drops of honey (for sweetness and abundance)
- A bowl of water (for cleansing and renewal)
- A small piece of paper and a pen

Instructions:

1. Begin by lighting the white or yellow candle and setting the bouquet of flowers in front of you. Take a moment to admire their beauty and reflect on the joy and abundance they symbolize.
2. On the small piece of paper, write down a blessing or intention for your home. This could be something like "I bless my home with peace and love" or "May joy and abundance fill my space."
3. Place the paper in the bowl of water, symbolizing the flow of blessings into your life. As you place the paper in the water, say:

"Water of life, clear and pure,
May blessings flow and joy endure.
As these words dissolve, may they bring,
Abundance and peace in everything."

1. Hold the bouquet of flowers in your hands and focus on your intention to fill your home with joy and blessings. Visualize the energy of the flowers radiating throughout your space, bringing light, happiness, and abundance. Say:

"Flowers of autumn, vibrant and bright,
Bless my home with love and light.
With each bloom, joy will grow,
And blessings will come, this I know."

1. Place a few drops of honey into the bowl of water, symbolizing the sweetness of life and abundance. As you do this, say:

"Honey for sweetness, joy, and grace,
May love and abundance fill this place."

1. Let the candle burn for at least 15 minutes, allowing the energy of the flowers and water to fill your home with blessings. When you are ready, extinguish the candle and place the bouquet in a central location in your home as a symbol of the blessings you have invited in.
2. You can pour the water from the bowl into the earth or at the base of a tree, offering the blessings back to nature in gratitude.

This Autumnal Flower Blessing Ritual is perfect for creating a joyful and abundant atmosphere in your home during Thanksgiving and beyond.

Spell 4: Acorn Prosperity Spell

Acorns are symbols of potential, growth, and prosperity, carrying the energy of new beginnings and the promise of future abundance. In this spell, we will use acorns to manifest financial success and opportunities, planting the seeds of wealth for the year ahead.

Ingredients:

- Three acorns (for prosperity and new beginnings)
- A small pot or patch of soil (for planting)
- A few coins (for wealth and financial success)
- A green candle (for prosperity)
- A small piece of citrine (for abundance)

Instructions:

1. Begin by lighting the green candle and setting up your space with the acorns, coins, and a small pot of soil.
2. Hold the acorns in your hands and focus on your intention to attract prosperity and financial success. Visualize the acorns as seeds of abundance that will grow and flourish in your life. Say:

"Acorns of potential, growth, and might,
I plant you now in prosperity's light.
With each seed, I call forth wealth,
Financial success, and vibrant health."

1. Place the acorns into the pot of soil, burying them gently. As you plant each acorn, place a coin in the soil with it, saying:

"With this coin, I plant my desire,
To manifest abundance and raise it higher.

May prosperity grow strong and true,
Bringing wealth in all I do."

1. Hold the small piece of citrine in your hands and focus on your financial goals. Visualize yourself achieving success and attracting wealth into your life. Say:

"Citrine of gold, bright and clear,
Bring me abundance, wealth, and cheer.
With this spell, I manifest,
Financial blessings and all the rest."

1. Place the citrine in the pot or near the base of the plant as a symbol of wealth and success.
2. Allow the candle to burn for at least 20 minutes, focusing on the energy of growth and prosperity. When you are ready, extinguish the candle and keep the pot in a sunny location, watering it regularly as a symbol of the growing prosperity in your life.

This Acorn Prosperity Spell helps to plant the seeds of financial success, allowing you to manifest wealth and opportunities in the year ahead.

Daily Nature Offering Ritual for Gratitude

In addition to specific spells, you can incorporate nature offerings into your daily routine to maintain a consistent connection with gratitude and abundance. This simple daily ritual uses leaves, flowers, or other natural elements to express thanks and invite blessings into your life.

Spell 5: Daily Nature Offering Ritual for Gratitude

This daily ritual involves creating a simple nature offering using leaves, flowers, or other natural materials. It can be performed each morning or evening to align your energy with gratitude and abundance.

Ingredients:

- A few leaves, flowers, or small stones from nature
- A small bowl or dish (for holding the offering)
- A quiet space for reflection

Instructions:

1. Begin by gathering a few leaves, flowers, or small stones from your surroundings. As you collect each item, focus on something you are grateful for.
2. Place the natural elements in the small bowl or dish, saying:

"With this offering, I give thanks,
For the blessings that fill my life.
May gratitude grow, and joy expand,
As I honor the gifts of the land."

1. Take a few moments to reflect on the things you are grateful for, focusing on the feeling of thankfulness in your heart.
2. Leave the bowl or dish in a special place as a reminder of the blessings in your life. You can refresh the offering daily by adding new leaves, flowers, or stones.

By incorporating this simple ritual into your daily routine, you can maintain a strong connection to gratitude and invite continuous blessings into your life.

In this chapter, we have explored how to use elements from nature—such as leaves, pine cones, acorns, and autumnal flowers—in Thanksgiving spells and rituals. Nature offerings allow you to connect deeply with the earth's energy and align your intentions with the cycles of the natural world. Whether you are creating a gratitude grid, planting acorns for prosperity, or offering leaves back to nature, these spells help you express thanks, attract abundance, and honor the blessings of the season. By working with nature, you can create powerful magical connections and invite more joy, love, and success into your life.

Chapter 12: Feasting Rituals

The Thanksgiving feast is the heart of the holiday, a time when friends and family gather to share food, gratitude, and the bounty of the season. In many cultures, food has always been deeply intertwined with ritual and magic. By incorporating spells and rituals into the preparation and serving of your Thanksgiving feast, you can infuse each dish with love, abundance, and blessings. These rituals not only enhance the flavor and enjoyment of the meal but also create an atmosphere of warmth, gratitude, and connection, strengthening bonds among those gathered.

In this chapter, we will explore various feasting rituals that you can perform before, during, and after the Thanksgiving meal. These include blessings for each dish, rituals to honor the harvest, and spells to invite abundance and prosperity into your home. By blessing the food, you transform the act of eating into a sacred celebration of life, love, and gratitude.

The Power of Feasting Rituals

Feasting rituals have been a part of human tradition for centuries, spanning cultures and belief systems. In ancient times, people understood that food was more than just sustenance—it was a gift from the Earth, and preparing and sharing meals was a sacred act. By blessing your Thanksgiving feast, you acknowledge the abundance in your life and honor the natural cycles that brought the food to your table.

Feasting rituals focus on gratitude, abundance, love, and community. Each dish becomes a vessel for your intentions, allowing you to share those blessings with others. Whether you are cooking for a large gathering or preparing a small meal, these rituals help you channel positive energy into the food, ensuring that everyone who partakes feels nourished not just in body, but in spirit.

Preparing the Feast: Blessing Your Ingredients

The magic of the Thanksgiving feast begins with the ingredients themselves. Each item you use, from vegetables to grains to spices, carries its own energy and symbolism. Before you begin cooking, take a moment to bless the ingredients, infusing them with love, abundance, and gratitude. This not only enhances the energy of the food but also ensures that every dish carries the intention of nourishment and blessing.

Spell 1: Blessing the Ingredients

This simple ritual is designed to bless the ingredients for your Thanksgiving feast, ensuring that each dish is filled with love, abundance, and gratitude. It can be performed before you begin cooking or as you prepare each dish.

Ingredients:

- A white or green candle (for purity and abundance)
- A pinch of salt (for purification)
- A bowl of water (for cleansing and renewal)
- Your ingredients for the feast (vegetables, grains, meats, spices, etc.)

Instructions:

1. Begin by setting up your space with the white or green candle, bowl of water, and a small dish of salt. Light the candle, symbolizing the light and warmth of the harvest.
2. Take a moment to reflect on the journey each ingredient has taken to reach your kitchen—from the seeds planted in the earth, to the farmers who harvested the crops, to the stores where you bought them. As you reflect, say:

"I honor the earth that has provided this food,
And the hands that have brought it to my table.

May each ingredient be blessed with love,
And may abundance fill our hearts and home."

1. Sprinkle a pinch of salt into the bowl of water, stirring it gently with your finger. As you do, say:

"Salt and water, cleanse and renew,
Purify this food in all I do.
May it bring joy, health, and grace,
To all who gather in this place."

1. Take each ingredient in your hands (or if you have too many, place your hands over them), and visualize them glowing with a warm, golden light. Imagine that this light is filling the food with love, abundance, and gratitude. Say:

"With love and thanks, I bless this food,
May it nourish body, heart, and mood.
With each bite, may joy increase,
And may we gather in love and peace."

1. When you have blessed all of the ingredients, extinguish the candle and begin cooking, knowing that each dish you prepare is infused with magical energy.

This ritual helps to set a positive and loving tone for the meal, ensuring that every dish is prepared with intention and gratitude.

Cooking with Intention: Infusing Your Dishes with Magic

As you prepare each dish, you have the opportunity to infuse it with specific intentions. Whether you are cooking turkey, roasting vegetables, or baking pies, you can channel different types of energy into each dish. For example, you might infuse your main dish with abundance, your side dishes with love and harmony, and your desserts with sweetness and joy. Cooking with intention transforms each recipe into a spell, making the act of preparing food a magical experience.

Spell 2: Cooking with Love and Abundance

This spell focuses on infusing your dishes with specific magical intentions, ensuring that each bite carries the energy of love, abundance, and joy. It can be used for any recipe, from savory dishes to sweet treats.

Ingredients:

- Your ingredients for a specific dish
- A spoon, whisk, or other kitchen utensil (to stir the energy)
- A green candle (for abundance) and a pink candle (for love)
- A pinch of cinnamon (for prosperity) and a pinch of sugar (for sweetness)

Instructions:

1. Begin by lighting the green and pink candles. These represent the energies of abundance and love, which you will be infusing into your dish. As the candles burn, visualize the kitchen filling with warm, loving energy.
2. Hold your hands over the ingredients, focusing on the specific intention you want to infuse into the dish. For example, if you are making a side dish, you might want to focus on harmony among your guests, or if you are baking a dessert, you might focus on bringing joy and sweetness into the lives of those eating it.

3. As you stir, mix, or prepare the dish, say aloud or in your mind:

"As I prepare this meal with care,
I fill it with love, joy, and abundance rare.
With each stir, my intention grows,
Bringing blessings to those this meal bestows."

1. Sprinkle a pinch of cinnamon into the dish (for abundance and prosperity), saying:

"Cinnamon of wealth and grace,
Bring abundance into this space."

1. Add a pinch of sugar (for sweetness and joy), saying:

"Sugar sweet, bring joy anew,
Let happiness flow through all we do."

1. Continue to prepare the dish as you normally would, but keep your focus on the intention. Imagine the energy of the candles infusing the food with light and love. When you are finished, say:

"This dish is blessed with love and cheer,
Bringing joy to all who gather here."

1. When the dish is ready, extinguish the candles and serve the meal with the knowledge that you have created a feast of love and abundance.

This simple spell transforms the act of cooking into a magical experience, ensuring that the energy of love and abundance is present in every bite.

Blessing the Feast: A Ritual for Thanksgiving Dinner

Once the feast has been prepared, it's time to bless the table and the food, inviting abundance, love, and gratitude into the meal. This ritual is perfect for performing just before the meal begins, allowing everyone present to participate in the magic. It honors the harvest, the Earth, and the community that has gathered to share the feast.

Spell 3: Blessing the Feast

This ritual is designed to bless the entire Thanksgiving feast, filling the table with love, gratitude, and abundance. It can be performed by the host, or everyone can take turns offering their blessings.

Ingredients:

- A white or gold candle (for blessings and abundance)
- A small bowl of salt (for purification)
- A sprig of rosemary or sage (for blessings)
- The Thanksgiving feast, set on the table

Instructions:

1. Begin by lighting the white or gold candle, symbolizing the light of gratitude and abundance that fills the meal.
2. Take the sprig of rosemary or sage and hold it over the table. As you do, focus on the blessings you want to infuse into the meal. Say:

"With this herb, I bless this food,
May it bring love, health, and joy to all who partake.
We give thanks for the harvest, for the Earth,
And for the abundance that fills our lives."

1. Sprinkle a pinch of salt over the table and the food, saying:

"Salt of the Earth, pure and true,
Bless this feast and all we do.
Let this meal nourish body and soul,
And may our hearts be ever full."

1. If you are dining with others, invite each person to say one thing they are thankful for before beginning the meal. This can be done by going around the table or allowing individuals to speak freely. As each person speaks, imagine the energy of gratitude filling the room.
2. When everyone has expressed their gratitude, say:

"With grateful hearts, we share this feast,
Giving thanks for love, for joy, for peace.
May this food bring abundance near,
And may our blessings grow each year."

1. Allow the candle to burn throughout the meal as a symbol of the light and love that fills the gathering. Once the meal is over, extinguish the candle with gratitude for the blessings received.

This Blessing the Feast ritual helps to create a sacred atmosphere for your Thanksgiving meal, allowing everyone to participate in the magic of gratitude and abundance.

Dessert Magic: Sweetening Life with Gratitude

Desserts are the perfect way to end a Thanksgiving feast, symbolizing the sweetness of life and the joy of sharing abundance with others. By performing a simple spell while preparing or serving dessert, you can infuse the final course with extra love and gratitude, ensuring that everyone leaves the table with a full heart as well as a full belly.

Spell 4: Sweet Gratitude Dessert Ritual

This spell is designed to infuse your Thanksgiving dessert with love, joy, and gratitude. Whether you are baking a pie, cookies, or another sweet treat, this ritual will ensure that the dessert carries the energy of sweetness and thankfulness.

Ingredients:

- Your dessert (pie, cookies, cake, etc.)
- A small bowl of honey or sugar (for sweetness)
- A pink candle (for love and gratitude)
- A small piece of rose quartz (optional, for love and emotional healing)

Instructions:

1. Begin by lighting the pink candle and placing the dessert in front of you. As the candle burns, focus on the feelings of gratitude, love, and joy that you want to infuse into the dessert.
2. Hold your hands over the dessert and visualize a warm pink light surrounding it. Imagine that this light represents the love and gratitude that fills your heart and home. Say:

"With love and joy, I bless this sweet,
May its magic make life complete.

As we eat, let gratitude grow,
And may our blessings overflow."

1. Drizzle a small amount of honey or sprinkle a pinch of sugar over the dessert, saying:

"Honey (or sugar) for sweetness, joy, and grace,
Let love and gratitude fill this place."

1. If you have a piece of rose quartz, place it next to the dessert to enhance the energy of love. As you do, say:

"Rose quartz of love, soft and true,
I give thanks for all we do.
With this dessert, let sweetness reign,
And may love and joy remain."

1. When the dessert is ready, serve it with a smile, knowing that it carries the energy of gratitude, sweetness, and love.

This Sweet Gratitude Dessert Ritual adds an extra layer of magic to your Thanksgiving meal, ensuring that the final course is filled with love and joy.

Post-Feast Ritual: Giving Thanks and Clearing the Energy

After the meal, it's important to give thanks for the food, the company, and the abundance that has been shared. A simple post-feast ritual can help clear the energy and express gratitude for the blessings received, ensuring that the positive energy of the day lingers long after the meal is over.

Spell 5: Post-Feast Gratitude Ritual

This ritual is designed to give thanks after the Thanksgiving feast, clearing the energy and ensuring that the abundance and love continue to flow into your life.

Ingredients:

- A white or green candle (for gratitude and abundance)
- A small bowl of water (for cleansing)
- A handful of dried herbs (such as rosemary, sage, or lavender)

Instructions:

1. After the meal, gather around the table or in a central area of your home. Light the white or green candle and take a moment to reflect on the meal and the blessings that have been shared.
2. Hold the bowl of water and the dried herbs, saying:

"Water of life, cleanse and renew,
We give thanks for all we've been given.
May abundance continue to flow,
And may love and joy forever grow."

1. Sprinkle the herbs into the water, visualizing the energy of the meal being cleared and refreshed. As you do, say:

"With these herbs, I clear the way,
For more blessings to come each day.
We give thanks for food, for love, for light,
And welcome abundance, pure and bright."

1. Pass the bowl of water around, inviting each person to take a small sip or sprinkle a few drops onto their hands as a symbol of gratitude and cleansing.
2. Once everyone has participated, extinguish the candle and pour the remaining water into the earth or at the base of a tree as an offering of thanks.

This Post-Feast Gratitude Ritual helps to clear the energy after the meal and express thanks for the abundance that has been shared.

Conclusion

In this chapter, we have explored the powerful connection between food, magic, and gratitude. Feasting rituals allow you to infuse your Thanksgiving meal with love, abundance, and joy, transforming the act of eating into a sacred celebration. By blessing your ingredients, cooking with intention, and performing rituals before, during, and after the meal, you can create a magical atmosphere that nourishes both body and spirit.

Whether you are sharing a feast with family, friends, or simply preparing a meal for yourself, these rituals help you connect more deeply with the energies of gratitude and abundance, ensuring that the blessings of the Thanksgiving season flow into every aspect of your life.

Chapter 13: Ancestor Blessings

Honoring our ancestors is a sacred tradition that spans cultures and generations. During Thanksgiving, a time for reflecting on gratitude and abundance, it is especially fitting to pay homage to those who came before us. Our ancestors have paved the way for our existence, and their wisdom, guidance, and love continue to influence our lives in unseen ways. By incorporating ancestor blessings into your Thanksgiving rituals, you can invoke their presence, receive their blessings, and strengthen your connection to your lineage.

In this chapter, we will explore various spells and rituals to honor your ancestors, express gratitude for their lives and sacrifices, and invite their guidance and protection into your life. These rituals can be performed individually, with family, or as part of a larger Thanksgiving celebration. By invoking your ancestors during this time of gratitude, you not only honor their memory but also align yourself with their wisdom and spiritual support.

The Importance of Ancestor Reverence

Ancestor reverence is a practice found in many cultures, from the Day of the Dead in Mexico to Samhain in Celtic traditions. It is based on the belief that our ancestors continue to watch over us, offering protection, guidance, and blessings from the spirit realm. By honoring them, we acknowledge the connection between past, present, and future, and recognize that we are part of a larger lineage that stretches across time.

Thanksgiving is an ideal time to invoke ancestor blessings, as it is a celebration of family, heritage, and the bounty of the harvest. Through these rituals, you can express gratitude for the lessons, sacrifices, and love of your ancestors, while also seeking their guidance for the future.

Creating a Sacred Space for Ancestors

Before performing ancestor blessings, it's important to create a sacred space that invites their presence and honors their memory. This can be as simple as setting up an ancestor altar with photos, mementos, or offerings, or as elaborate as creating a designated area for rituals and meditation. The key is to create a space that feels respectful, peaceful, and inviting to your ancestors.

Creating an Ancestor Altar

An ancestor altar serves as a focal point for honoring your ancestors. It can be set up temporarily for Thanksgiving or maintained year-round as a place of reverence. Here's how to create a simple yet powerful ancestor altar.

Items for Your Ancestor Altar:

- Photos of ancestors or family heirlooms
- Candles (white or red for protection, guidance, and love)
- Offerings (such as food, wine, water, or flowers)
- Incense or sage (for purification)
- Crystals (such as amethyst for spiritual connection or black tourmaline for protection)
- A piece of paper and a pen (for writing messages or blessings)

Instructions:

1. Choose a quiet, undisturbed place in your home to set up the altar. This could be a table, shelf, or any flat surface.
2. Place photos of your ancestors on the altar, along with any mementos or family heirlooms that have special meaning to you.
3. Light one or more candles to symbolize the presence of your ancestors. You may also burn incense or sage to cleanse the space and invite positive energy.
4. Offerings are an important part of ancestor reverence. Choose items that your ancestors may have enjoyed in life, such as favorite

foods, wine, water, or flowers. Place these offerings on the altar as a gesture of gratitude.

5. Finally, take a moment to sit in front of the altar, reflecting on your ancestors and the legacy they have passed down to you. You can speak aloud, saying something like:

"I honor the spirits of my ancestors,
Those known and unknown,
Who have walked before me.
I give thanks for your wisdom,
Your protection,
And your love that endures beyond time."

1. You can use the altar as a place for meditation, reflection, or performing the ancestor spells described below.

This ancestor altar will serve as a sacred space where you can connect with your lineage, offer gratitude, and seek guidance.

Spell 1: Ancestral Guidance Invocation

This spell is designed to invoke the wisdom and guidance of your ancestors, inviting them to offer their support and protection during the Thanksgiving season and beyond. It is a simple yet powerful ritual that can be performed in front of your ancestor altar or in any quiet space where you feel connected to their presence.

Ingredients:

- A white or black candle (for protection and spiritual guidance)
- A bowl of water (for purification)
- A small dish of salt (for grounding)
- A photo or memento of an ancestor (optional)
- A piece of paper and a pen

Instructions:

1. Begin by lighting the candle, symbolizing the light of your ancestors and their presence in your life. Place the bowl of water and the dish of salt in front of the candle to ground and purify the space.
2. If you have a photo or memento of an ancestor, place it beside the candle. Take a moment to reflect on the connection you share with your ancestors and the wisdom they hold.
3. On the piece of paper, write down a question or area of your life where you would like guidance. This could be something related to family, career, health, or any other issue where you seek their wisdom.
4. Hold the paper in your hands and close your eyes. Focus on your intention to connect with your ancestors, and visualize their presence around you. Imagine them offering their support, guidance, and protection.

5. As you hold the paper, say the following invocation:

"Spirits of my ancestors, wise and strong,
I call upon you to guide me along.
With love and light, your wisdom I seek,
To help me find the answers I speak.
Ancestors of old, hear my plea,
And share your guidance and love with me."

1. Place the paper under the candle and let the candle burn for at least 15-20 minutes while you meditate on your connection to your ancestors.
2. Once you feel a sense of peace or have received insights, extinguish the candle and keep the paper in a safe place. You may repeat this ritual whenever you need guidance or feel the need to connect with your ancestors.

This Ancestral Guidance Invocation is a powerful way to seek your ancestors' wisdom and protection, especially during times of uncertainty or decision-making.

Spell 2: Thanksgiving Ancestral Blessing

This spell is designed to honor your ancestors during the Thanksgiving celebration, inviting their blessings upon your family and home. It can be performed before or after the Thanksgiving feast, either privately or with the participation of family members.

Ingredients:

- A white or red candle (for ancestral blessings and protection)
- A plate of food from the Thanksgiving feast (as an offering)
- A small glass of wine, water, or juice (as a libation)
- A piece of paper and a pen (optional)
- A photo or memento of an ancestor (optional)

Instructions:

1. Begin by lighting the white or red candle, symbolizing the presence of your ancestors and their protective blessings over your home.
2. Prepare a small plate of food from the Thanksgiving feast, along with a glass of wine, water, or juice. These offerings represent your gratitude and respect for your ancestors, symbolizing the continuation of the harvest and abundance they once knew.
3. If you have a photo or memento of an ancestor, place it near the candle as a focal point for the ritual.
4. Take a moment to reflect on the legacy your ancestors have passed down to you. If you wish, you can write down a message of gratitude on the piece of paper, such as:

"I honor my ancestors for the strength,
The love, and the wisdom they have given.
May their spirits bless this home,
And may their guidance continue to shine."

1. Place the plate of food and the glass of wine on your ancestor altar or another designated space, saying:

"With this food and drink, I give thanks,
To the ancestors who came before me.
May their spirits be honored this day,
And may their blessings continue to flow."

1. Take a few moments to sit quietly, imagining the presence of your ancestors around the table, offering their love, protection, and blessings to all who are gathered.
2. When you feel ready, extinguish the candle. You may leave the food and drink offerings out overnight as a sign of respect, then return them to the earth the next day by pouring the drink into the ground and placing the food in a natural space (such as a garden or under a tree) as a symbolic offering to nature.

This Thanksgiving Ancestral Blessing ritual helps to honor your ancestors and invites their continued blessings over your home and family during the holiday season.

Spell 3: Ancestor Gratitude Jar

This spell is designed to create a physical representation of your gratitude for your ancestors, filling a jar with messages of thanks, love, and appreciation. It can be done individually or as a group activity with family members, creating a beautiful symbol of ancestral love and connection.

Ingredients:

- A small glass jar or container with a lid
- Strips of paper and pens
- A white or red candle (for ancestral blessings)
- Dried flowers or herbs (such as rosemary for remembrance, lavender for love, or sage for cleansing)

Instructions:

1. Begin by lighting the white or red candle to invite the presence of your ancestors and create a sacred space for the ritual.
2. Place the jar in front of the candle and set out the strips of paper and pens. If you are performing this ritual with family, invite everyone to participate.
3. On each strip of paper, write a message of gratitude to your ancestors. This could be a simple "Thank you for your love and protection" or something more personal, such as thanking a specific ancestor for their influence on your life. If you don't know much about your ancestors, you can still express gratitude for the unknown relatives who have shaped your family's lineage.
4. Once you have written your messages, roll up or fold each strip of paper and place it into the jar. As you do, say:

"With this message, I give thanks,
To the ancestors who came before me.

May their spirits be honored and loved,
And may their blessings continue to grow."

1. After placing all the messages in the jar, sprinkle the dried flowers or herbs into the jar, symbolizing the continuation of life and the love that flows through your lineage.
2. Seal the jar with the lid and hold it in your hands, focusing on the energy of gratitude and connection. Visualize your ancestors surrounding you with their blessings, protection, and love.
3. Place the jar on your ancestor altar or in a special place in your home as a physical reminder of your connection to your ancestors. You can add new messages to the jar throughout the year, especially during significant family events or holidays.

This Ancestor Gratitude Jar serves as a beautiful way to honor your ancestors and keep their memory alive, allowing you to continually express thanks for their presence in your life.

Spell 4: Ancestor Candle Ceremony for Protection and Guidance

This candle ceremony is designed to invoke the protection and guidance of your ancestors, creating a spiritual shield over your home and loved ones. It can be performed during Thanksgiving or any time you feel the need for ancestral support and protection.

Ingredients:

- A black or red candle (for protection and ancestral power)
- A small dish of salt (for grounding and protection)
- A small bowl of water (for cleansing)
- A sprig of rosemary or sage (for blessing)
- A photo or memento of an ancestor (optional)

Instructions:

1. Begin by lighting the black or red candle, symbolizing the strength and protection of your ancestors.
2. Place the dish of salt and the bowl of water in front of the candle, representing the grounding and cleansing energy of the Earth and Water elements.
3. If you have a photo or memento of an ancestor, place it near the candle as a focal point for the ceremony.
4. Take the sprig of rosemary or sage and hold it over the candle, focusing on your intention to invoke the protection and guidance of your ancestors. Say:

"Spirits of my ancestors, strong and wise,
I call upon you to protect and guide.
With love and strength, your presence I seek,
To shield my home and family this week.
Ancestors of old, hear my plea,
And watch over those dear to me."

1. Sprinkle a pinch of salt around the candle, creating a protective circle, and say:

"Salt of the Earth, pure and true,
Protect this home in all we do."

1. Dip the rosemary or sage in the bowl of water and sprinkle a few drops around the candle and the room, saying:

"Water of life, cleanse and renew,
Let the blessings of my ancestors flow through."

1. Sit quietly for a few moments, meditating on the presence of your ancestors. Visualize their protective energy surrounding your home, creating a shield of love and strength.
2. When you feel ready, extinguish the candle and keep the rosemary or sage on your ancestor altar as a symbol of their protection.

This Ancestor Candle Ceremony for Protection and Guidance is a powerful way to invoke the spiritual strength of your ancestors, ensuring that their protective energy surrounds you and your loved ones.

Daily Ancestor Gratitude Practice

In addition to specific spells and rituals, you can incorporate a daily gratitude practice to honor your ancestors and invite their blessings into your life. This simple practice takes only a few moments each day but helps to strengthen your connection to your lineage and keep their memory alive.

Daily Ancestor Gratitude Practice

This practice involves lighting a candle each morning or evening and taking a moment to express gratitude to your ancestors for their presence, love, and guidance.

Ingredients:

- A small white or red candle (for ancestral blessings)
- A quiet space for reflection

Instructions:

1. Each morning or evening, light the white or red candle in a quiet space where you won't be disturbed.
2. Take a few deep breaths and focus on the presence of your ancestors. Visualize them surrounding you with love, wisdom, and protection.
3. Say a simple prayer or message of gratitude, such as:

"I give thanks to my ancestors for their guidance and love.
May their spirits continue to watch over me,
And may their blessings flow into my life."

1. Let the candle burn for a few minutes while you reflect on the ways your ancestors have influenced your life. When you feel

ready, extinguish the candle and carry the energy of gratitude with you throughout the day.

This Daily Ancestor Gratitude Practice is a simple yet meaningful way to honor your ancestors each day, ensuring that their blessings and wisdom remain a constant presence in your life.

Conclusion

In this chapter, we have explored the powerful magic of ancestor blessings and the various ways you can honor your ancestors during the Thanksgiving season. By creating ancestor altars, performing invocation spells, and offering gratitude through rituals, you strengthen your connection to your lineage and invite the wisdom, protection, and blessings of your ancestors into your life.

Whether you are seeking guidance, protection, or simply wishing to honor your family's legacy, these rituals help you align with the powerful energies of those who came before you. By incorporating ancestor blessings into your Thanksgiving celebrations, you not only deepen your connection to the past but also create a stronger foundation for the future, knowing that you are supported by the love and wisdom of your ancestors.

Chapter 14: Gratitude Journaling

Gratitude journaling is a powerful and transformative practice that blends mindfulness, intention-setting, and magic. By regularly writing down what you are thankful for, you align your mind, body, and spirit with the frequency of gratitude, which in turn helps attract more blessings, opportunities, and positive energy into your life. When combined with magical practices, journaling becomes a potent tool for manifesting not only gratitude but also your deepest desires.

In this chapter, we will explore how to incorporate spells and rituals into your gratitude journaling practice to amplify its effects. Whether you want to manifest abundance, strengthen your relationships, or attract new opportunities, gratitude journaling can help you bring those desires into reality. You will learn about specific gratitude journaling spells, daily writing practices, and how to create a personalized gratitude journal that serves as both a magical tool and a reflective space.

The Magic of Gratitude Journaling

Gratitude journaling is rooted in the principle that "like attracts like." By focusing on what you already have and giving thanks for it, you open yourself to receiving more of the same energy. Writing down your blessings anchors your gratitude in the physical world, making it easier to attract more positive experiences. Beyond its psychological benefits, gratitude journaling can also serve as a foundation for magical work.

When you write with intention, you combine the magic of words with the energy of manifestation. Each time you put pen to paper, you are engaging in a form of spellwork, channeling your desires and aligning them with universal energies. In gratitude journaling, your words become powerful affirmations that amplify the energy of thankfulness and attract blessings into your life.

Creating Your Gratitude Journal

Before we dive into specific spells and practices, it's essential to create a gratitude journal that resonates with your energy and intentions. While any notebook can serve as a gratitude journal, crafting one with purpose and intention will elevate your journaling practice.

Materials for Your Gratitude Journal:

- A blank notebook or journal (preferably with a design or color that inspires you)
- A pen dedicated to your journaling practice
- Crystals (such as clear quartz for clarity, rose quartz for love, or citrine for abundance)
- Dried herbs (such as lavender for peace or bay leaves for manifestation)
- Stickers, images, or symbols that represent your desires and goals
- A small pouch to keep your journal and magical tools in

Instructions:

1. **Choosing Your Journal:** Select a journal that feels special to you. It can have a cover that resonates with your personal style or be a simple notebook that you decorate yourself. The key is to choose something that inspires you and makes you want to return to it regularly.

2. **Cleansing and Preparing the Journal:** Before using your journal, cleanse it with sage or incense to remove any residual energy. Hold the journal in your hands and focus on your intention to use it as a tool for gratitude and manifestation. You can say something like:

"I cleanse this journal with love and light,
May it be filled with gratitude bright.
As I write, my intentions grow,
Manifesting blessings that flow."

1. **Decorating the Journal (Optional):** If you wish, you can decorate the cover of your journal with stickers, symbols, or images that represent your goals and desires. For example, if you are manifesting abundance, you might include images of coins, trees, or symbols of prosperity. For love, you might include hearts or flowers.

2. **Adding Magical Enhancements:** Place a crystal, dried herbs, or a sigil inside the journal to enhance its energy. Clear quartz can amplify your intentions, while lavender can bring peace and clarity to your thoughts. As you place these items in your journal, say:

"With crystals, herbs, and sacred light,
I charge this journal to bring delight.
May my words bring blessings near,
And manifest abundance here."

1. **Setting Your Intention:** Before you begin writing, take a few moments to set your intention for the journal. What do you hope to achieve through gratitude journaling? Whether it's attracting abundance, strengthening relationships, or finding inner peace, clarify your intention and visualize it as you hold the journal.

Now that you have prepared your journal, it's ready to serve as a tool for manifesting gratitude and your desires.

Spell 1: Gratitude Manifestation Ritual

This spell combines gratitude journaling with a manifestation ritual, helping you focus on the blessings you already have while attracting your desires. By expressing gratitude and setting clear intentions, you open the door to receiving more of what you seek.

Ingredients:

- Your gratitude journal
- A green candle (for abundance and growth)
- A few drops of lavender or rosemary essential oil (for clarity and focus)
- A small piece of clear quartz (for amplifying intentions)
- A pinch of cinnamon (for success and abundance)

Instructions:

1. **Prepare Your Space:** Begin by setting up your space with the green candle, essential oil, and clear quartz. Light the candle to symbolize abundance and the energy of growth.
2. **Anoint the Journal:** Place a few drops of lavender or rosemary essential oil on your hands and gently rub them over the cover of your journal. As you do this, say:

"With this oil, I bless these pages,
May they manifest my dreams through all stages.
Gratitude flows from my heart and hand,
Bringing abundance upon this land."

1. **Write Your Gratitude List:** Open your journal and write a list of at least five things you are grateful for. These can be small or large blessings, ranging from the people in your life to the comforts you enjoy daily. As you write, focus on the feeling of gratitude filling your heart.

2. **Set Your Intentions:** After you have written your gratitude list, write down one or more intentions that you wish to manifest. These could be specific goals (such as "I attract financial abundance into my life") or general desires (such as "I welcome more love and joy into my relationships").

3. **Charge the Journal:** Hold the journal in your hands and place the piece of clear quartz on top. Sprinkle a pinch of cinnamon over the journal, symbolizing success and abundance. As you hold the journal, visualize your intentions coming to fruition and say:

"With gratitude and love, I call it near,
Abundance and blessings, without fear.
May my words manifest and grow,
As the seeds of my desires I sow."

1. **Seal the Spell:** Allow the candle to burn for at least 15 minutes while you meditate on your gratitude and desires. When you are ready, extinguish the candle and place the clear quartz inside your journal as a reminder of the energy you've created.

Repeat this ritual whenever you feel the need to manifest specific desires, using the power of gratitude as a foundation for your intentions.

Spell 2: Daily Gratitude Writing Ritual

This spell is a simple daily practice that combines gratitude journaling with a quick ritual to align your energy with abundance and positivity each day. It's perfect for incorporating gratitude into your morning or evening routine and setting a positive tone for the day ahead.

Ingredients:

- Your gratitude journal
- A white or yellow candle (for positivity and clarity)
- A small dish of salt (for grounding)
- A feather or piece of clear quartz (for lightness and focus)

Instructions:

1. **Light the Candle:** Begin by lighting the white or yellow candle to symbolize positivity, clarity, and the light of gratitude.
2. **Write Three Things You Are Grateful For:** Open your gratitude journal and write down three things you are grateful for today. These can be anything that brings you joy, from the food on your table to a kind word from a friend. As you write, focus on the feeling of gratitude filling your heart.
3. **Affirm Your Gratitude:** After writing your list, hold the feather or clear quartz in your hands and focus on the feeling of lightness and positivity. Say aloud or in your mind:

"With gratitude, I open the way,
For love and blessings to fill my day.
I am thankful for all I receive,
And in abundance, I believe."

1. **Ground the Energy:** Sprinkle a pinch of salt around your journal to ground the energy of gratitude and create a stable founda-

tion for the day ahead. Visualize your gratitude grounding you and anchoring positive energy in your life.

2. **Close the Ritual:** Allow the candle to burn for a few minutes as you reflect on the blessings in your life. When you are ready, extinguish the candle and carry the positive energy with you throughout the day.

By performing this daily ritual, you create a consistent flow of gratitude in your life, helping you attract more blessings and opportunities.

Spell 3: Full Moon Gratitude Journaling Ritual

The full moon is a time of heightened energy and manifestation, making it a powerful period for gratitude journaling. This ritual harnesses the energy of the full moon to amplify your gratitude and set intentions for the coming month.

Ingredients:

- Your gratitude journal
- A silver or white candle (for the moon's energy and illumination)
- A small bowl of water (to represent the moon's connection to water)
- A piece of moonstone or selenite (for lunar energy)
- A moon phase chart (optional, for timing)

Instructions:

1. **Prepare for the Full Moon:** Perform this ritual on the night of the full moon, when the energy of illumination and manifestation is at its peak. Set up your space with the silver or white candle, bowl of water, and moonstone or selenite.
2. **Light the Candle:** Light the silver or white candle to symbolize the full moon's energy, bringing clarity, illumination, and insight to your gratitude practice.
3. **Write Your Gratitude List:** In your journal, write a list of things you are grateful for that have come to fruition since the last full moon. Reflect on the growth, opportunities, and blessings you've received. As you write, focus on the energy of completion and fulfillment.
4. **Set Full Moon Intentions:** After expressing your gratitude, write down your intentions for the next lunar cycle. What do you hope to manifest before the next full moon? Be specific in your

desires, and focus on what you are ready to welcome into your life.

5. **Charge Your Journal:** Hold the journal in your hands and place the moonstone or selenite on top. Visualize the energy of the full moon infusing your intentions with power and light. Say:

"Under the full moon, I give thanks and release,
Welcoming abundance, joy, and peace.
My intentions grow, bright and clear,
As the light of the moon draws blessings near."

1. **Close the Ritual:** Allow the candle to burn for 10-15 minutes as you reflect on the energy of the full moon. When you are ready, extinguish the candle and keep the moonstone or selenite near your journal to amplify your intentions throughout the lunar cycle.

This Full Moon Gratitude Journaling Ritual is perfect for deepening your connection to the moon's cycles and using its energy to manifest gratitude and desires.

Daily Practices for Gratitude Journaling

In addition to specific spells, incorporating daily gratitude journaling into your routine can have lasting positive effects on your mindset, well-being, and ability to manifest desires. Below are a few daily practices to enhance your gratitude journaling experience:

1. Morning Gratitude Affirmations

Each morning, write three things you are grateful for and follow them with an affirmation such as, *"I am open to receiving more blessings today."* This simple practice sets a positive tone for the day and aligns your mind with abundance.

2. Evening Reflection and Gratitude

Before bed, reflect on the day and write down at least one thing that went well or brought you joy. This practice helps shift your focus from any challenges you faced to the positive moments, no matter how small.

3. Weekly Gratitude Check-In

At the end of each week, review your gratitude journal and note any patterns or recurring blessings. This helps you see the ongoing flow of abundance in your life and keeps you motivated to continue the practice.

4. Gratitude Letters

Occasionally, write a letter of gratitude to a specific person, even if you don't intend to send it. This practice helps you focus on the impact that others have had on your life and deepens your sense of connection.

Conclusion

Gratitude journaling is a simple yet profound way to cultivate positivity, manifest desires, and align your energy with abundance. When combined with spells and rituals, it becomes a powerful magical practice that can transform your life. By consistently writing down what you are thankful for and setting clear intentions, you create a ripple effect that invites more blessings and opportunities into your life.

Whether you are performing daily gratitude rituals, harnessing the energy of the full moon, or simply reflecting on your blessings at the end of the day, gratitude journaling serves as a powerful tool for manifestation and spiritual growth. Through the act of writing, you solidify your intentions, deepen your connection to the universe, and align yourself with the energy of gratitude, love, and abundance.

Chapter 15: Thanksgiving Altar Magic

An altar is a sacred space where magic is focused and amplified, serving as both a physical and spiritual center for your spellwork. Setting up a Thanksgiving altar is a powerful way to honor the season, express gratitude for the abundance in your life, and channel magical energy for love, harmony, and prosperity. Altars help bridge the gap between the material and spiritual worlds, offering a dedicated place to focus your intentions, connect with divine energies, and perform rituals.

In this chapter, we will explore the creation of a Thanksgiving altar, focusing on how to set it up, the tools and items you'll need, and how to use the altar to cast spells for love, harmony, and abundance. Whether you have an altar already or are creating one for the first time, these rituals will enhance your Thanksgiving celebration and help you align with the energies of gratitude, love, and prosperity.

The Power of an Altar

An altar acts as a focal point for your magical practice, providing a dedicated space for your tools, intentions, and offerings. By setting up an altar specifically for Thanksgiving, you create a space that embodies the themes of the holiday—gratitude, abundance, love, and community. It is a place where you can honor the harvest, express thanks for your blessings, and perform spells that invite love, harmony, and financial prosperity into your life.

The items you place on your altar serve as symbolic representations of your intentions, helping to channel your energy toward your goals. Whether you are performing a spell, offering thanks, or simply meditating, the altar anchors your energy and enhances your connection to the spiritual forces you are working with.

Setting Up Your Thanksgiving Altar

Creating a Thanksgiving altar is a personal and intuitive process. There is no right or wrong way to set it up, as long as it reflects your intentions and resonates with you. Your altar can be small or large, simple or elaborate, indoors or outdoors. The key is to fill it with items that embody the energy of gratitude, love, harmony, and abundance.

Items for Your Thanksgiving Altar:

- **Candles:** Use colors that represent your intentions. Green for abundance, gold for prosperity, pink for love, and white for gratitude and harmony.
- **Crystals:** Citrine for abundance, rose quartz for love, amethyst for spiritual clarity, and clear quartz to amplify all intentions.
- **Natural Elements:** Include items that reflect the season, such as autumn leaves, acorns, pine cones, and pumpkins. These elements symbolize the harvest, growth, and the cycles of nature.
- **Offerings:** Place offerings such as fruit, nuts, wine, or bread on the altar to honor the Earth and give thanks for the abundance in your life.
- **Photos or Symbols:** Include photos of loved ones or symbols that represent love, harmony, and prosperity, such as hearts, a cornucopia, or a pentacle.
- **Incense or Sage:** Burning incense or sage helps cleanse the space, invite divine energies, and raise the vibration of your altar.
- **A Cloth or Scarf:** Choose a cloth to cover your altar, ideally in warm autumn colors like red, orange, gold, or brown, to reflect the energy of Thanksgiving.
- **A Bowl or Chalice of Water:** This represents the element of water, symbolizing emotions, healing, and intuition.

Once you've gathered your items, follow these steps to set up your Thanksgiving altar:

Step-by-Step Guide to Setting Up Your Thanksgiving Altar

1. **Choose the Location:** Select a space where your altar will be undisturbed. It can be a small corner of a room, a table, a shelf, or even a spot outdoors. Ensure the area is clean and free of distractions.

2. **Cleanse the Space:** Before setting up your altar, cleanse the space with sage, incense, or another purifying method. This helps clear any stagnant or negative energy and ensures that the space is open to receiving positive vibrations. As you cleanse, say:

"I cleanse this space with light and love,
Opening the way for blessings from above.
May this altar be a place of peace and power,
Guiding my magic from this hour."

1. **Lay the Cloth:** Cover the surface of your altar with a cloth or scarf that reflects the autumn season or your personal style. This cloth will act as the foundation for the items you place on it.

2. **Place the Candles:** Position the candles on your altar, using colors that correspond to your intentions. You might place a green candle in the center for abundance, flanked by pink candles for love and harmony. White candles can be added to represent purity and gratitude.

3. **Add Crystals:** Place your chosen crystals around the candles. Citrine and pyrite are perfect for abundance, while rose quartz invites love and harmony. Clear quartz can amplify all your intentions, and amethyst adds a spiritual connection.

4. **Incorporate Natural Elements:** Arrange autumn leaves, pine cones, pumpkins, acorns, and other natural elements around your altar to symbolize the harvest and the abundance of nature.

These items ground your altar in the season of Thanksgiving and honor the cycles of growth and renewal.

5. **Place Offerings:** Add offerings of food and drink to your altar, such as a plate of fruit, bread, or a chalice of wine. These offerings are given in gratitude to the Earth and the divine forces that sustain your life. Say:

"I offer these gifts in thanks and praise,
For the blessings that fill my days.
May abundance continue to flow,
And love and harmony forever grow."

1. **Add Photos or Symbols:** If you have photos of loved ones or symbols that represent love, harmony, and abundance, place them on the altar as a way of connecting your intentions to the people or energies you are honoring.
2. **Light the Incense:** Light incense or sage to purify the altar and invite spiritual energy into the space. The smoke serves as an offering to the divine and carries your intentions to the spiritual realm.
3. **Bless the Altar:** Finally, take a moment to bless the altar. Stand before it, close your eyes, and visualize it glowing with golden light. Say:

"With love and light, I bless this space,
Filled with harmony, joy, and grace.
May this altar be a beacon of power,
Blessing my life from this hour."

Your Thanksgiving altar is now set up and ready to serve as a sacred space for your spells, rituals, and meditations.

Using Your Thanksgiving Altar for Magic

Now that your altar is prepared, you can use it to perform spells that focus on love, harmony, and abundance. The altar serves as a powerful conduit for your magical work, amplifying your intentions and anchoring them in the physical world.

Spell 1: Thanksgiving Love and Harmony Ritual

This ritual is designed to invite love and harmony into your relationships, both with family and friends. It is perfect for enhancing the energy of Thanksgiving gatherings, ensuring that the bonds between loved ones grow stronger and more peaceful.

Ingredients:

- Two pink candles (for love and harmony)
- A rose quartz crystal (for love and emotional healing)
- A small dish of salt (for protection and grounding)
- A piece of paper and a pen

Instructions:

1. **Light the Candles:** Begin by lighting the two pink candles on your altar, symbolizing love and harmony between yourself and others.

2. **Write Down Your Intentions:** On the piece of paper, write down the names of family members or friends with whom you would like to strengthen your bond. Next to each name, write a short affirmation, such as, *"I am grateful for the love and peace we share."*

3. **Charge the Rose Quartz:** Hold the rose quartz in your hands and focus on your desire to cultivate love and harmony. Visualize a soft pink light surrounding the crystal and growing larger, filling the entire room. Say:

"With this rose quartz, I call forth love,
Bringing peace and harmony from above.
May our bonds be strong and true,
Filled with love in all we do."

1. **Bless the Names:** Place the paper with the names on your altar, near the candles. Sprinkle a pinch of salt over the paper to protect and ground the relationships. Say:

"Salt of the Earth, pure and strong,
Protect these bonds as we move along.
May love and harmony always remain,
And may peace be ours again and again."

1. **Meditate on Love and Peace:** Take a few moments to meditate on the energy of love and harmony flowing into your relationships. Visualize any tension or misunderstandings dissolving into peace. Allow the candles to burn for at least 15-20 minutes, focusing on the warmth of love filling the space.
2. **Close the Ritual:** When you feel ready, extinguish the candles. Keep the rose quartz on your altar as a symbol of love and harmony, and revisit this ritual anytime you wish to strengthen your relationships.

This Thanksgiving Love and Harmony Ritual helps create a peaceful and loving atmosphere during family gatherings and strengthens emotional connections.

Spell 2: Abundance and Prosperity Thanksgiving Spell

This spell focuses on attracting abundance and financial prosperity into your life, using the energy of Thanksgiving to amplify your intentions for wealth and success.

Ingredients:

- A green candle (for abundance)
- A citrine crystal (for prosperity and wealth)
- A pinch of cinnamon (for success)
- A small bowl of coins or money (for financial energy)
- A piece of paper and a pen

Instructions:

1. **Light the Green Candle:** Begin by lighting the green candle on your altar, symbolizing growth, wealth, and abundance. Place the bowl of coins or money in front of the candle as a focal point for financial prosperity.
2. **Write Your Intention:** On the piece of paper, write down your financial or career goals. Be specific about the type of abundance you wish to attract, whether it's a new job, a raise, or financial stability. As you write, focus on the feeling of already having achieved these goals.
3. **Charge the Citrine Crystal:** Hold the citrine in your hands and visualize a bright golden light surrounding it. Imagine this light expanding, filling your life with prosperity and success. Say:

"Citrine of gold, bright and clear,
Bring me abundance, wealth, and cheer.
With this spell, I manifest,
Prosperity, growth, and all the rest."

1. **Bless the Coins:** Sprinkle a pinch of cinnamon over the bowl of coins or money, symbolizing success and the flow of financial energy. Place the citrine in the bowl as a conduit for prosperity. Say:

"Cinnamon of wealth, success, and gain,
Let abundance flow like gentle rain.
As I give thanks for all I receive,
May more prosperity be achieved."

1. **Visualize Your Abundance:** Close your eyes and visualize wealth and prosperity flowing into your life. Imagine doors opening, opportunities coming your way, and financial success growing in your life. Hold this vision for a few minutes, focusing on gratitude for what you already have and what is coming.
2. **Close the Ritual:** Allow the candle to burn for at least 15-20 minutes, letting the energy of abundance fill the space. When you are ready, extinguish the candle and keep the bowl of coins on your altar as a symbol of the wealth you are attracting.

This Abundance and Prosperity Thanksgiving Spell helps manifest financial growth and success, aligning your energy with the flow of abundance.

Spell 3: Gratitude Altar Blessing

This simple yet powerful spell is designed to express gratitude for the blessings in your life, amplifying the energy of Thanksgiving. By giving thanks and offering your gratitude to the universe, you open yourself to receiving even more abundance and joy.

Ingredients:

- A white candle (for gratitude and purity)
- A small bowl of water (for renewal and blessings)
- A pinch of dried rosemary (for remembrance)
- A piece of paper and a pen

Instructions:

1. **Light the White Candle:** Begin by lighting the white candle on your altar to symbolize purity, gratitude, and the blessings you are giving thanks for.
2. **Write Your Gratitude List:** On the piece of paper, write down five things you are grateful for. These can be people, experiences, opportunities, or material blessings. As you write, focus on the feeling of gratitude filling your heart.
3. **Bless the Water:** Hold the small bowl of water in your hands and visualize it glowing with a bright light. Say:

"Water of life, pure and clear,
I give thanks for the blessings near.

As I honor all I've received,
May more abundance be achieved."

1. **Sprinkle the Rosemary:** Sprinkle a pinch of dried rosemary into the water, symbolizing remembrance and gratitude for the past. Say:

"Rosemary for the blessings of old,
I give thanks for the stories told.
May my gratitude continue to grow,
And may abundance forever flow."

1. **Meditate on Gratitude:** Take a few moments to meditate on the blessings in your life. Visualize each one growing stronger and filling your life with joy. Imagine new opportunities and blessings flowing into your life as a result of your gratitude.
2. **Close the Ritual:** Allow the candle to burn for a few minutes while you reflect on your gratitude. When you are ready, extinguish the candle and pour the water into the earth or at the base of a tree as an offering of thanks to nature.

This Gratitude Altar Blessing helps you express thanks for the blessings in your life, amplifying the energy of gratitude and inviting even more abundance.

Daily Thanksgiving Altar Practice

In addition to performing specific spells, you can incorporate daily practices into your Thanksgiving altar magic. This helps maintain the energy of gratitude, love, and abundance throughout the season and beyond.

Daily Thanksgiving Altar Practice

This simple daily practice allows you to reconnect with the energy of gratitude and abundance each day, using your Thanksgiving altar as a focal point for reflection and intention-setting.

Ingredients:

- A small white or green candle (for gratitude and abundance)
- A piece of clear quartz or rose quartz (for clarity and love)
- A quiet space for reflection

Instructions:

1. **Light the Candle:** Each morning or evening, light the white or green candle on your altar, symbolizing the energy of gratitude and abundance.
2. **Hold the Crystal:** Hold the clear quartz or rose quartz in your hands and take a few deep breaths. Focus on the energy of gratitude filling your heart.
3. **Reflect on Your Blessings:** Take a few moments to reflect on one or two things you are grateful for that day. Say aloud or in your mind:

"I give thanks for the blessings I've known,
For the love, the joy, the seeds I've sown.

May gratitude guide my way,
And bring more blessings each day."

1. **Close the Practice:** Let the candle burn for a few minutes while you meditate on gratitude. When you feel ready, extinguish the candle and carry the energy of thankfulness with you throughout the day.

This Daily Thanksgiving Altar Practice helps maintain a positive and grateful mindset, ensuring that the energy of abundance and love flows consistently into your life.

Conclusion

In this chapter, we have explored the power of creating and using a Thanksgiving altar to focus your magical energy on love, harmony, and abundance. By setting up a sacred space filled with items that represent your intentions, you create a powerful environment for spells and rituals that enhance your life during the Thanksgiving season and beyond.

Whether you are performing specific spells for love and prosperity or simply meditating on gratitude at your altar, this practice deepens your connection to the energies of the Earth, the divine, and your own intentions. Through Thanksgiving altar magic, you align yourself with the flow of abundance, strengthen your relationships, and invite blessings into your life with an open and thankful heart.

Chapter 16: Wishing Cornucopia

The cornucopia, also known as the "Horn of Plenty," is a symbol of abundance, prosperity, and the bounty of the harvest. During Thanksgiving, it represents the blessings we have received throughout the year and the gratitude we offer for those gifts. However, the cornucopia can also be a magical tool for manifesting future blessings. By creating a Wishing Cornucopia, you infuse it with enchanted objects that symbolize your desires, wishes, and goals for the upcoming year. This magical practice is a powerful way to blend the energies of gratitude and manifestation, ensuring that the blessings continue to flow into your life.

In this chapter, we will explore the magical art of creating a Wishing Cornucopia, filling it with enchanted objects that represent your dreams, goals, and aspirations. You'll learn how to charge the cornucopia with your intentions, align it with the energies of abundance, and use it as a focal point for manifesting your wishes over the next year.

The Symbolism of the Cornucopia

The cornucopia has ancient origins, often depicted as a curved horn overflowing with fruits, grains, flowers, and other symbols of plenty. In Greek mythology, it was associated with the horn of Amalthea, the goat who nursed Zeus and provided endless nourishment. The cornucopia became a symbol of abundance, fertility, and sustenance, representing an endless flow of blessings.

In magical terms, the cornucopia is a vessel that can hold your intentions for prosperity, growth, and fulfillment. When filled with enchanted objects that symbolize your wishes, it becomes a tool for manifestation, drawing your desires into reality. By creating a Wishing Cornucopia during Thanksgiving, you honor the blessings of the past year while actively working to manifest new opportunities and abundance for the future.

Creating Your Wishing Cornucopia

The Wishing Cornucopia is a physical representation of your goals, dreams, and desires for the upcoming year. Each object you place inside is enchanted with a specific wish, symbolizing what you want to attract into your life. These wishes can be related to love, career, health, finances, or any area where you seek growth and abundance.

Materials for Your Wishing Cornucopia:

- A cornucopia basket or horn (available at craft stores or online)
- A collection of objects representing your wishes (such as crystals, herbs, fruits, coins, charms, or written intentions)
- Green, gold, or white ribbon (for prosperity and blessings)
- Candles (green for abundance, white for clarity, and gold for success)
- A small dish of water (for purification)
- Incense or sage (for cleansing)
- Optional: natural elements like autumn leaves, pine cones, and acorns (to represent the season and Earth's abundance)

Once you have gathered your materials, follow these steps to create and charge your Wishing Cornucopia:

Step-by-Step Guide to Creating a Wishing Cornucopia

1. **Cleansing the Cornucopia:** Begin by cleansing the cornucopia basket or horn with sage or incense to remove any stagnant or negative energy. As you do this, visualize the cornucopia glowing with a soft light, open to receiving the blessings of the universe. Say:

"I cleanse this vessel with love and light,
May it hold my dreams so bright.

With gratitude, I prepare this space,
To manifest abundance, joy, and grace."

1. **Choosing Your Objects:** Select objects that symbolize your wishes and goals for the upcoming year. These can be small items like crystals, herbs, charms, coins, or even written intentions on slips of paper. Each object should be chosen with a specific wish in mind. For example:
   - **Citrine or coins** for financial prosperity
   - **Rose quartz** for love and relationships
   - **Amethyst** for spiritual growth and clarity
   - **Small fruits or grains** for health and vitality
   - **A key charm** for new opportunities or unlocking doors
   - **A feather** for travel or freedom
2. **Charging the Objects:** Before placing each object into the cornucopia, hold it in your hands and focus on the wish or intention it represents. Visualize the object glowing with energy, charged with your desire. As you hold the object, say aloud or in your mind:

"With this [name the object], I call forth [state your wish],
May abundance flow and blessings be rich.
As this object rests in the horn,
May my dreams manifest, newly born."

1. **Placing the Objects in the Cornucopia:** Once each object is charged with your intention, place it inside the cornucopia. Arrange the items thoughtfully, allowing them to layer and interweave, symbolizing how your wishes will come together in the coming year.
2. **Wrapping the Cornucopia with Ribbon:** After filling the cornucopia with your enchanted objects, wrap green, gold, or white ribbon around the outside of the basket or horn. These colors

represent prosperity, success, and clarity. As you wrap the ribbon, say:

"Ribbon of gold, green, and white,
Wrap my dreams in abundant light.
As this cornucopia holds my desire,
May my wishes come to life and inspire."

1. **Charging the Cornucopia with Candlelight:** Place green, gold, and white candles around the cornucopia. Light the candles to activate the energy of your wishes. As the candles burn, focus on the feeling of gratitude for the blessings you've received and the wishes you are manifesting. Say:

"With fire and flame, I now ignite,
My wishes carried on beams of light.
May love, abundance, and joy draw near,
And may these blessings grow this year."

1. **Purifying with Water:** Dip your fingers into the dish of water and sprinkle a few drops over the cornucopia. Water represents the flow of energy and the cleansing of any obstacles that might prevent your wishes from manifesting. As you sprinkle the water, say:

"Water of life, pure and true,
Clear the way for dreams anew.
As this cornucopia holds my will,
May the universe my wishes fulfill."

1. **Final Meditation:** Take a few moments to meditate in front of the cornucopia. Visualize each of your wishes coming true, one by one. See yourself living the life you desire, filled with love,

abundance, and success. Hold this vision as long as you feel comfortable, allowing the energy of the cornucopia to amplify your intentions.

Spell 1: Cornucopia of Abundance

This spell focuses on filling your Wishing Cornucopia with intentions for financial prosperity and material abundance. By enchanting objects that represent wealth and success, you align your energy with the flow of abundance for the upcoming year.

Ingredients:

- A small handful of coins or gold-colored charms
- A piece of citrine (for prosperity)
- A bay leaf (for wishes and success)
- A green candle (for growth and wealth)
- Cinnamon (for abundance)
- Your Wishing Cornucopia

Instructions:

1. **Light the Candle:** Begin by lighting the green candle, symbolizing the energy of growth, prosperity, and abundance.
2. **Charge the Coins:** Hold the handful of coins or gold charms in your hands and focus on your desire for financial prosperity. Visualize money and wealth flowing into your life easily and effortlessly. Say:

"Coins of gold and wealth so bright,
Bring abundance into my sight.
May prosperity flow with ease and grace,
Filling my life, a steady pace."

1. **Bless the Citrine:** Hold the citrine and charge it with your intention for financial success. Visualize opportunities coming your

way, new streams of income opening up, and financial security growing. Say:

"Citrine of gold, bright and true,
I call abundance, fresh and new.
With this stone, my wealth will grow,
As the seeds of prosperity I sow."

1. **Write Your Wish on the Bay Leaf:** Take the bay leaf and write a specific financial goal or wish on it, such as "I attract financial security" or "I succeed in my career." Place the bay leaf in the cornucopia with the coins and citrine.
2. **Sprinkle Cinnamon:** Sprinkle a pinch of cinnamon over the items in the cornucopia to symbolize success and the flow of wealth. As you do, say:

"Cinnamon for success and gain,
Let abundance flow like gentle rain.
With this cornucopia full of grace,
Prosperity flows into my space."

1. **Close the Spell:** Allow the green candle to burn for at least 20 minutes, focusing on the energy of abundance filling your life. When you feel ready, extinguish the candle and place the cornucopia in a prominent place where it can continue to attract prosperity throughout the year.

This Cornucopia of Abundance spell will help you manifest financial success and align with the flow of wealth in the year to come.

Spell 2: Cornucopia of Love and Harmony

This spell is designed to fill your Wishing Cornucopia with the energy of love, emotional healing, and harmonious relationships. By enchanting objects that represent love and connection, you invite these qualities into your life for the upcoming year.

Ingredients:

- A rose quartz crystal (for love and emotional healing)
- A small heart charm or pink ribbon (for romantic love)
- A lavender sprig or dried rose petals (for peace and harmony)
- A pink candle (for love and kindness)
- Honey or sugar (for sweetness and affection)
- Your Wishing Cornucopia

Instructions:

1. **Light the Pink Candle:** Begin by lighting the pink candle to invoke the energy of love, peace, and emotional healing.
2. **Charge the Rose Quartz:** Hold the rose quartz in your hands and focus on your desire for love, whether it's self-love, romantic love, or harmonious relationships with others. Visualize your heart opening to receive love and give love freely. Say:

"Rose quartz of love, gentle and true,
Open my heart to love anew.
May love and kindness fill my days,
Bringing peace and joy in endless ways."

1. **Enchant the Heart Charm:** Hold the heart charm or pink ribbon and charge it with your intention for romantic love or deep emotional connection. Visualize yourself in a loving, supportive relationship, or see your existing relationships deepening. Say:

"Heart of love, soft and bright,
Bring affection into my sight.
May love grow strong and always true,
And may harmony be renewed."

1. **Add Lavender or Rose Petals:** Place the lavender sprig or dried rose petals into the cornucopia to symbolize peace, harmony, and emotional healing. Say:

"Lavender (or rose) for peace and calm,
Bring love's soothing, healing balm.
With harmony and joy, let love expand,
Flowing freely through heart and hand."

1. **Sprinkle Honey or Sugar:** Sprinkle a small amount of honey or sugar into the cornucopia to represent sweetness, kindness, and affection in your relationships. As you do, say:

"Honey sweet, love so pure,
Bring affection that will endure.
May kindness flow in all I see,
And love fill my heart, endlessly."

1. **Close the Spell:** Allow the pink candle to burn for at least 15-20 minutes, focusing on the energy of love and harmony growing in your life. When you feel ready, extinguish the candle and place the cornucopia in a space where it can radiate love throughout the year.

This Cornucopia of Love and Harmony spell helps you manifest deeper connections, emotional healing, and harmonious relationships in the year to come.

Spell 3: Cornucopia of Health and Vitality

This spell focuses on filling your Wishing Cornucopia with the energy of health, vitality, and physical well-being. By enchanting objects that represent strength and vitality, you invite these qualities into your life, ensuring good health for the upcoming year.

Ingredients:

- A green or gold candle (for health and vitality)
- A small apple or pomegranate (for health and longevity)
- A sprig of rosemary or sage (for healing and protection)
- A piece of carnelian or bloodstone (for physical strength and energy)
- Your Wishing Cornucopia

Instructions:

1. **Light the Candle:** Begin by lighting the green or gold candle to symbolize health, vitality, and physical well-being.
2. **Bless the Apple or Pomegranate:** Hold the apple or pomegranate in your hands and focus on your desire for health and longevity. Visualize yourself in vibrant health, with strong energy and resilience. Say:

"Fruit of health, strong and true,
I call forth vitality, fresh and new.
May my body be strong and filled with light,
With energy and health shining bright."

1. **Enchant the Rosemary or Sage:** Hold the sprig of rosemary or sage and charge it with healing energy. Visualize any illnesses or weaknesses being healed and replaced with strength and vitality. Say:

"Herb of healing, pure and wise,
Bring me health in all I realize.
Protect my body, mind, and soul,
And make my spirit strong and whole."

1. **Charge the Carnelian or Bloodstone:** Hold the piece of carnelian or bloodstone and focus on your intention to boost your physical energy and strength. Visualize yourself filled with vitality, able to take on any challenges with ease. Say:

"Stone of strength, bold and bright,
Fill me with energy, day and night.
May vitality flow through all I do,
And keep my body strong and true."

1. **Place the Items in the Cornucopia:** Place the apple or pomegranate, the sprig of rosemary or sage, and the stone into the cornucopia, visualizing the energy of health and vitality filling the vessel. Say:

"With this cornucopia of health and light,
I call forth strength, day and night.
May vitality grow in body and mind,
And health and wellness may I find."

1. **Close the Spell:** Allow the candle to burn for 20 minutes, focusing on the energy of health and strength flowing into your life. When you feel ready, extinguish the candle and place the cornucopia where it can continue to radiate vitality and well-being.

This Cornucopia of Health and Vitality spell helps you maintain physical strength and well-being throughout the year, ensuring that your body remains strong and energized.

Daily Cornucopia Ritual for Manifestation

In addition to specific spells, you can incorporate a daily practice of working with your Wishing Cornucopia to keep your intentions active and manifest your wishes throughout the year.

Daily Cornucopia Ritual for Manifestation

This simple daily ritual helps you stay connected to the energy of your Wishing Cornucopia, keeping your intentions strong and ensuring that your wishes are actively manifesting.

Ingredients:

- A white or gold candle (for clarity and success)
- Your Wishing Cornucopia
- A quiet space for reflection

Instructions:

1. **Light the Candle:** Each morning or evening, light the white or gold candle near your Wishing Cornucopia, symbolizing clarity and the active manifestation of your desires.
2. **Focus on Your Intentions:** Take a few moments to look at the objects inside your cornucopia. Reflect on the wishes they represent and visualize those wishes coming true in your life. Say:

"Cornucopia of dreams and light,
Bring my wishes into sight.
May abundance flow and blessings grow,
As my intentions take root and glow."

1. **Hold the Energy:** Spend a few minutes meditating on your desires, focusing on how it will feel to have them manifest. Allow

yourself to feel the excitement, joy, and gratitude for these blessings.

2. **Close the Ritual:** Let the candle burn for a few minutes while you focus on the energy of manifestation. When you are ready, extinguish the candle and carry the energy of your intentions with you throughout the day.

By performing this daily ritual, you keep the energy of your Wishing Cornucopia active and ensure that your wishes are consistently attracting the energy they need to manifest.

Conclusion

In this chapter, we have explored the creation and use of a Wishing Cornucopia as a powerful magical tool for manifesting your desires. By filling the cornucopia with enchanted objects that represent your wishes for the upcoming year, you align your energy with the flow of abundance, love, health, and prosperity. Whether you are focusing on financial success, emotional healing, or physical vitality, the Wishing Cornucopia serves as a vessel for your dreams, helping you manifest your goals and maintain a connection to the magic of the season.

Through daily rituals and intentional spellwork, your Wishing Cornucopia becomes a source of continuous blessings, ensuring that the energy of Thanksgiving extends far beyond the holiday and into every area of your life.

Chapter 17: Gratitude Tokens

Gratitude is a powerful force that can transform your life by attracting positive energy, blessings, and opportunities. Crafting Gratitude Tokens—talismans and charms that carry the energy of gratitude and good fortune—allows you to harness this energy and carry it with you wherever you go. These tokens act as physical representations of your thankfulness, constantly reminding you of the blessings in your life while also helping to attract more abundance, love, and success.

In this chapter, we will explore how to create personalized Gratitude Tokens, each one infused with magical intent and gratitude. You'll learn the significance of these tokens, the materials you can use, and how to charge them with your intentions. Whether you carry these charms with you, gift them to loved ones, or place them in significant areas of your home or workspace, Gratitude Tokens will serve as conduits of positive energy and fortune.

The Power of Gratitude Tokens

Gratitude Tokens are magical objects created to amplify the energy of gratitude, which in turn attracts more blessings and good fortune into your life. These tokens act as personal talismans, each one charged with a specific intention of thankfulness. Whether crafted from natural elements, crystals, or symbolic charms, these tokens serve as reminders to focus on the positive aspects of your life.

When you actively engage in gratitude, you align your mind and spirit with abundance, positivity, and contentment. Gratitude Tokens help maintain this mindset by giving you a tangible object to hold or carry, reinforcing your focus on the blessings you've received and those yet to come. They are also powerful gifts, as they transfer the energy of gratitude and good fortune to others, helping to spread positivity.

Choosing Materials for Your Gratitude Tokens

The materials you choose for your Gratitude Tokens are significant because they each carry their own magical properties. By selecting materials that resonate with your intentions, you enhance the power of your tokens. You can create simple tokens from natural items, like stones or leaves, or craft more elaborate talismans from crystals, metals, and symbolic charms.

Here are some common materials you can use to craft Gratitude Tokens and their associated meanings:

- **Crystals:** Crystals are excellent for gratitude tokens because they naturally amplify energy. Some of the best crystals for gratitude include:
    - **Citrine:** For abundance, joy, and financial blessings.
    - **Rose Quartz:** For love, emotional healing, and kindness.
    - **Clear Quartz:** For clarity and amplification of your intentions.
    - **Amethyst:** For spiritual growth, intuition, and inner peace.
- **Coins or Charms:** Coins can symbolize wealth and prosperity, while charms with symbolic shapes (like hearts, keys, or leaves) can represent specific wishes or blessings.
- **Natural Elements:** Leaves, acorns, pine cones, or small stones can be enchanted to carry the energy of the Earth and nature's abundance.
- **Herbs:** Dried herbs like rosemary (for remembrance), lavender (for peace), or cinnamon (for success) can be added to your tokens for extra magical potency.
- **Personal Items:** Items that hold personal significance, such as family heirlooms, jewelry, or small keepsakes, can be charged with gratitude to create powerful talismans.

Crafting Your Gratitude Tokens

Creating Gratitude Tokens is an intuitive and personal process. Each token should be crafted with a clear intention, focusing on the energy of gratitude and the specific blessings or goals you wish to attract. Below is a step-by-step guide to crafting a variety of tokens, from simple nature charms to crystal-empowered talismans.

Step-by-Step Guide to Crafting Gratitude Tokens

1. **Set Your Intention:** Before you begin crafting, take a few moments to focus on what you are grateful for and what you wish to attract. This could be love, financial prosperity, personal growth, or simply more blessings in general. As you reflect, hold the materials for your token and visualize the energy of gratitude filling them.

2. **Choose Your Materials:** Based on your intention, select the materials that resonate with the type of energy you want to carry in your Gratitude Token. For example, if you want to attract more love, you might choose a rose quartz crystal and a heart-shaped charm. For financial success, you could use a citrine stone and a gold coin.

3. **Cleanse Your Materials:** Before crafting your tokens, it's important to cleanse your materials of any unwanted or stagnant energy. You can do this by passing the items through sage or incense smoke, placing them in a bowl of salt, or holding them under running water (if the materials are water-safe). As you cleanse the materials, say:

"I cleanse this token, pure and bright,
Removing all shadows, darkness, and blight.
May this token now be free,
Filled with gratitude and light for me."

1. **Assemble Your Token:** Once your materials are cleansed, begin crafting your token. This could involve tying a ribbon around a crystal, creating a small charm bracelet, or simply placing an enchanted object inside a pouch to carry with you. As you assemble the token, focus on your intention and gratitude. Visualize the token glowing with a warm, golden light.

2. **Enchant the Token:** Hold the completed token in your hands and charge it with your gratitude and intention. Imagine your feelings of thankfulness flowing into the object, filling it with positive energy and light. Say:

"With love and gratitude, I now create,
A token of blessings, good fortune, and fate.
May this charm carry joy and peace,
And may the flow of abundance never cease."

1. **Seal the Energy:** To seal the energy of your token, you can pass it through the smoke of incense, sprinkle it with salt, or hold it in your hands while reciting a final blessing. Say:

"I seal this charm with gratitude pure,
For blessings abundant and good fortune sure.
May its magic grow day by day,
Bringing joy and love along my way."

1. **Use or Gift the Token:** Now that your Gratitude Token is complete, you can carry it with you, place it in a special location, or gift it to someone you love. Each time you hold or look at the token, allow it to remind you of the gratitude you feel and the blessings that are flowing into your life.

Types of Gratitude Tokens and Their Uses

Gratitude Tokens can take many forms, each serving a different purpose depending on the materials used and the intentions set during their creation. Below are examples of different types of Gratitude Tokens and how to use them in your everyday life.

1. Crystal Gratitude Token

Crystals are natural amplifiers of energy, making them ideal for Gratitude Tokens. A crystal token can help you stay connected to the energy of gratitude, attract abundance, or manifest love and joy in your life.

How to Make a Crystal Gratitude Token:

- Select a crystal that aligns with your intention (such as citrine for abundance, rose quartz for love, or amethyst for peace).
- Cleanse the crystal, then hold it in your hands and charge it with your gratitude. Focus on the specific blessings you are grateful for and the desires you wish to manifest.
- Carry the crystal with you in your pocket or wear it as a piece of jewelry to keep its energy close to you throughout the day.

Suggested Crystals for Gratitude Tokens:

- **Citrine:** For abundance, prosperity, and success.
- **Rose Quartz:** For love, kindness, and emotional healing.
- **Clear Quartz:** For clarity and amplifying intentions.
- **Amethyst:** For spiritual growth, peace, and intuition.

2. Nature Charm Token

A Nature Charm Token is crafted from natural elements like leaves, acorns, pine cones, or stones. These tokens connect you with the energy of the Earth and the natural flow of abundance.

How to Make a Nature Charm Token:

- Gather natural materials that resonate with the energy of gratitude and abundance, such as a fallen leaf (for release and renewal), an acorn (for potential and growth), or a stone (for grounding and stability).
- Cleanse the natural items by holding them under running water or passing them through incense smoke.
- Tie the items together with a ribbon, or place them in a small pouch to carry with you.
- Charge the charm by holding it and focusing on your gratitude for the blessings in your life. Say:

"Token of nature, strong and true,
I carry the blessings of Earth with you.
May abundance flow and love increase,
Bringing joy, prosperity, and peace."

Place your Nature Charm Token on your altar, carry it with you, or keep it in your workspace to stay grounded and connected to the energy of the Earth.

3. Gratitude Coin or Charm Token

Coins and charms are powerful symbols of wealth, luck, and protection. Creating a Gratitude Token from a coin or charm can help attract financial success, good fortune, and overall abundance.

How to Make a Gratitude Coin or Charm Token:

- Choose a coin or charm that represents wealth, prosperity, or protection. This could be an old coin, a lucky charm, or a symbolic piece of jewelry.
- Cleanse the coin or charm with sage, incense, or water to remove any previous energies.

- Hold the coin in your hands and charge it with gratitude for the financial and material blessings in your life. Visualize abundance flowing into your life. Say:

"Coin of fortune, bright and true,
I give thanks for all I accrue.
May abundance flow like a steady stream,
Filling my life with fortune's gleam."

- Carry the coin or charm in your wallet or purse, place it on your altar, or gift it to someone as a token of good fortune.

4. Gratitude Token for Others: A Gift of Blessings

Gratitude Tokens can also be gifted to loved ones as a way of sharing the energy of gratitude and good fortune. By giving a personalized token to someone you care about, you transfer the positive energy of your intention, creating a meaningful and magical gift.

How to Make a Gratitude Token Gift:

- Select a crystal, charm, or natural item that represents the energy you want to share with your loved one. This could be a rose quartz for love, a citrine for abundance, or a feather for freedom and lightness.
- Cleanse and charge the item with the energy of gratitude, focusing on your thankfulness for the person receiving the gift.
- Wrap the token in a small bag or box, and include a note explaining the intention behind the gift.
- When giving the token, say something like:

"I gift this token with love and light,
A symbol of gratitude pure and bright.
May it bring you joy and grace,
And bless your life in every place."

By gifting a Gratitude Token, you not only share your positive energy with someone else but also strengthen your connection to gratitude and the flow of blessings in your life.

Daily Gratitude Token Practice

Once you have created your Gratitude Tokens, it's important to use them regularly to keep the energy of gratitude active in your life. Here is a simple daily practice to help you stay connected to your tokens and the positive energy they carry.

Daily Gratitude Token Practice

Ingredients:

- Your Gratitude Token
- A small candle (white for purity, green for abundance, or pink for love)
- A quiet space for reflection

Instructions:

1. **Light the Candle:** Each morning or evening, light the candle and hold your Gratitude Token in your hands. Focus on the feeling of gratitude, allowing yourself to reflect on the blessings in your life.

2. **Set Your Intention for the Day:** As you hold the token, set a specific intention for the day. This could be something like "I am open to receiving love and kindness today" or "I attract abundance and success in all I do."

3. **Affirm Your Gratitude:** Speak a simple gratitude affirmation, such as:

"I carry this token of gratitude near,
A reminder of blessings that I hold dear.
May good fortune and joy flow through,
And may abundance be my due."

1. **Close the Practice:** Allow the candle to burn for a few minutes while you meditate on your gratitude. When you are ready, extinguish the candle and carry the energy of your Gratitude Token with you throughout the day.

This daily practice helps keep the energy of gratitude and good fortune active in your life, ensuring that the positive energy of your Gratitude Tokens continues to grow and manifest blessings.

Conclusion

Gratitude Tokens are powerful magical tools that allow you to carry the energy of gratitude and good fortune with you wherever you go. By crafting talismans and charms infused with positive intentions, you align yourself with the flow of abundance, love, and success. Whether you use crystals, coins, nature charms, or personalized tokens, these objects serve as reminders of the blessings in your life and the limitless potential for new opportunities.

By engaging in the process of creating, charging, and using your Gratitude Tokens, you reinforce the powerful connection between gratitude and manifestation. These tokens become conduits for attracting more joy, prosperity, and harmony, helping you maintain a mindset of thankfulness and abundance in everything you do.

Chapter 18: Circle of Love

The Thanksgiving season is a time for gathering with loved ones, celebrating the bonds of family and friendship, and expressing gratitude for the connections that enrich our lives. One of the most powerful ways to strengthen these bonds is through group rituals and spells that focus on love, harmony, and unity. When performed in a group setting, magical rituals amplify the energy of intention, creating a powerful circle of love that can deepen emotional connections and bring a sense of togetherness to those involved.

In this chapter, we will explore a variety of group rituals and spells that can be performed with family or friends to cultivate love, harmony, and mutual understanding. These rituals are designed to strengthen relationships, heal emotional wounds, and create a sacred space for expressing gratitude and affection. Whether you're gathering around a dinner table, enjoying an evening together, or hosting a special family ritual, these spells will help foster love and unity.

The Power of Group Rituals

Group rituals are deeply transformative because they harness the collective energy and intentions of everyone involved. When a group of people comes together with a shared focus—whether it's love, gratitude, or harmony—their combined energy is much more powerful than individual efforts. This amplified energy creates a "circle of love," where participants can experience deeper emotional connections, open lines of communication, and heal any existing tensions within relationships.

These rituals are perfect for family gatherings during Thanksgiving or any other time when you wish to foster love, unity, and mutual support. They can be performed with both family and friends, bringing a sense of sacredness to the time you spend together and helping everyone feel more connected and loved.

Preparing for a Group Ritual: Setting the Space

Before performing any group ritual, it's important to create a sacred space where the energy can flow freely and where everyone feels safe and comfortable. Preparing the space enhances the power of the ritual and helps participants focus on their intentions.

Step-by-Step Guide to Preparing the Space:

1. **Cleanse the Space:** Start by cleansing the space where the ritual will take place. This can be done with sage, incense, or any purifying method you prefer. Walk around the room or space, allowing the smoke to clear away any negative or stagnant energy. As you cleanse, say:

"I cleanse this space with light and love,
Removing all that does not serve.
May only love and peace reside,
As we gather here, side by side."

1. **Arrange Seating in a Circle:** Set up the seating in a circle, which symbolizes unity, equality, and the flow of energy between all participants. The circle allows everyone to be seen and heard, and it creates a sense of connection. If seating isn't possible, participants can stand in a circle.

2. **Create a Central Altar or Focal Point:** In the center of the circle, create a small altar or focal point where you can place symbols of love and unity. This might include:
   - A candle (pink for love, white for unity, or gold for harmony)
   - Crystals (such as rose quartz for love, amethyst for peace, or clear quartz for amplifying intentions)
   - Flowers (roses or other flowers that symbolize love and friendship)

    ◦ A bowl of water (for cleansing and emotional healing)

3. **Invite Participation:** Before the ritual begins, invite everyone to contribute an item to the altar that represents their personal intention for the ritual. This could be a small object, a flower, or even a written affirmation. This act of contribution helps everyone feel connected and invested in the ritual.

Once the space is prepared, the group is ready to begin the ritual. Below are a variety of spells and group rituals that can be performed to deepen connections, strengthen love, and create a powerful sense of unity.

Ritual 1: The Circle of Gratitude

This ritual is designed to help participants express their gratitude for one another, deepening bonds and fostering appreciation. It is perfect for family gatherings, as it encourages open communication and allows each person to be seen and acknowledged for their contributions.

Ingredients:

- A pink or white candle (for love and unity)
- A small bowl of salt (for protection and grounding)
- A crystal or symbolic item for each participant (such as rose quartz or a heart charm)
- A piece of paper and pen for each participant

Instructions:

1. **Light the Candle:** Begin by lighting the pink or white candle in the center of the circle, symbolizing the love and unity shared among the participants.
2. **Pass the Salt:** Each participant takes a pinch of salt and sprinkles it into the bowl of water, symbolizing the cleansing and protection of the circle. As each person does this, they say:

"I contribute my energy to this circle of love,
Protecting it with peace from above."

1. **Express Gratitude:** Give each participant a piece of paper and a pen. Ask everyone to write down something they are grateful for about each person in the circle. These can be qualities they admire, kind actions they've witnessed, or ways in which the person has enriched their life. After everyone has written their notes, fold the papers.

2. **Sharing Gratitude:** Once the notes are written, each participant takes turns reading aloud the notes they wrote about others in the circle. This is done in a loving and positive way, focusing on affirmations, kindness, and the ways each person brings joy and value to the group.

3. **Offer a Token of Love:** As the final part of the ritual, each participant is invited to take a crystal, charm, or heart-shaped object from the altar. They can carry this token with them as a reminder of the love and appreciation shared during the ritual. As they take the token, everyone in the circle says together:

"With love and light, I honor you,
Our bond is strong, our hearts are true."

1. **Close the Ritual:** Extinguish the candle to symbolize the end of the ritual, but encourage everyone to carry the energy of gratitude with them. End with a group affirmation, such as:

"Together we stand in love and grace,
Our circle is blessed, our bonds embrace."

This Circle of Gratitude ritual creates a powerful space for expressing love and appreciation, helping to deepen relationships and foster a sense of community.

Ritual 2: The Ribbon of Connection

This ritual is designed to strengthen emotional connections between family members or friends, using a simple ribbon as a symbol of the bond that unites the group. It's perfect for healing relationships, resolving conflicts, or simply reinforcing the love that already exists.

Ingredients:

- A long ribbon (pink for love, red for strength, or gold for unity)
- A pink candle (for love)
- A small bowl of water (for healing)
- A rose quartz crystal (for love and emotional healing)

Instructions:

1. **Prepare the Ribbon:** Begin by holding the ribbon in your hands and charging it with the intention of connection, love, and healing. Visualize the ribbon glowing with pink or golden light, symbolizing the bond between all participants. Say:

"Ribbon of love, connection, and light,
Strengthen our bonds, pure and bright."

1. **Light the Candle:** Light the pink candle in the center of the circle, calling in the energy of love and healing. As the candle burns, visualize the love between each participant growing stronger and more harmonious.
2. **Tie the Ribbon Around the Circle:** The ribbon is passed around the circle, with each participant holding a part of it. As they hold the ribbon, they are encouraged to silently reflect on the love they have for each person in the group and the ways they can support one another.

3. **Speak an Affirmation of Connection:** Once everyone is holding the ribbon, each person takes turns saying an affirmation of connection and love. This could be something like:

"I honor the love we share,
Our bond is strong and will always be there."

1. **Dip the Ribbon in Water:** After the affirmations are spoken, the ribbon is dipped in the small bowl of water to symbolize emotional healing and the purification of the bond. As the ribbon touches the water, say:

"With this water, we cleanse and renew,
Our love grows strong, pure, and true."

1. **Cut the Ribbon:** Once the ribbon has been dipped, each participant cuts a small piece of the ribbon to keep as a token of the connection they share with the group. The piece can be tied around their wrist, carried in a pocket, or placed on an altar as a reminder of the bond.
2. **Close the Ritual:** Extinguish the candle to symbolize the end of the ritual, and encourage everyone to carry the energy of connection and love with them. End with a group affirmation, such as:

"Our circle is bound by love so true,
In harmony and light, we stand anew."

This Ribbon of Connection ritual is a powerful way to reinforce the emotional bonds between family and friends, creating a shared experience of love, healing, and unity.

Ritual 3: The Heart of Healing

This ritual focuses on healing emotional wounds within a group, whether between family members or friends. It's particularly useful for resolving conflicts, clearing misunderstandings, and fostering forgiveness. By creating a space for open communication and mutual understanding, this ritual helps participants release past hurts and move forward in love.

Ingredients:

- A heart-shaped object or charm (for each participant)
- A white or blue candle (for peace and healing)
- A bowl of water (for cleansing)
- A small dish of salt (for protection)
- Lavender or rose petals (for love and peace)

Instructions:

1. **Light the Candle:** Begin by lighting the white or blue candle to invite peace and healing into the circle. As the candle burns, visualize a soft, calming light filling the space, creating an atmosphere of safety and understanding.

2. **Pass the Salt:** Each participant takes a pinch of salt and sprinkles it into the bowl of water, symbolizing the protection and cleansing of the emotional wounds being addressed. As each person does this, they say:

"With this salt, I cleanse our bond,
Protecting our love, peaceful and strong."

1. **Share Feelings Openly:** Each participant is given the opportunity to speak openly about any unresolved issues, misunderstandings, or emotional wounds they have experienced within the group. This part of the ritual is done with respect and kind-

ness, allowing everyone to express their feelings without judgment or interruption. Encourage participants to focus on healing and moving forward, rather than dwelling on the past.

2. **Offer Forgiveness:** After each person has spoken, invite the group to offer forgiveness and understanding. This can be done silently or verbally, with participants saying something like:

"I release all pain and misunderstanding,
In love, our hearts are expanding."

1. **Add Lavender or Rose Petals to the Water:** Each participant then adds lavender or rose petals to the bowl of water, symbolizing the love and peace they are bringing into the circle. As they add the petals, they silently focus on healing and releasing any lingering negativity.

2. **Gift the Heart-Shaped Token:** Give each participant a heart-shaped charm or object to symbolize the love and healing shared during the ritual. As they receive the token, say:

"This heart I give with love and light,
A symbol of healing, pure and bright.
May our bond be strong and whole,
Filled with love in every soul."

1. **Close the Ritual:** Extinguish the candle to symbolize the end of the ritual, and encourage everyone to carry the energy of forgiveness and healing with them. End with a group affirmation, such as:

"Together we heal, together we grow,
In love and peace, our bond will show."

This Heart of Healing ritual is a powerful way to resolve conflicts and emotional wounds within a group, creating a space for forgiveness and understanding.

Ritual 4: The Circle of Unity and Love

This is a celebratory ritual designed to create a deep sense of unity and love within a group. It's perfect for Thanksgiving gatherings, family reunions, or any time you want to emphasize the strength of your relationships and the love you share.

Ingredients:

- A gold or pink candle (for unity and love)
- A circle of rose petals or autumn leaves (to symbolize connection)
- A crystal or small charm for each participant (such as rose quartz or a heart)
- A bowl of honey or sugar (for sweetness and joy)

Instructions:

1. **Create a Circle of Petals or Leaves:** Begin by laying a circle of rose petals or autumn leaves on the floor, large enough for everyone to sit around or stand within. This circle represents the unity of the group and the beauty of the relationships within it.
2. **Light the Candle:** Light the gold or pink candle in the center of the circle, symbolizing the love and unity that binds the group together. As the candle burns, visualize the light of love flowing between all participants.
3. **Hold Hands and Affirm Unity:** Invite everyone to hold hands as a symbol of connection and unity. As you hold hands, each person takes turns speaking an affirmation of love and unity, such as:

"In this circle, we are one,
Bound by love, under the sun."
"Our hearts are connected, strong and true,
In unity and love, we stand renewed."

1. **Pass the Honey or Sugar:** Pass the bowl of honey or sugar around the circle, inviting each participant to take a small taste. This symbolizes the sweetness and joy of your relationships. As each person tastes the honey or sugar, they say:

"With this sweetness, I honor our bond,
May our love grow bright and strong."

1. **Gift the Crystal or Charm:** Each participant receives a crystal or charm from the altar as a symbol of the love and unity shared in the circle. As they receive the charm, everyone says together:

"With love and unity, our bond will grow,
In strength and joy, as we all know."

1. **Close the Ritual:** Allow the candle to burn for a few minutes longer, focusing on the unity and love within the group. When you feel ready, extinguish the candle and end with a group affirmation, such as:

"Together we stand, in love and light,
Our bond is strong, pure, and bright."

This Circle of Unity and Love ritual celebrates the strength of your relationships, creating a powerful sense of togetherness and joy.

Daily Practices for Group Love and Connection

In addition to performing these group rituals, you can incorporate daily practices that foster love, connection, and unity within your family or group of friends. These simple practices help maintain the positive energy created during group rituals and ensure that love and harmony continue to grow.

Daily Practices for Group Love and Connection:

1. **Daily Gratitude Circle:** At the end of each day, gather as a family or group and share one thing you are grateful for about one another. This helps reinforce positive feelings and creates a habit of appreciation.

2. **Affirmation Sharing:** Before parting ways for the day, take a moment to offer a positive affirmation to each person in your group. This could be as simple as "I appreciate your kindness" or "I love how you make me laugh."

3. **Unity Token Exchange:** Create small tokens of love or unity (such as crystals, charms, or notes) and exchange them with family members or friends throughout the day or week. Each time you give or receive a token, take a moment to acknowledge the connection you share.

4. **Group Meditation or Reflection:** Set aside time once a week to meditate together as a group. Focus on the energy of love, connection, and peace, allowing the positive energy to flow between you.

Conclusion

The rituals and spells in this chapter are designed to deepen the connections between family and friends, fostering love, unity, and mutual support. By creating sacred spaces for open communication, emotional healing, and shared gratitude, these group rituals help strengthen the bonds that hold us together. Whether you are resolving conflicts, celebrating your relationships, or simply reinforcing the love that exists, these practices create lasting, meaningful connections that enrich every aspect of your life.

By performing these group rituals during gatherings like Thanksgiving or whenever you want to cultivate a deeper sense of connection, you ensure that your relationships continue to grow in love, harmony, and unity.

Chapter 19: Seasonal Divination

Divination is a powerful practice for gaining insight, clarity, and guidance from the unseen forces that influence our lives. During Thanksgiving, a time of reflection, gratitude, and renewal, divination can help us explore the deeper meaning of our experiences, identify areas of growth, and prepare for the future. Seasonal divination aligns our personal insights with the energies of the harvest, gratitude, and abundance, offering profound guidance as we enter the holiday season and prepare for a new year.

In this chapter, we will explore Thanksgiving-themed divination practices using tarot, runes, and other tools. These practices will help you tap into the wisdom of the season, offering insights into your personal growth, relationships, and future opportunities. You'll also learn how to create and interpret Thanksgiving-themed tarot spreads, use runes for seasonal guidance, and work with other divination tools to connect with the energies of gratitude, harvest, and abundance.

The Significance of Seasonal Divination

Seasonal divination allows you to align your spiritual insights with the natural cycles of the year, making your readings more powerful and relevant to the energies around you. Thanksgiving is a time for reflecting on abundance, gratitude, and the harvest—both literal and metaphorical. It's an ideal season to perform divination, as the energies of completion, reflection, and renewal are particularly strong.

Divination during this time helps you focus on what you've harvested throughout the year—whether it's personal growth, relationships, career achievements, or spiritual insights. It also provides guidance on how to navigate the remaining months of the year, preparing you for a prosperous and fulfilling future.

Thanksgiving-Themed Tarot Spreads

Tarot cards are one of the most popular and effective tools for divination, offering insight into your current situation and the energies surrounding your life. Thanksgiving-themed tarot spreads are designed to help you reflect on the blessings you've received, areas where you can express more gratitude, and how to cultivate abundance moving forward.

Below are a few Thanksgiving-themed tarot spreads that can be used during the holiday season for personal reflection or group readings.

1. The Gratitude Harvest Spread

This spread focuses on the blessings you've harvested throughout the year, the lessons learned, and the areas where you can express more gratitude. It's perfect for reflecting on the past year and preparing for the abundance that lies ahead.

The Spread Layout:

```css
Copy code
[2] [5]
[1] [3] [6]
[4] [7]
```

Card Positions and Meanings:

1. **The Seed:** What you planted at the beginning of the year—a goal, desire, or intention that has grown. This card represents the root of your current circumstances.
2. **The Growth:** How this seed has grown or evolved over time. What progress have you made? What personal growth or development have you experienced?
3. **The Harvest:** The blessings you are currently receiving as a result of your efforts. What have you achieved or gained from your actions this year?

4. **The Lesson:** A key lesson you've learned over the past year. What has your journey taught you? How can you apply this lesson moving forward?

5. **The Gratitude:** Where you need to express more gratitude in your life. This card highlights areas where you may have overlooked blessings or taken things for granted.

6. **The Challenge:** Any remaining challenges or obstacles you face. What's standing in the way of your abundance or growth?

7. **The Abundance:** How you can attract more abundance into your life. This card offers guidance on cultivating future success, prosperity, and gratitude.

How to Use the Spread:

- Begin by cleansing your tarot deck and setting your intention for the reading. Focus on gratitude, abundance, and personal growth.

- As you lay out the cards, reflect on the meaning of each position and how it relates to your current life.

- Take notes on the insights you receive, especially in areas where you can express more gratitude or focus on your future abundance.

2. The Circle of Thanks Spread

This spread is designed for group readings, where participants gather to reflect on the blessings they share and the connections they've cultivated. It's perfect for family or friends during Thanksgiving gatherings and fosters a deeper sense of connection and gratitude.

The Spread Layout:

css

Copy code

```
[1]
[4] [2]
[5] [6] [3]
[7]
```

Card Positions and Meanings:

1. **The Center (Card 1):** The shared energy of the group. This card represents the collective spirit of those gathered, the energy that connects everyone together.
2. **The Blessing (Card 2):** A blessing the group has received this year. What shared success or joy can the group give thanks for?
3. **The Challenge (Card 3):** A challenge or obstacle the group has faced together. How did the group overcome this challenge, and what lessons were learned?
4. **The Individual Blessing (Cards 4-6):** Each participant draws a card to represent a personal blessing they've received this year. This can be something they are thankful for or a way they've grown.
5. **The Future Abundance (Card 7):** Guidance for the group's future. What abundance or success can the group collectively work toward in the coming months or year?

How to Use the Spread:

- Each person in the group can participate by drawing a card and sharing their insights with the others.
- Focus on creating a warm, supportive atmosphere where everyone feels comfortable expressing their gratitude and reflections.
- This spread is ideal for fostering emotional connections, celebrating shared blessings, and discussing the group's collective future.

3. The Abundance Path Spread

This spread helps you focus on how to cultivate abundance in all areas of your life—whether financial, emotional, or spiritual. It provides guidance on what's blocking your abundance and how to unlock it for the future.

The Spread Layout:

css
Copy code
[1]
[2] [3] [4]
[5]

Card Positions and Meanings:

1. **The Current State of Abundance:** This card represents your current level of abundance—whether it's financial, emotional, or spiritual. Are you feeling prosperous, or are you experiencing lack?

2. **The Block:** This card reveals what is blocking you from experiencing greater abundance. What is standing in your way—fear, limiting beliefs, external circumstances?

3. **The Opportunity:** This card highlights where you can focus your energy to attract more abundance. What opportunities are available to you right now that you may not be seeing?

4. **The Action:** What specific actions can you take to increase your abundance? This card provides practical advice for moving forward.

5. **The Future Abundance:** This card offers a glimpse of the abundance that lies ahead if you follow the guidance provided in the spread. What can you look forward to in the coming months?

How to Use the Spread:

- Focus on a specific area of your life where you wish to attract abundance—this could be finances, love, career, or spiritual growth.
- As you lay out the cards, reflect on the guidance they offer and how you can take action to remove blocks and cultivate abundance.
- Take note of any opportunities or actions suggested by the cards and make a plan to integrate them into your life.

Using Runes for Seasonal Guidance

Runes are another powerful tool for divination, offering insight through ancient symbols that carry specific meanings. During Thanksgiving, runes can help you tap into the energies of harvest, gratitude, and reflection, providing clarity on where you stand in your life and how to move forward.

Below is a simple rune reading designed for the Thanksgiving season:

The Harvest Rune Reading

This rune reading focuses on the harvest—the fruits of your labor, the lessons you've learned, and the guidance you need for the future. You can cast three to five runes, depending on the level of insight you seek.

How to Perform the Reading:

1. **Set Your Intention:** Focus on the theme of the harvest and what you wish to gain insight on. This could be your personal growth, relationships, or future opportunities.
2. **Cast the Runes:** Draw three to five runes from your rune set, placing them in a row or in a small circle.

Rune Meanings for the Harvest Reading:

- **Rune 1 (The Seed):** What you planted at the beginning of the year. This rune represents your intentions, goals, or desires that have grown over time.

- **Rune 2 (The Growth):** How your efforts have grown and evolved. This rune highlights your personal development or progress in specific areas.
- **Rune 3 (The Harvest):** The results of your efforts. What have you achieved or gained from your actions? This rune reveals your current blessings.
- **Rune 4 (The Lesson):** The key lesson you've learned from your experiences. What wisdom have you gained, and how can it guide you in the future?
- **Rune 5 (The Next Step):** Guidance for the future. This rune offers insight into what's next for you and how you can cultivate more abundance moving forward.

Interpreting the Runes:

- Reflect on how each rune's meaning connects to your personal journey this year.
- Pay attention to any runes that seem to indicate challenges or lessons you still need to address.
- Use the guidance of the final rune to plan your next steps for achieving future success.

Other Divination Tools for Thanksgiving

In addition to tarot and runes, there are several other divination tools you can use for Thanksgiving-themed insights. Here are a few options:

1. Pendulum Divination for Gratitude

A pendulum is a simple yet powerful tool for receiving yes/no answers or guidance on specific questions. During Thanksgiving, you can use your pendulum to ask questions about gratitude, blessings, and future abundance.

How to Use the Pendulum:

- Begin by holding your pendulum still and asking a question related to gratitude, such as "Am I focusing enough on the blessings in my life?" or "Is there an opportunity I need to be more grateful for?"
- Watch how the pendulum swings—clockwise for "yes" and counterclockwise for "no."
- Use the answers to reflect on where you can deepen your gratitude or take action to attract more blessings.

2. Oracle Cards for Reflection

Oracle cards provide gentle and intuitive guidance, often focusing on themes of personal growth, spiritual insights, and emotional healing. Use an oracle deck that resonates with the energy of Thanksgiving, such as a deck focused on abundance, gratitude, or harvest.

Thanksgiving-Themed Oracle Reading:

- Draw three cards from your oracle deck, asking for insight into the blessings you've received, the lessons you've learned, and the guidance you need for the future.
- Reflect on the messages of each card and how they relate to your personal journey this year.

Seasonal Divination Ritual

To make the most of your Thanksgiving-themed divination practice, you can perform a ritual that helps you align with the energies of the season and deepen your connection to the insights you receive.

Ingredients for the Ritual:

- A white or gold candle (for clarity and abundance)
- A small dish of water (for emotional clarity)
- A crystal (such as citrine for abundance or amethyst for spiritual insight)
- Your tarot deck, rune set, or oracle cards

Instructions for the Ritual:

1. **Set Your Intention:** Begin by lighting the candle and focusing on your intention for the divination session. This could be gaining clarity on a specific situation, reflecting on your blessings, or seeking guidance for the future.
2. **Cleanse Your Tools:** Hold your divination tools over the candle or pass them through the smoke of incense to cleanse them of any previous energy.
3. **Cast Your Reading:** Use one of the Thanksgiving-themed tarot spreads, rune casts, or other divination tools described earlier in the chapter.
4. **Reflect on Your Insights:** Take a few moments to meditate on the messages you've received. What insights have been revealed, and how can you apply them to your life? Write down your reflections in a journal.

5. **Close the Ritual:** Extinguish the candle and thank the universe (or your chosen spiritual guides) for the guidance you've received. Keep your divination tools in a special place, ready for future use.

Conclusion

Thanksgiving-themed divination is a beautiful way to align your spiritual practice with the energies of the season. By using tarot, runes, pendulums, and other divination tools, you can gain valuable insights into your personal growth, express gratitude for the blessings you've received, and prepare for the abundance that lies ahead. Whether you're performing these readings for yourself or sharing them with loved ones, divination helps you connect with the deeper wisdom of the universe, guiding you on your path to a prosperous and fulfilling future.

Chapter 20: Grateful Heart Spells

A grateful heart is a powerful tool for manifesting happiness, inner peace, and fulfillment. When we cultivate gratitude in our daily lives, we align ourselves with the energy of abundance and love, opening our hearts to receive more blessings. Grateful Heart Spells are designed to foster a sense of contentment, self-love, and serenity by focusing on the positive aspects of life and embracing the present moment. These daily spells help you develop a deeper connection to yourself, nurture your emotional well-being, and attract more joy into your life.

In this chapter, we will explore a series of daily spells that can be easily incorporated into your routine to cultivate gratitude, inner peace, and self-love. Whether you are looking to start your day with a positive mindset, soothe your emotions in difficult times, or enhance your sense of fulfillment, these spells will guide you toward a heart-centered approach to life.

The Power of Gratitude in Spellwork

Gratitude is more than just a feeling—it's a powerful energetic force that can transform your life. When you practice gratitude, you shift your focus from what you lack to what you already have, and this mindset of abundance attracts even more blessings. In spellwork, gratitude serves as the foundation for manifesting inner peace, contentment, and self-love. By expressing thankfulness for yourself, your experiences, and the world around you, you open your heart to receive even greater joy and fulfillment.

Grateful Heart Spells tap into this energy by helping you align your thoughts, emotions, and actions with the vibration of gratitude. These spells encourage you to honor yourself, find peace in the present moment, and cultivate a deep sense of contentment. When practiced regularly, they can shift your perspective, reduce stress and anxiety, and help you develop a more loving relationship with yourself and others.

Daily Grateful Heart Spell Practices

The following Grateful Heart Spells are simple but powerful rituals that you can incorporate into your daily routine. Each spell is designed to help you cultivate gratitude, inner peace, and self-love, transforming your mindset and energy over time. You can perform these spells individually or combine them to create a daily gratitude practice.

1. Morning Gratitude Spell for a Positive Start

This simple morning spell helps you start your day with a sense of gratitude, setting a positive tone for everything that follows. By focusing on the blessings you already have, you attract more abundance and joy throughout the day.

Ingredients:

- A white or yellow candle (for clarity and positivity)
- A small bowl of water (for emotional balance)
- A clear quartz crystal (for amplifying gratitude)

Instructions:

1. **Light the Candle:** Begin by lighting the white or yellow candle to symbolize the light of gratitude that will guide your day. As the candle burns, visualize its light filling your heart with warmth and positivity.
2. **Hold the Crystal:** Hold the clear quartz crystal in your hands and focus on the feeling of gratitude. Think of three things you are grateful for in this moment—these could be people, experiences, or simple pleasures like the sunrise or a good night's sleep.
3. **Affirm Your Gratitude:** As you hold the crystal, say aloud or in your mind:

"With gratitude, I begin this day,
Filled with love and light in every way.

I honor the blessings I hold dear,
And invite more joy to draw near."

1. **Dip Your Fingers in Water:** Dip your fingers in the bowl of water and gently sprinkle a few drops over your heart, symbolizing emotional balance and peace. As you do this, say:

"With peace in my heart, I start anew,
Grateful for all that I will do."

1. **Carry the Energy with You:** Allow the candle to burn for a few moments as you focus on the feeling of gratitude. When you're ready, extinguish the candle and carry the clear quartz crystal with you throughout the day as a reminder of your gratitude.

This Morning Gratitude Spell helps you set a positive intention for the day, aligning your energy with abundance and joy.

2. Evening Self-Love Spell for Emotional Healing

This spell is perfect for the end of the day, when you want to unwind, reflect, and nurture your emotional well-being. It focuses on cultivating self-love and releasing any negative emotions or self-judgment that may have accumulated throughout the day.

Ingredients:

- A pink candle (for self-love and compassion)
- A rose quartz crystal (for emotional healing and love)
- Lavender essential oil or dried lavender (for peace and relaxation)

Instructions:

1. **Light the Candle:** Light the pink candle to invoke the energy of self-love and compassion. As the candle burns, imagine its warm, pink light surrounding you in a protective and loving embrace.
2. **Anoint with Lavender:** Dab a small amount of lavender essential oil on your wrists and heart center, or sprinkle dried lavender around your space. Lavender helps calm the mind and promote emotional healing. As you apply the lavender, say:

"Lavender's scent, gentle and kind,
I release all worries from my mind."

1. **Hold the Rose Quartz:** Hold the rose quartz crystal in your hands and focus on feelings of self-love and acceptance. Visualize any negative thoughts or emotions melting away, replaced by unconditional love for yourself. Say:

"With love and light, I honor me,
Releasing all that doesn't serve, I'm free.
My heart is filled with gentle grace,
In self-love's arms, I find my space."

1. **Reflect on the Day:** Spend a few moments reflecting on your day, acknowledging any challenges you faced without judgment. Focus on what you did well, even in difficult situations, and express gratitude for your efforts.
2. **Close the Spell:** When you're ready, extinguish the candle and place the rose quartz near your bed. As you fall asleep, let the energy of self-love and peace fill your heart, ensuring that you wake up refreshed and emotionally balanced.

This Evening Self-Love Spell helps you release stress and cultivate compassion for yourself, making it easier to rest and rejuvenate.

3. Daily Peace and Contentment Spell

This spell is designed to bring a sense of inner peace and contentment, no matter what challenges or stresses you may be facing. It helps you ground yourself in the present moment and find joy in simplicity, nurturing a grateful heart.

Ingredients:

- A green candle (for balance and peace)
- A small stone or pebble (for grounding and stability)
- A sprig of rosemary or sage (for clarity and wisdom)

Instructions:

1. **Light the Green Candle:** Light the green candle to symbolize balance and peace. As the flame flickers, focus on the calming energy of the candle and allow any stress or tension to dissolve.
2. **Hold the Stone:** Pick up the stone or pebble and hold it in your hands. Feel its solid, grounded energy and let it connect you to the Earth. As you hold the stone, visualize yourself becoming more balanced and centered. Say:

"Earth beneath me, strong and true,
Bring me peace in all I do.
With grounded heart and steady mind,
I find contentment in life's kind."

1. **Wave the Sprig of Rosemary or Sage:** Gently wave the sprig of rosemary or sage around your body, clearing away any lingering doubts or negativity. These herbs are known for their wisdom and clarity, helping you see the blessings in even the smallest things. As you do this, say:

"With clarity and peace, I now embrace,
Contentment fills this sacred space."

1. **Take a Deep Breath:** Inhale deeply and focus on the present moment. Feel the peace and contentment that come from being fully present in your body, mind, and spirit.
2. **Close the Spell:** Allow the candle to burn for a few more minutes while you enjoy the feeling of peace. When you're ready, extinguish the candle and carry the stone with you as a reminder to stay grounded and content throughout the day.

This Peace and Contentment Spell helps you remain calm and balanced, even in challenging situations, by grounding you in gratitude and the present moment.

4. Mirror Spell for Self-Acceptance

This daily mirror spell is designed to foster self-love and acceptance by helping you see yourself through the lens of compassion and gratitude. It's especially helpful if you struggle with self-doubt or negative self-image, as it shifts your focus to your inner beauty and strengths.

Ingredients:

- A hand mirror or bathroom mirror
- A pink candle (for love and acceptance)
- A small bowl of rose petals or a rose quartz crystal

Instructions:

1. **Light the Candle:** Light the pink candle and place it near the mirror. The flame represents the light of self-love and acceptance that you are calling into your life.
2. **Look into the Mirror:** Stand or sit in front of the mirror and look into your own eyes. Take a moment to really see yourself, without judgment or criticism. As you gaze into the mirror, repeat the following affirmation:

"I see myself with love and grace,
I honor the beauty within this face.
With every breath, I love me more,
Grateful for the light I hold at my core."

1. **Hold the Rose Petals or Rose Quartz:** As you continue to look into the mirror, hold the rose petals or rose quartz crystal in your

hands. Focus on the loving, gentle energy of the rose or the crystal, allowing it to fill your heart with warmth and compassion.

2. **Speak Words of Gratitude:** Speak aloud or in your mind about the things you are grateful for within yourself. These could be physical traits, personality qualities, or strengths that have helped you overcome challenges. For example:
   - "I am grateful for my resilience."
   - "I honor my creativity and passion."
   - "I love my kind and caring heart."

3. **Close the Spell:** When you feel complete, extinguish the candle and place the rose quartz or rose petals on your altar or in a special place. Carry the energy of self-acceptance and love with you throughout the day, remembering to see yourself through the lens of gratitude.

This Mirror Spell for Self-Acceptance helps you develop a more loving relationship with yourself by focusing on the qualities that make you unique and valuable.

5. Gratitude Breath Spell for Stress Relief

This simple breathing spell helps you release stress and anxiety while focusing on gratitude. It's a quick and effective way to shift your energy from tension to calm, grounding you in the present moment.

Ingredients:

- A quiet space where you won't be disturbed
- A small token or object that represents gratitude (such as a leaf, crystal, or charm)

Instructions:

1. **Hold the Gratitude Token:** Find a comfortable place to sit and hold the small token or object in your hands. This item will act as a focal point for your gratitude and peace.
2. **Inhale Gratitude:** Close your eyes and take a deep breath in through your nose, focusing on the feeling of gratitude. Imagine your breath filling you with peace, love, and contentment.
3. **Exhale Stress:** Slowly exhale through your mouth, releasing any stress, tension, or worries you may be holding onto. As you exhale, visualize these negative feelings leaving your body and dissolving into the air.
4. **Repeat the Process:** Continue to inhale gratitude and exhale stress for several breaths, focusing on the feeling of peace growing within you. As you breathe, silently repeat the affirmation:

"With every breath, I welcome peace,
With every exhale, my worries cease.
Gratitude fills my heart and mind,
In this moment, I am aligned."

1. **Close the Spell:** When you're ready, open your eyes and place the gratitude token somewhere visible as a reminder of the peace you've cultivated. Carry this sense of calm and gratitude with you throughout the day.

This Gratitude Breath Spell is perfect for moments when you feel overwhelmed or stressed, helping you quickly reconnect with your inner peace.

Daily Gratitude Journaling Spell

In addition to these spells, a powerful daily practice to cultivate a grateful heart is gratitude journaling. Writing down your blessings each day reinforces the energy of gratitude and helps you stay focused on the positive aspects of life.

How to Perform the Gratitude Journaling Spell:

1. **Choose a Special Journal:** Select a journal that is dedicated to your gratitude practice. This could be a beautifully designed notebook or something simple that you decorate yourself.
2. **Set Your Intention:** Each day, take a few moments to write down three things you are grateful for. These can be big or small—anything from a delicious meal to a meaningful conversation with a friend.
3. **Affirm Your Gratitude:** As you write, silently or aloud, affirm your gratitude for these blessings. Say something like:

"I am grateful for the blessings I see,
I welcome more abundance to flow to me.
With every word, my heart expands,
As gratitude guides my mind and hands."

1. **Reflect on Your Blessings:** After writing, spend a few moments reflecting on the feelings of gratitude you've expressed. Allow yourself to feel content and fulfilled by the blessings you've acknowledged.
2. **Close the Practice:** When you're ready, close your journal and carry the energy of gratitude with you for the rest of the day.

Gratitude journaling is a powerful way to incorporate the magic of gratitude into your daily life, helping you stay mindful of the blessings that surround you.

Conclusion

Grateful Heart Spells are a transformative way to bring more love, peace, and contentment into your life. By focusing on the energy of gratitude through daily spells and rituals, you align yourself with the flow of abundance and joy. These spells help you nurture your emotional well-being, foster self-love, and maintain a positive, heart-centered approach to life.

Whether you're starting your day with a Morning Gratitude Spell, reflecting on your blessings in a gratitude journal, or performing a Mirror Spell for self-acceptance, these practices will help you develop a deeper connection with yourself and the world around you. As you cultivate a grateful heart, you open the door to even greater joy, peace, and fulfillment in every aspect of your life.

Chapter 21: Weather Magic for Thanksgiving

Thanksgiving often brings families and friends together for outdoor gatherings, feasts, and celebrations. The beauty of nature during this season—cool breezes, vibrant leaves, and crisp air—adds to the festive spirit. However, unfavorable weather conditions can sometimes interfere with plans. In these moments, weather magic can be a powerful tool to invite favorable weather for your Thanksgiving gatherings and ensure that your outdoor celebrations proceed smoothly.

Weather magic involves using spellwork and intention to align with the natural elements and influence the weather. Whether you're hoping for clear skies, gentle winds, or mild temperatures, weather magic taps into the forces of nature to help you create an ideal environment for your outdoor events. In this chapter, we'll explore various spells and rituals to summon favorable weather, protect gatherings from storms or cold, and work harmoniously with the elements to bring balance and calm to the skies.

The Power of Weather Magic

Weather magic, like any form of elemental magic, is about working in harmony with nature rather than trying to control or force it. The weather is influenced by vast and complex forces, and while we may not be able to alter major weather patterns, we can use magic to invite cooperation from the elements. By aligning our intentions with the energy of the Earth, air, fire, and water, we can gently nudge the weather toward favorable conditions.

Thanksgiving weather magic focuses on creating balance in the elements, ensuring that outdoor celebrations are comfortable and enjoyable. Whether you're hoping for clear skies, preventing rain from disrupting a gathering, or calling for mild temperatures, these spells help you work with the natural forces to influence the atmosphere around your event.

Preparing for Weather Magic

Before casting any weather spells, it's essential to prepare yourself and the space where you'll be working. Weather magic requires a deep connection to the elements, so grounding yourself and tuning into the natural world is an important first step.

Step-by-Step Guide to Preparing for Weather Magic:

1. **Grounding and Centering:** Begin by grounding yourself. Stand barefoot on the earth, close your eyes, and take a few deep breaths. Imagine roots extending from your feet deep into the Earth, connecting you to its energy. Feel the stability and power of the Earth beneath you.

2. **Connecting with the Elements:** Tune into the natural elements around you. Feel the air moving around you, sense the warmth of the sun or the coolness of the breeze, and listen to the sounds of nature. Visualize yourself as part of this natural world, in harmony with the elements.

3. **Setting Your Intention:** Clearly define the weather conditions you are hoping to manifest. Be specific and realistic in your request, focusing on favorable weather for your gathering rather than attempting to control large-scale weather patterns. For example, "I invite clear skies and gentle breezes for our outdoor celebration" or "May the rain hold off until after the feast is complete."

4. **Choose a Time and Place:** Weather magic is best performed outdoors, where you can directly connect with the elements. Choose a quiet, natural setting for your spellwork, preferably in the early morning or evening, when the energy is calm.

Once you've grounded yourself and set your intention, you are ready to begin working your weather magic. Below are a variety of spells to invite favorable weather, protect your gathering from storms, and ensure that your Thanksgiving celebration is filled with comfort and joy.

Weather Spells for Thanksgiving

The following spells focus on summoning favorable weather conditions for outdoor gatherings. Whether you need clear skies, mild temperatures, or protection from storms, these spells help you work in harmony with nature to influence the weather.

1. Clear Skies Spell

This spell is designed to invite clear, sunny skies for an outdoor Thanksgiving gathering. It's perfect if you're planning a picnic, barbecue, or feast under the open sky and want to ensure that the weather stays dry and pleasant.

Ingredients:

- A blue or white candle (for clarity and calm skies)
- A small dish of water (to represent the clouds)
- A feather (for gentle winds)
- A piece of sunstone or citrine (for the energy of the sun)

Instructions:

1. **Light the Candle:** Begin by lighting the blue or white candle to symbolize the clear sky you are inviting. As the candle burns, focus on the image of a bright, open sky free of clouds.
2. **Charge the Water:** Hold the dish of water in your hands and imagine it as the clouds in the sky. As you focus on the water, visualize the clouds parting and dissolving, leaving a bright, clear sky behind. Say:

"Waters of the sky, pure and bright,
Part the clouds, bring forth the light.
Clear skies above, calm and clear,
To bless this day as we gather near."

1. **Use the Feather:** Gently wave the feather over the candle and water, representing the gentle winds that will carry the clouds away. As you do this, say:

"Winds of the air, soft and light,
Guide the clouds far from sight.
Bring clear skies, open and bright,
For our gathering under the sun's light."

1. **Charge the Sunstone or Citrine:** Hold the sunstone or citrine in your hands, focusing on the warmth and energy of the sun. Visualize the sun shining brightly in the sky, warming the Earth and illuminating your gathering. Say:

"Sunstone bright, bring your rays,
Shine upon us through the days.
Clear skies above, calm and clear,
With your light, joy draws near."

1. **Close the Spell:** Allow the candle to burn for a few minutes while you visualize the weather being favorable. When you're ready, extinguish the candle, and place the sunstone or citrine outside or on your altar to continue drawing the energy of the sun. Keep the feather with you as a reminder of the gentle winds you've invited.

This Clear Skies Spell works best when performed a day or two before the gathering, giving the natural elements time to align with your request.

2. Mild Temperature Spell

If you're hosting a gathering during cooler or unpredictable weather, this spell can help invite mild, comfortable temperatures. It focuses on balancing the elements to create a pleasant, temperate atmosphere for outdoor celebrations.

Ingredients:

- A green candle (for balance and harmony)
- A small bowl of earth or sand (for grounding)
- A sprig of rosemary or sage (for warmth)
- A clear quartz crystal (for amplifying balance)

Instructions:

1. **Light the Candle:** Light the green candle to symbolize balance and harmony in the elements. As the candle burns, focus on the feeling of comfort and mild temperatures, neither too hot nor too cold.
2. **Ground with the Earth:** Place your hands over the bowl of earth or sand and feel its grounding energy. Visualize the Earth stabilizing the weather, bringing calm and temperate conditions. Say:

"Earth below, strong and steady,
Bring balance to the weather, ready.
Mild and calm, perfect and bright,
For our gathering filled with delight."

1. **Use the Rosemary or Sage:** Wave the sprig of rosemary or sage over the candle and the bowl of earth, inviting warmth and comfort. These herbs represent protection and clarity, ensuring that the weather remains pleasant. Say:

"Herbs of warmth, gentle and bright,
Bring comfort to the day and night.
Let the air be mild and sweet,
As we gather and share this feast."

1. **Charge the Clear Quartz:** Hold the clear quartz crystal in your hands, focusing on the energy of balance and amplification. Visualize the temperature being just right—warm enough for comfort but cool enough for enjoyment. Say:

"Quartz of clarity, balance the air,
Bring mild weather, perfect and fair.
Neither too hot nor too cold,
As we gather, young and old."

1. **Close the Spell:** Allow the candle to burn for a few minutes, holding the vision of balanced, mild weather. When you're ready, extinguish the candle and place the clear quartz outside or on your altar. Keep the sprig of rosemary or sage near your gathering space to continue inviting warmth and comfort.

This Mild Temperature Spell is ideal for gatherings where you want to ensure that the weather remains comfortable for everyone, especially during cooler seasons.

3. Rain Delay Spell

If rain threatens to disrupt your outdoor celebration, this spell helps delay or lessen the intensity of rain during the time of your gathering. It's not about stopping rain entirely (as rain is often necessary and beneficial), but rather asking for cooperation from the elements to ensure your event remains dry.

Ingredients:

- A gray or blue candle (to represent rain clouds)
- A small mirror (for reflection)
- A bowl of saltwater (to represent the rain)
- A piece of aquamarine or blue lace agate (for calming the weather)

Instructions:

1. **Light the Candle:** Light the gray or blue candle to represent the rain clouds. As the candle burns, visualize the clouds gathering but remaining calm, holding off on releasing rain until after your event.

2. **Hold the Mirror:** Hold the small mirror in your hands and imagine it reflecting the rain away from your event. Visualize the rain being delayed, passing by your gathering without causing disruption. Say:

"Mirror bright, reflect the rain,
Guide it away until we're done again.
Hold the storm, delay the fall,
Keep the skies calm over all."

1. **Charge the Saltwater:** Dip your fingers into the bowl of saltwater and swirl it gently, representing the rain. As you do this, vi-

sualize the rain slowing down or stopping, holding off until your event is complete. Say:

"Waters of the sky, gentle and clear,
Delay your fall, bring no fear.
After our feast, you may fall,
But until then, remain calm over all."

1. **Hold the Aquamarine or Blue Lace Agate:** Hold the aquamarine or blue lace agate in your hands, focusing on its calming energy. Visualize the clouds remaining soft and light, with no heavy downpours. Say:

"Stone of water, calm and bright,
Bring peace to the clouds, soft and light.
Delay the rain, hold it tight,
Until our gathering ends in light."

1. **Close the Spell:** Allow the candle to burn for a few minutes while you focus on delaying the rain. When you're ready, extinguish the candle and place the mirror near a window or outside. Keep the aquamarine or blue lace agate with you during the event as a calming talisman.

This Rain Delay Spell helps ensure that rain does not disrupt your gathering by delaying the storm until after your event.

4. Wind Taming Spell

If strong winds are expected and could interfere with your outdoor event, this spell helps calm the winds and invite a gentle breeze instead. It's perfect for ensuring that decorations stay in place and that the atmosphere remains calm and enjoyable.

Ingredients:

- A green or white candle (for balance and calm)
- A feather (for representing the wind)
- A small dish of sand or soil (for grounding)
- A piece of jade or aventurine (for balance and harmony)

Instructions:

1. **Light the Candle:** Light the green or white candle to symbolize balance and calmness in the air. As the candle burns, focus on the feeling of gentle winds and calm skies.
2. **Wave the Feather:** Hold the feather and gently wave it around, symbolizing the wind. As you do this, imagine the wind softening, becoming a gentle breeze rather than a forceful gust. Say:

"Winds of air, calm and bright,
Tame your strength, gentle your might.
A breeze so soft, light and sweet,
For our gathering where we meet."

1. **Ground with the Sand or Soil:** Place your hands over the dish of sand or soil, representing the grounding energy that will an-

chor the wind. Visualize the winds calming and settling as they are balanced by the Earth. Say:

"Earth below, hold the air,
Ground the winds, calm and fair.
Bring balance to the breeze today,
Let it be gentle in every way."

1. **Hold the Jade or Aventurine:** Hold the jade or aventurine in your hands, focusing on the energy of harmony and balance. Visualize the winds being perfectly tempered—enough to keep the air fresh but not strong enough to cause disruption. Say:

"Stone of balance, bring the air,
Gentle winds, calm and fair.
With this spell, I call the breeze,
To bless our gathering with ease."

1. **Close the Spell:** Allow the candle to burn for a few minutes while you focus on the wind becoming gentle and calm. When you're ready, extinguish the candle and place the feather outside or near the entrance to your gathering space. Keep the jade or aventurine with you as a talisman to maintain balance.

This Wind Taming Spell helps ensure that the wind remains gentle and calm, creating a peaceful atmosphere for your outdoor event.

Seasonal Weather Magic Ritual for Thanksgiving

If you want to perform a more comprehensive weather magic ritual to ensure favorable conditions for your Thanksgiving gathering, you can combine the elements of the spells above into a larger ritual.

Ingredients for the Ritual:

- A white or blue candle (for clear skies)
- A green candle (for mild temperatures)
- A gray candle (for rain delay, if needed)
- A feather (for calming the wind)
- A small bowl of earth or sand (for grounding)
- A sunstone or citrine (for sunlight)
- A piece of jade or aventurine (for balance)

Instructions for the Ritual:

1. **Set Your Intention:** Begin by setting your intention for the weather on the day of your gathering. Be specific about what you want—clear skies, mild temperatures, or calm winds. Visualize the perfect weather conditions for your event.

2. **Create a Sacred Circle:** Create a circle in your outdoor space, either physically (with stones or leaves) or energetically. This space will be where you call in the elements and invite their cooperation.

3. **Light the Candles:** Light the white or blue candle for clear skies, the green candle for mild temperatures, and the gray candle (if you need to delay rain). As each candle burns, focus on the energy of that element and how it will contribute to your ideal weather.

4. **Work with the Elements:**
   - Hold the feather and wave it gently, inviting calm winds.
   - Place your hands over the bowl of earth or sand to ground the weather and stabilize the elements.
   - Hold the sunstone or citrine to invite warm sunlight, and the jade or aventurine to balance the overall energy.
5. **Speak Your Intention:** Say aloud your intention for the weather, such as:

"By the light of sun and earth below,
I call the elements to ebb and flow.
Clear skies, calm winds, and mild air,
Bless our gathering with your care.
No rain shall fall, the skies are bright,
Our celebration filled with light."

1. **Close the Ritual:** Allow the candles to burn for a few more minutes, visualizing the perfect weather for your gathering. When you're ready, extinguish the candles and thank the elements for their cooperation. Leave the sunstone, jade, or aventurine outside as offerings to continue attracting favorable weather.

This Seasonal Weather Magic Ritual combines multiple elements to ensure that your outdoor Thanksgiving celebration is blessed with ideal weather.

Conclusion

Weather magic for Thanksgiving is a beautiful and harmonious way to invite favorable conditions for your outdoor gatherings and celebrations. By working with the elements through clear intention, spells, and rituals, you align yourself with nature's forces, helping to ensure that the weather cooperates for your event. Whether you're calling for clear skies, delaying rain, or taming the wind, these weather spells will enhance the comfort and joy of your Thanksgiving festivities.

Remember, weather magic is about working with nature, not against it. Approach your spellwork with respect, gratitude, and a willingness to adapt to the natural rhythms of the Earth. By doing so, you'll create a magical space where the elements support your gathering, allowing you to celebrate Thanksgiving with peace, love, and favorable skies.

Chapter 22: Herbal Teas and Potions

Herbal teas and potions have been used for centuries to promote healing, relaxation, and well-being. During Thanksgiving, when loved ones gather to celebrate gratitude and abundance, these teas and potions can create a warm and soothing environment that encourages relaxation, deepens bonds, and fosters a sense of peace and gratitude. The right blend of herbs and natural ingredients can elevate your celebration, helping everyone relax, unwind, and connect on a deeper level.

In this chapter, we'll explore a variety of herbal tea and potion recipes designed to enhance the Thanksgiving experience. Whether you want to create a calming tea to soothe holiday stress, a gratitude-infused potion to share with family, or a bonding brew to foster connection, these recipes will bring a touch of magic and tranquility to your holiday gathering.

The Power of Herbal Teas and Potions

Herbal teas and potions offer more than just nourishment for the body; they work on a spiritual and emotional level to soothe the soul, calm the mind, and bring people together. Each herb has its own magical properties, and when combined thoughtfully, these ingredients can create powerful brews that encourage relaxation, gratitude, and bonding.

During Thanksgiving, herbal teas and potions can be used to:

- Help guests relax and release holiday stress.
- Promote feelings of gratitude and abundance.
- Foster deeper connections between family and friends.
- Create a calming atmosphere during busy holiday preparations.
- Bring a sense of warmth and comfort to gatherings.

By incorporating herbal teas and potions into your Thanksgiving celebration, you invite the energy of nature and magic into your home, transforming your gathering into a peaceful and harmonious event.

Herbs for Relaxation, Gratitude, and Bonding

Before we dive into the recipes, it's important to understand the key herbs that will be featured in these teas and potions. Each of these herbs carries specific properties that align with the themes of Thanksgiving: relaxation, gratitude, and bonding.

Herbs for Relaxation:

- **Lavender:** Known for its calming and soothing effects, lavender promotes relaxation and reduces stress and anxiety.
- **Chamomile:** A gentle and calming herb, chamomile is perfect for promoting sleep, relaxation, and a peaceful state of mind.
- **Lemon Balm:** A mild sedative, lemon balm helps ease tension, anxiety, and restlessness, making it ideal for winding down after a busy day.
- **Valerian Root:** A strong sedative, valerian root is often used to relieve stress and promote deep relaxation and sleep.

Herbs for Gratitude and Grounding:

- **Rose:** Symbolizing love, gratitude, and emotional healing, rose petals are often used in teas to foster a sense of appreciation and gratitude.
- **Hibiscus:** This tart, vibrant flower represents abundance, gratitude, and joy, helping to uplift the spirit.
- **Ginger:** A warming herb that stimulates circulation and energy flow, ginger promotes gratitude by encouraging feelings of warmth and appreciation.

Herbs for Bonding and Connection:

- **Rosemary:** An herb of remembrance and clarity, rosemary enhances memory and helps deepen emotional bonds.
- **Cinnamon:** A warming, spicy herb, cinnamon promotes emotional warmth, connection, and love between people.
- **Cardamom:** With its exotic, sweet flavor, cardamom fosters love, friendship, and closeness.

Herbal Tea and Potion Recipes for Thanksgiving

Now that we understand the key herbs, let's dive into the recipes. These herbal teas and potions are designed to encourage relaxation, promote gratitude, and strengthen bonds during Thanksgiving. Each recipe includes step-by-step instructions for brewing, along with suggested magical intentions to enhance the experience.

1. Gratitude and Abundance Tea

This herbal tea blend is designed to evoke feelings of gratitude and appreciation for the blessings in your life. With a combination of heart-warming herbs like rose and hibiscus, this tea is perfect for sipping before or after a Thanksgiving meal, allowing everyone to reflect on the abundance in their lives.

Ingredients:

- 1 tablespoon dried rose petals (for love and gratitude)
- 1 tablespoon hibiscus petals (for abundance and joy)
- 1 teaspoon dried ginger (for warmth and appreciation)
- 1 teaspoon cinnamon chips (for connection and sweetness)
- Honey (optional, for sweetness and love)

Instructions:

1. **Boil Water:** Begin by boiling a pot of water, about 4 cups, for a small group. Once the water reaches a rolling boil, remove it from heat.
2. **Mix the Herbs:** In a large teapot or tea infuser, combine the dried rose petals, hibiscus, ginger, and cinnamon chips. As you mix the herbs, focus on your intention to cultivate gratitude and appreciate the blessings in your life. Say:

"With love and joy, this tea I brew,
To give thanks for all I have and do.
Abundance flows and gratitude grows,
As I sip, my heart knows."

1. **Steep the Tea:** Pour the hot water over the herb blend and let it steep for 5-7 minutes. As the tea steeps, visualize your heart filling with gratitude for the love, abundance, and blessings in your life.
2. **Sweeten and Serve:** If desired, add honey to taste for sweetness and love. Serve the tea in small cups, and invite guests to reflect on what they are grateful for as they sip.

This Gratitude and Abundance Tea is perfect for sharing with loved ones as part of a Thanksgiving ritual of reflection and appreciation.

2. Calm and Cozy Tea for Relaxation

After a busy day of preparations and celebrations, this herbal tea is ideal for helping you and your guests relax and unwind. With calming herbs like lavender and chamomile, this blend promotes a sense of peace, making it perfect for winding down in the evening.

Ingredients:

- 1 tablespoon dried lavender flowers (for relaxation and peace)
- 1 tablespoon dried chamomile flowers (for calming and soothing)
- 1 teaspoon lemon balm (for stress relief)
- 1 teaspoon dried valerian root (optional, for deep relaxation)
- Lemon slices (optional, for brightness)

Instructions:

1. **Boil Water:** Bring 4 cups of water to a boil, then remove it from the heat.
2. **Combine the Herbs:** In a teapot or tea infuser, combine the lavender, chamomile, lemon balm, and valerian root. As you mix the herbs, set the intention of inviting peace and relaxation. Say:

"Herbs of calm and peaceful grace,
Bring stillness to this sacred space.
As we sip, stress melts away,
Peace and rest fill this day."

1. **Steep the Tea:** Pour the hot water over the herb blend and let it steep for 5-7 minutes. As the tea steeps, visualize any stress or tension dissolving and being replaced by calm and tranquility.

2. **Serve with Lemon (Optional):** Add a slice of lemon to each cup for brightness, if desired. Serve the tea warm, encouraging everyone to take slow sips and relax deeply.

This Calm and Cozy Tea is ideal for creating a peaceful atmosphere after a long day, helping your guests unwind and enjoy the rest of the evening.

3. Bonding Brew for Connection

This spicy and aromatic tea blend is perfect for encouraging deeper connections and fostering bonding between family and friends. With warming spices like cinnamon and cardamom, this tea promotes feelings of love, friendship, and emotional warmth, making it ideal for sharing during Thanksgiving gatherings.

Ingredients:

- 2 cinnamon sticks (for warmth and connection)
- 1 tablespoon dried rosemary (for remembrance and bonding)
- 1 teaspoon cardamom pods (for love and friendship)
- 1 teaspoon dried orange peel (for joy and positivity)
- Honey or maple syrup (optional, for sweetness)

Instructions:

1. **Boil Water:** Bring 4 cups of water to a boil.
2. **Prepare the Herbs:** In a teapot or large saucepan, combine the cinnamon sticks, dried rosemary, cardamom pods, and dried orange peel. As you mix the herbs, focus on your intention to foster love, warmth, and connection between everyone present. Say:

"With spices warm and love so bright,
We share this tea in friendship's light.
Bonding strong, hearts open wide,
In joy and love, we do abide."

1. **Simmer the Tea:** Pour the boiling water over the herb blend and let it simmer on low heat for 10 minutes. As the tea simmers, visualize the bonds between you and your loved ones growing stronger, filled with warmth and love.

2. **Sweeten and Serve:** If desired, add honey or maple syrup for sweetness. Serve the tea in large mugs, encouraging guests to enjoy the warming, spicy flavors while engaging in meaningful conversation.

This Bonding Brew is perfect for sharing during moments of connection, whether around the dinner table or during cozy post-meal conversations.

4. Hearthside Potion for Gratitude and Comfort

This special potion is a rich, warming brew designed to evoke feelings of gratitude, comfort, and abundance. It combines spiced herbs with milk (or a milk alternative) to create a creamy, nourishing drink that's perfect for sipping by the fire or after a meal.

Ingredients:

- 2 cups milk or milk alternative (such as almond or oat milk)
- 1 cinnamon stick (for warmth and connection)
- 1 teaspoon dried ginger (for grounding and gratitude)
- 1 teaspoon ground nutmeg (for abundance and comfort)
- 1 teaspoon honey or maple syrup (for sweetness)
- A pinch of ground cloves (for protection)

Instructions:

1. **Heat the Milk:** In a small saucepan, gently heat the milk or milk alternative over low heat until warm, but not boiling.
2. **Add the Spices:** Add the cinnamon stick, dried ginger, ground nutmeg, and a pinch of ground cloves to the milk. Stir slowly, infusing the spices into the milk. As you stir, focus on your intention of creating gratitude and comfort. Say:

"Hearth and home, warm and bright,
We drink this potion, filled with light.
Gratitude flows, comfort grows,
As we share in love's sweet glow."

1. **Simmer and Sweeten:** Let the potion simmer for 5-7 minutes, stirring occasionally. Remove from heat, strain out the cinnamon stick, and stir in honey or maple syrup for added sweetness.
2. **Serve Warm:** Pour the Hearthside Potion into mugs and serve warm. Encourage everyone to sip slowly and reflect on the feelings of gratitude and abundance that surround them.

This Hearthside Potion is perfect for cozy moments by the fire, offering warmth and comfort during Thanksgiving gatherings.

5. Tranquil Sleep Potion for Post-Feast Relaxation

After a long day of celebration, this sleep potion helps guests relax and drift off into peaceful slumber. With calming herbs like valerian root and chamomile, this brew is perfect for sipping just before bed, promoting restful and rejuvenating sleep.

Ingredients:

- 1 tablespoon dried chamomile flowers (for relaxation and sleep)
- 1 teaspoon valerian root (for deep sleep and calm)
- 1 teaspoon lemon balm (for stress relief)
- 1 teaspoon dried lavender flowers (for peace and tranquility)
- A splash of milk or honey (optional, for sweetness and comfort)

Instructions:

1. **Boil Water:** Bring 2 cups of water to a boil.
2. **Mix the Herbs:** In a small teapot or infuser, combine the chamomile, valerian root, lemon balm, and lavender flowers. As you mix the herbs, set the intention of promoting deep, peaceful sleep and relaxation. Say:

"Herbs of rest and gentle sleep,
Into dreamland I now leap.
With peace and calm, this potion brings,
Restful sleep on soft wings."

1. **Steep the Potion:** Pour the boiling water over the herb blend and let it steep for 5-7 minutes. As the potion steeps, visualize yourself or your guests drifting into a deep, restful sleep.
2. **Serve Warm:** Pour the potion into mugs and add a splash of milk or honey for extra comfort. Encourage everyone to drink slowly, allowing the calming effects of the herbs to take hold.

This Tranquil Sleep Potion is perfect for winding down after a busy Thanksgiving day, ensuring that everyone sleeps peacefully and wakes up refreshed.

Creating a Thanksgiving Tea Ceremony

In addition to these individual recipes, you can create a Thanksgiving Tea Ceremony to incorporate these herbal teas and potions into your celebration. A tea ceremony is a mindful and magical way to bring people together, share blessings, and foster a deeper sense of gratitude and connection.

How to Create a Thanksgiving Tea Ceremony:

1. **Prepare the Space:** Set up a cozy, quiet space where you and your guests can gather. Light candles, arrange comfortable seating, and set out the tea or potion you've brewed. Create a calming atmosphere with soft music or nature sounds.
2. **Set the Intention:** Before serving the tea, invite everyone to set an intention for the ceremony. This could be gratitude, relaxation, or simply enjoying the moment together. Encourage each person to reflect on what they are thankful for.
3. **Serve the Tea:** Serve the tea or potion in small cups, allowing everyone to take a moment to breathe deeply and focus on their intention before taking a sip.
4. **Share Gratitude:** After sipping the tea, invite each guest to share something they are grateful for, whether it's a personal experience, a relationship, or a moment from the day.
5. **Close the Ceremony:** Once everyone has shared, close the ceremony with a group affirmation or blessing, such as:

"With hearts full of love and gratitude,
We give thanks for this moment shared.
May the bonds we've strengthened continue to grow,
And may love and peace always flow."

A Thanksgiving Tea Ceremony is a beautiful way to honor the themes of gratitude and connection, making your celebration even more magical and meaningful.

Conclusion

Herbal teas and potions are a delightful and magical addition to your Thanksgiving celebration, offering relaxation, gratitude, and deeper connection for all who gather. These recipes blend the healing properties of herbs with the power of intention, creating a space where guests can unwind, reflect, and bond.

Whether you're sipping a warm Hearthside Potion by the fire, enjoying a calming cup of Chamomile-Lavender tea after dinner, or sharing a Gratitude and Abundance tea with family, these brews will enhance the warmth and magic of your Thanksgiving gathering. By incorporating herbal teas and potions into your celebration, you foster a deeper sense of connection to yourself, your loved ones, and the abundance that surrounds you.

Through these simple yet powerful recipes, you can transform your Thanksgiving into a magical, heartwarming experience that nurtures the body, mind, and soul.

Chapter 23: Harvest Moon Rituals

The Harvest Moon, the full moon that occurs closest to the autumn equinox, has long been associated with abundance, gratitude, and the culmination of efforts. As the last full moon before the cold winter months, it represents the final harvest—both literally and metaphorically. This powerful lunar event is an ideal time for performing rituals and spells that focus on giving thanks for the blessings received throughout the year and manifesting future abundance. The energies of the Harvest Moon encourage reflection, completion, and preparing for the quieter, introspective season ahead.

In this chapter, we'll explore a variety of rituals and spells aligned with the energies of the autumn moon. These practices will help you harness the power of the Harvest Moon to express gratitude, manifest your desires, and prepare for the next phase of your life with intention and clarity.

The Significance of the Harvest Moon

The Harvest Moon carries unique energy that amplifies themes of abundance, gratitude, and completion. Traditionally, this full moon illuminated the night for farmers during the harvest season, allowing them to work late into the night to gather their crops. Spiritually, this moon represents a time to reflect on what you've harvested in your own life—whether it's personal growth, career achievements, relationships, or creative projects.

Key themes associated with the Harvest Moon include:

- **Gratitude:** Recognizing and giving thanks for the blessings and abundance in your life.
- **Manifestation:** Focusing on what you want to attract in the future, using the moon's energy to set powerful intentions.
- **Completion:** Reviewing the goals and projects you've worked on throughout the year and bringing them to completion.
- **Release:** Letting go of anything that no longer serves you, clearing space for new growth and opportunities in the future.

By performing rituals and spells during the Harvest Moon, you align with these energies, allowing you to embrace abundance, express gratitude, and prepare for a new chapter.

Preparing for Harvest Moon Rituals

Before performing any Harvest Moon rituals, it's important to prepare your space and yourself. Lunar magic is deeply connected to the natural cycles, so creating a sacred, harmonious environment will enhance your connection to the moon's energy.

Step-by-Step Guide to Preparing for Harvest Moon Rituals:

1. **Cleanse the Space:** Begin by cleansing the space where you will perform your ritual. You can do this by burning sage, palo santo, or incense, or by sprinkling salt around the area. As you cleanse, say:

"I cleanse this space with love and light,
Preparing for the moon's insight.
May all be clear, may all be bright,
As I call forth the Harvest Moon's might."

1. **Create a Sacred Altar:** Set up a small altar to honor the Harvest Moon. You can include items such as:
    - **Candles:** White, gold, or orange candles to represent the moon and the harvest.
    - **Crystals:** Citrine (for abundance), moonstone (for lunar connection), and clear quartz (for manifestation).
    - **Harvest Symbols:** Autumn leaves, pumpkins, corn, or wheat to symbolize the season.
    - **Offerings:** Place offerings of food or drink (such as apples, bread, or wine) as a symbol of gratitude.
2. **Ground and Center Yourself:** Spend a few moments grounding yourself by standing barefoot on the earth or sitting in a comfortable position. Close your eyes, take deep breaths, and visualize roots extending from your feet deep into the Earth, anchoring

you. Allow yourself to feel connected to the natural cycles of the Earth and the moon.

3. **Set Your Intention:** Clearly define the purpose of your ritual or spell. Whether it's expressing gratitude, manifesting abundance, or releasing old patterns, your intention will guide the energy of the ritual. Take a few moments to focus on what you wish to achieve and invite the moon's energy to support you.

Once your space is prepared and your intention is set, you're ready to begin your Harvest Moon rituals.

Harvest Moon Rituals and Spells for Gratitude and Manifestation

The following rituals and spells are designed to align with the powerful energies of the Harvest Moon. Each practice focuses on themes of gratitude, abundance, and manifestation, helping you make the most of this special lunar event.

1. Full Moon Gratitude Ritual

This ritual is designed to help you express gratitude for the blessings and abundance you've received throughout the year. By offering thanks to the universe and the Harvest Moon, you invite even more blessings into your life and align yourself with the energy of abundance.

Ingredients:

- A white or gold candle (for lunar energy and gratitude)
- A small bowl of water (to represent the moon's connection to water and emotions)
- A piece of paper and pen
- A moonstone or citrine crystal (for lunar connection and abundance)

Instructions:

1. **Light the Candle:** Begin by lighting the white or gold candle to represent the light of the Harvest Moon. As the flame flickers, visualize the moon shining brightly above you, illuminating all the blessings in your life.
2. **Reflect on Your Blessings:** Take a few moments to reflect on the blessings and abundance you've received throughout the year.

Think about the people, opportunities, experiences, and personal growth that have enriched your life.

3. **Write Down Your Gratitude:** On the piece of paper, write down at least three things you are deeply grateful for. These can be large or small—anything that has brought you joy, growth, or fulfillment. As you write, feel your heart expanding with gratitude. Say:

"With this moon's light, I give thanks,
For all the blessings in my ranks.
Abundance flows, love grows strong,
I honor the gifts I've had all along."

1. **Charge the Water:** Hold the bowl of water in your hands and visualize the moon's light filling the water with its energy. Say:

"Water of the moon, pure and bright,
Carry my thanks on this sacred night.
I honor the flow of love and grace,
As I stand in this blessed space."

1. **Offer Your Gratitude:** Place the paper with your gratitude list under the bowl of water as an offering to the Harvest Moon. Allow the candle to burn for a few minutes while you focus on the feeling of gratitude.
2. **Close the Ritual:** When you're ready, extinguish the candle and pour the water onto the earth as a final offering to the moon and the universe. Keep the moonstone or citrine on your altar to continue attracting abundance and gratitude.

This Full Moon Gratitude Ritual helps you align with the energy of the Harvest Moon by focusing on thankfulness for the blessings in your life.

2. Manifestation Spell for Abundance

The Harvest Moon is an ideal time to set powerful intentions for future abundance. This manifestation spell focuses on attracting prosperity, success, and new opportunities, helping you bring your desires to fruition in the coming months.

Ingredients:

- A green or gold candle (for abundance and prosperity)
- A small bowl of seeds or grains (to represent the harvest and potential)
- A piece of paper and pen
- A citrine or clear quartz crystal (for amplifying abundance)

Instructions:

1. **Light the Candle:** Light the green or gold candle to symbolize abundance and prosperity. As the flame flickers, visualize your intention for abundance growing stronger, fueled by the energy of the Harvest Moon.
2. **Set Your Intention:** On the piece of paper, write down a specific intention for abundance. This could be financial prosperity, career success, creative opportunities, or any other form of abundance you wish to manifest. Be clear and specific in your wording.
3. **Hold the Seeds or Grains:** Take the bowl of seeds or grains in your hands and focus on the potential for growth and abundance within them. As you hold the bowl, visualize your intention growing, just like the seeds, into a bountiful harvest. Say:

"Seeds of abundance, strong and true,
I plant my intentions and watch them grow.
With the moon's light, my dreams take flight,
Abundance flows, shining bright."

1. **Charge the Crystal:** Hold the citrine or clear quartz crystal in your hands and visualize it amplifying your intention for abundance. Imagine it glowing with golden light, radiating prosperity and success. Place the crystal on top of the paper with your intention written on it.

2. **Close the Spell:** Allow the candle to burn for a few minutes while you focus on your intention manifesting. When you're ready, extinguish the candle and keep the crystal on your altar or carry it with you to continue attracting abundance.

This Manifestation Spell for Abundance helps you harness the energy of the Harvest Moon to bring your desires for prosperity and success into reality.

3. Harvest Moon Release Ritual

As the year comes to a close, the Harvest Moon offers an opportunity to release anything that no longer serves you, making room for new growth and opportunities. This ritual focuses on letting go of old patterns, fears, or obstacles, allowing you to enter the next phase of your life with clarity and freedom.

Ingredients:

- A black or gray candle (for release and transformation)
- A small fireproof bowl or cauldron
- A piece of paper and pen
- A sage or palo santo bundle (for cleansing)
- A clear quartz crystal (for clarity)

Instructions:

1. **Light the Candle:** Light the black or gray candle to symbolize the energy of release and transformation. As the flame burns, visualize anything you need to let go of being drawn into the flame and transformed into light.
2. **Reflect on What No Longer Serves You:** Take a few moments to reflect on any patterns, fears, or obstacles that have been holding you back. These could be limiting beliefs, toxic relationships, habits, or anything else that no longer aligns with your highest good.
3. **Write Down What You're Releasing:** On the piece of paper, write down what you wish to release. Be honest and specific, focusing on the things that you are ready to let go of. As you write, imagine the weight of these things lifting off your shoulders.

4. **Burn the Paper:** Carefully light the paper with the candle flame and place it in the fireproof bowl or cauldron. As the paper burns, visualize the things you are releasing being transformed and dissolved. Say:

"With this flame, I release and clear,
All that holds me back, all that I fear.
The moonlight shines, I'm free at last,
I let go of the burdens of the past."

1. **Cleanse with Sage or Palo Santo:** Once the paper has burned completely, light the sage or palo santo bundle and use the smoke to cleanse yourself and your space. As you cleanse, say:

"I cleanse my spirit, pure and bright,
With the moon's glow, I'm filled with light.
I release the old, I welcome the new,
My heart is clear, my soul renewed."

1. **Close the Ritual:** Allow the candle to burn for a few more minutes as you focus on the feeling of release and freedom. When you're ready, extinguish the candle and place the clear quartz crystal on your altar to continue inviting clarity and transformation.

This Harvest Moon Release Ritual helps you let go of what no longer serves you, clearing space for new growth and opportunities in the coming months.

4. Group Harvest Moon Ritual for Gratitude and Bonding

This group ritual is perfect for celebrating the Harvest Moon with family or friends. It focuses on expressing gratitude, fostering connection, and creating a sense of community. This ritual helps deepen bonds while honoring the abundance and blessings of the season.

Ingredients:

- A large white or gold candle (to represent the Harvest Moon)
- A bowl of seasonal fruits or vegetables (for sharing abundance)
- A piece of paper and pen for each participant
- A small token or crystal for each participant (such as a clear quartz or rose quartz)
- A bell or chime (optional)

Instructions:

1. **Create a Sacred Circle:** Arrange seating in a circle, with the large candle placed in the center. This symbolizes the light of the Harvest Moon and the shared abundance of the group.
2. **Light the Candle:** Light the white or gold candle and invite each participant to take a moment to focus on their gratitude for the blessings they've received this year. As the candle burns, say:

"By the light of this moon so bright,
We gather here in love's pure light.
Grateful hearts, we share our cheer,
Honoring the blessings of this year."

1. **Reflect on Gratitude:** Give each participant a piece of paper and a pen, and ask them to write down one thing they are grateful for. This could be a personal blessing, a relationship, or a meaningful experience from the past year.

2. **Share Gratitude:** Once everyone has written their gratitude, invite each person to share what they've written with the group. As each person shares, pass the bowl of seasonal fruits or vegetables around the circle, offering a small piece to each participant as a symbol of shared abundance and connection.

3. **Gift the Tokens:** After sharing, give each participant a small token or crystal, such as a clear quartz or rose quartz, to carry with them as a reminder of the group's shared gratitude and connection.

4. **Close the Ritual:** If desired, ring a bell or chime to signify the end of the ritual. Thank the Harvest Moon for its energy and light, and allow the candle to burn for a few minutes longer before extinguishing it.

This Group Harvest Moon Ritual fosters gratitude, connection, and a sense of community, making it perfect for celebrating with loved ones during the autumn season.

Conclusion

The Harvest Moon is a time of deep reflection, gratitude, and manifestation. By aligning with the energies of this powerful lunar event, you can express thanks for the blessings you've received, set intentions for future abundance, and release anything that no longer serves you. Through these rituals and spells, you strengthen your connection to the cycles of nature, allowing the magic of the moon to guide you toward greater fulfillment and prosperity.

Whether you're performing a personal gratitude ritual, setting intentions for abundance, or celebrating the Harvest Moon with a group, these practices help you harness the full power of this special time. Embrace the energies of completion, gratitude, and renewal as you prepare for the quieter, introspective months ahead, knowing that the seeds of your intentions will continue to grow and bear fruit in the future.

Chapter 24: Blessing the Home

As the heart of family life and the center of celebration, the home plays an essential role in creating a peaceful, joyful environment during the holiday season. Blessing and cleansing your home with intention can enhance its energy, inviting peace, protection, and prosperity into every corner. As you prepare for holiday gatherings and the warmth of shared moments with loved ones, taking time to bless the home ensures that your space is harmonious, protected, and filled with positive energy.

In this chapter, we'll explore a variety of spells and rituals designed to cleanse and bless your home for the holidays. Whether you're focusing on removing negative energy, protecting your space from harm, or inviting abundance into your home, these practices will help you create an atmosphere of peace, love, and prosperity. By performing these blessings, you infuse your home with magic, making it a sanctuary of joy and well-being for all who enter.

The Importance of Blessing the Home

The energy of a home reflects the energy of those who live within it. Over time, the space can accumulate negativity, tension, or stagnant energy, especially during stressful times or after difficult experiences. Blessing and cleansing your home helps to clear out this unwanted energy, creating a fresh, vibrant environment that promotes peace and prosperity.

Blessing your home before the holidays is particularly beneficial, as it sets the tone for gatherings, encourages positive interactions, and protects against any negative influences. It also invites prosperity and abundance, ensuring that your home is filled with warmth and success throughout the season.

Key themes for home blessings during the holidays include:

- **Cleansing:** Removing negative or stagnant energy from the space.
- **Protection:** Creating a shield around the home to guard against negativity or harm.
- **Peace:** Promoting a calm, harmonious atmosphere where love and joy can thrive.
- **Prosperity:** Inviting abundance and success into the home, ensuring that all who live there are blessed with wealth and good fortune.

Preparing for Home Blessing Rituals

Before performing a home blessing, it's important to prepare both yourself and the space to ensure that the energy flows smoothly. Cleansing the home, setting clear intentions, and gathering the necessary tools will help you create a powerful and effective blessing.

Step-by-Step Guide to Preparing for Home Blessing Rituals:

1. **Clean and Declutter the Space:** Start by physically cleaning and decluttering your home. Remove any unnecessary items, sweep and dust, and create a tidy, welcoming environment. Physical cleanliness supports the flow of positive energy and makes the space feel fresh and inviting.

2. **Set Your Intention:** Clearly define the purpose of your home blessing. Are you focusing on cleansing negative energy, protecting your home from harm, or inviting peace and prosperity? Set a clear intention before beginning the ritual. For example: "I cleanse and bless this home for peace, protection, and abundance."

3. **Gather Your Tools:** You'll need a few key tools to perform your home blessing rituals. These might include:
   - **Sage or Palo Santo:** For cleansing negative energy.
   - **A white candle:** To represent purity and light.
   - **Salt or a bowl of water:** For protection and grounding.
   - **Crystals:** Such as black tourmaline for protection, rose quartz for love, or citrine for abundance.
   - **Essential oils or incense:** Lavender, frankincense, or rosemary to promote peace and positivity.

4. **Create a Sacred Space:** Find a quiet, comfortable place in your home where you can begin the ritual. If possible, set up an altar with the tools you'll be using. Light a candle, and take a few deep

breaths to ground yourself and connect with the energy of your home.

Once you've prepared yourself and your space, you're ready to begin blessing your home. The following spells and rituals will guide you through the process of cleansing, protecting, and blessing your home for the holiday season.

Spells and Rituals for Blessing the Home

The following home blessing rituals are designed to cleanse your space of unwanted energy, invite peace and prosperity, and protect your home from harm. You can perform these rituals individually or combine them to create a comprehensive home blessing.

1. Sage and Salt Cleansing Ritual

This simple but powerful ritual uses sage and salt to cleanse your home of negative energy, leaving it clear, vibrant, and ready to welcome positive influences. It's an excellent way to reset the energy of your space before a holiday gathering or any time you feel your home could use a fresh start.

Ingredients:

- A bundle of sage or palo santo (for cleansing)
- A bowl of salt or water (for grounding and protection)
- A white candle (for purity and light)

Instructions:

1. **Light the Sage:** Begin by lighting the sage or palo santo bundle. Allow the smoke to rise and swirl around you, and take a moment to connect with the cleansing energy of the herb. As the smoke rises, say:

"With this smoke, I cleanse and clear,
All negativity, disappear.
Pure and bright, this space I make,
Only love and light may wake."

1. **Walk Through the Home:** Starting at the entrance, slowly walk through each room of your home, allowing the sage smoke to fill the space. Be sure to waft the smoke into corners, closets, and any

areas where energy might feel stagnant or heavy. As you do this, visualize the smoke clearing away any negative or unwanted energy.

2. **Use the Salt or Water:** Once you've saged each room, return to the center of your home and sprinkle a small amount of salt or water around the perimeter of your space, focusing on doors and windows. This helps protect your home by creating a boundary of purification. As you do this, say:

"With salt (or water) pure, I shield this place,
Protecting all who fill this space.
No harm may enter, none shall stay,
Only peace will find its way."

1. **Light the Candle:** To complete the ritual, light the white candle in a central location in your home, such as your living room or kitchen. Allow the flame to symbolize the purity and light that now fills your home. As the candle burns, say:

"By flame's light, I bless this home,
With peace and love, no fear to roam.
From this moment, pure and bright,
My home is safe, filled with light."

1. **Close the Ritual:** Allow the candle to burn for at least 30 minutes, filling your home with positive energy. Extinguish the candle when you feel the space is fully cleansed and protected.

This Sage and Salt Cleansing Ritual is a powerful way to reset the energy of your home, making it a clean and welcoming space for the holiday season.

2. Protection Spell for the Home

This spell creates a protective shield around your home, guarding it from negative influences, unwanted visitors, or harmful energy. It's ideal for ensuring that your home remains a sanctuary of safety and well-being during the holidays and beyond.

Ingredients:

- A black or white candle (for protection)
- A bowl of salt (for grounding and protection)
- Black tourmaline or obsidian (for protective energy)
- Lavender or rosemary incense (for peace and protection)

Instructions:

1. **Light the Candle:** Begin by lighting the black or white candle to symbolize the protective energy you are invoking. As the flame flickers, visualize your home surrounded by a bright, protective shield of light. Say:

"By this flame, I call a shield,
Protect my home, all harm is healed.
Only love and light may stay,
All else must leave, far away."

1. **Place the Crystals:** Hold the black tourmaline or obsidian in your hands and focus on its protective properties. Place one crystal at each corner of your home (or each room, if you prefer) to anchor the protective energy. As you place each crystal, say:

"With this stone, protection grows,
My home is safe from head to toe.
No harm may pass this sacred line,
Only peace and love divine."

1. **Use the Salt:** Sprinkle a small amount of salt at each entrance to your home, such as doorways and windows. This creates a barrier that prevents negative energy from entering. As you do this, say:

"Salt of Earth, strong and true,
Protect this space, as I ask of you.
All who enter, pure must be,
This home is safe, blessed by me."

1. **Burn the Incense:** Light the lavender or rosemary incense and allow the smoke to rise and fill your space. Walk through each room of your home, focusing on the protective energy that now surrounds your space. As you do this, say:

"By air and flame, by Earth and sea,
Protection fills this home for me.
No harm shall come, no fear remain,
My home is blessed and safe again."

1. **Close the Spell:** Allow the candle and incense to burn for a few minutes, filling your home with protective energy. When you're ready, extinguish the candle and thank the elements for their support.

This Protection Spell for the Home ensures that your space remains a sanctuary of safety, guarding against any negative influences or unwanted visitors.

3. Peace and Harmony Blessing

This spell is designed to promote peace, harmony, and positive interactions within the home. It's especially useful for fostering loving communication and reducing tension during family gatherings or holidays.

Ingredients:

- A pink or white candle (for love and peace)
- A bowl of water (for emotional balance)
- Rose petals or lavender (for love and calm)
- A clear quartz crystal (for amplifying peace)

Instructions:

1. **Light the Candle:** Light the pink or white candle to symbolize love and peace filling your home. As the flame flickers, visualize a soft, calming light spreading throughout your space, promoting harmony and positive interactions. Say:

"By this flame, I call for peace,
May love and joy never cease.
Harmony flows, tensions dissolve,
With this blessing, all problems resolve."

1. **Prepare the Water:** Hold the bowl of water in your hands and visualize it being filled with calm, balanced energy. Add a few rose petals or lavender to the water for an extra boost of love and tranquility. As you do this, say:

"Water pure, gentle and bright,
Bring peace to this home tonight.
With love and calm, this space I bless,
Filling all hearts with happiness."

1. **Sprinkle the Water:** Dip your fingers in the bowl of water and gently sprinkle a few drops around each room of your home, focusing on areas where family or guests will gather. As you sprinkle the water, visualize any lingering tension or conflict being washed away. Say:

"Peace flows in, all stress flows out,
Harmony fills this home throughout.
With love and light, I bless this space,
May joy and calm fill every face."

1. **Charge the Crystal:** Hold the clear quartz crystal in your hands and focus on amplifying the energy of peace and harmony. Place the crystal in a central location, such as the dining room or living room, where family or guests will gather. Say:

"Crystal clear, amplify peace,
Let love and joy only increase.
May harmony fill this space with light,
Blessing all who gather tonight."

1. **Close the Ritual:** Allow the candle to burn for a few more minutes while you focus on the feeling of peace and harmony filling your home. When you're ready, extinguish the candle and thank the energy of love and calm for blessing your space.

This Peace and Harmony Blessing is perfect for fostering positive interactions and reducing tension during family gatherings, ensuring that your home remains a sanctuary of love and joy.

4. Prosperity Blessing for the Home

This spell invites abundance, wealth, and prosperity into your home. It's ideal for ensuring that your home is filled with financial security, success, and good fortune during the holidays and into the new year.

Ingredients:

- A green or gold candle (for abundance and prosperity)
- A bowl of coins, rice, or grains (for wealth and abundance)
- Cinnamon sticks or cloves (for prosperity)
- Citrine or pyrite crystal (for attracting wealth)

Instructions:

1. **Light the Candle:** Light the green or gold candle to represent abundance and prosperity flowing into your home. As the flame burns, visualize your home being filled with financial security, success, and good fortune. Say:

"By this flame of golden light,
Prosperity flows, clear and bright.
Wealth and success I call to stay,
Blessing this home in every way."

1. **Prepare the Bowl:** Hold the bowl of coins, rice, or grains in your hands, focusing on the energy of abundance. As you hold the bowl, visualize it overflowing with wealth, symbolizing the prosperity that is now flowing into your home. Say:

"Abundance flows, wealth is near,
Prosperity fills this home so dear.

By these grains and coins I see,
Success and fortune come to me."

1. **Place the Cinnamon or Cloves:** Place cinnamon sticks or cloves around your home, focusing on areas where financial energy flows, such as near your desk, cash registers, or areas where money is stored. As you place them, say:

"By spice of wealth and fortune's call,
Prosperity comes to bless us all.
With every step, success will grow,
Into this home, abundance flows."

1. **Charge the Crystal:** Hold the citrine or pyrite crystal in your hands and focus on attracting wealth and success. Place the crystal near the bowl of coins or grains, symbolizing the continuous flow of abundance. Say:

"Citrine bright (or pyrite's glow),
Bring wealth and fortune, let it grow.
With this blessing, my home shall be,
Filled with abundance, rich and free."

1. **Close the Spell:** Allow the candle to burn for a few more minutes while you focus on the energy of prosperity filling your home. When you're ready, extinguish the candle and keep the bowl of coins or grains in a central location to continue attracting wealth.

This Prosperity Blessing invites financial abundance, success, and good fortune into your home, ensuring that you and your family are blessed with wealth throughout the holiday season and beyond.

Conclusion

Blessing your home with intention and care transforms your living space into a sanctuary of peace, protection, and prosperity. Whether you're cleansing away negative energy, creating a protective shield, promoting harmony during family gatherings, or inviting wealth into your home, these rituals empower you to infuse your space with positive, supportive energy.

By performing these home blessings before the holidays, you ensure that your home is a welcoming, joyful place for all who enter. The energy of peace, love, and abundance will fill your space, creating a harmonious environment where meaningful connections, celebrations, and prosperity can thrive.

Through these rituals and spells, you take an active role in shaping the energy of your home, transforming it into a sacred space of light, love, and security for the holiday season and beyond.

Chapter 25: Autumn Equinox Reflections

The Autumn Equinox, also known as Mabon, marks a time of perfect balance between day and night. It is one of the two points in the year when the hours of light and darkness are equal, making it a powerful moment to pause, reflect, and align your intentions with the natural cycles of the Earth. As the season transitions from the warmth of summer to the cooler, quieter months of autumn, the equinox serves as a reminder to seek balance in our own lives, to reflect on what we've harvested throughout the year, and to prepare for the inward focus that winter brings.

In this chapter, we will explore a series of reflective rituals and spells that harness the unique energy of the Autumn Equinox. These practices help you align with the earth's natural rhythms, balance your energy, and set intentions for the months ahead. The Autumn Equinox is a time to reflect on the past, acknowledge what you've achieved, and decide what you need to release or continue cultivating as you prepare for the end of the year.

The Significance of the Autumn Equinox

The Autumn Equinox is a point of equilibrium in the natural world, where day and night stand in perfect balance before the darkness of winter overtakes the light. It represents the culmination of the harvest season, a time to gather the fruits of our labor—whether literal or metaphorical—and prepare for the colder months ahead.

The key themes of the Autumn Equinox include:

- **Balance:** Seeking harmony between light and dark, activity and rest, external action and inner reflection.
- **Reflection:** Looking back on the year's progress and considering what you've accomplished, what needs more attention, and what you may need to release.
- **Gratitude:** Recognizing and giving thanks for the abundance and blessings you've received.
- **Preparation:** Setting intentions for the quieter, introspective months of winter, deciding what you will cultivate or continue working on.

The energy of the Autumn Equinox encourages you to pause, take stock, and find balance within yourself and your life. It's an ideal time for rituals that promote equilibrium, reflection, and a sense of peaceful acceptance as you move toward the final months of the year.

Preparing for Autumn Equinox Rituals

As with any spellwork or ritual, it's important to prepare both your space and yourself before working with the energy of the Autumn Equinox. This preparation ensures that you are fully aligned with the earth's natural cycles and that your intentions are clear and focused.

Step-by-Step Guide to Preparing for Autumn Equinox Rituals:

1. **Cleanse and Ground Yourself:** Before performing an equinox ritual, take time to cleanse and ground yourself. This can be done through meditation, a cleansing bath, or simply spending time in nature. Focus on releasing any chaotic or unbalanced energy and connecting deeply with the earth beneath you.

2. **Create a Sacred Space:** Set up a sacred space or altar where you can focus on your ritual. Include items that symbolize the season of autumn and balance, such as:
   - **Candles:** Use white, black, or gold candles to represent balance and the transition between light and dark.
   - **Crystals:** Clear quartz (for clarity and balance), citrine (for abundance), and amethyst (for reflection).
   - **Harvest Items:** Apples, pumpkins, wheat, corn, or autumn leaves to represent the harvest season.
   - **Balance Symbols:** You may also want to include symbols of balance, such as a set of scales, or place two candles side by side to represent the equal balance of day and night.

3. **Set Your Intention:** As you prepare for the ritual, take a few moments to set a clear intention. This could be to seek balance in a

specific area of your life, reflect on your achievements, or set goals for the remainder of the year. Your intention will guide the energy of the ritual.

Once you've grounded yourself, created your sacred space, and set your intention, you're ready to begin your Autumn Equinox ritual.

Autumn Equinox Rituals and Spells for Reflection and Balance

The following rituals and spells are designed to help you align with the energy of the Autumn Equinox. Each practice focuses on themes of balance, reflection, and gratitude, allowing you to tap into the power of the season and bring harmony to your life.

1. Equinox Balance Ritual

This ritual is centered around achieving balance in your life. By focusing on the equal energies of light and dark during the equinox, you can restore balance to areas that feel out of alignment, whether they are emotional, physical, or spiritual.

Ingredients:

- Two candles: one black (for darkness and rest) and one white (for light and action)
- A piece of paper and pen
- A small bowl of water (for emotional balance)
- A crystal or stone that represents balance (such as clear quartz or a balancing stone like tourmaline)
- A small scale or two similar objects to represent balance

Instructions:

1. **Light the Candles:** Place the black and white candles on either side of your sacred space or altar, symbolizing the balance between light and dark, action and rest. Light both candles, and as you do so, focus on the balance of energies within your own life.

2. **Reflect on Areas of Imbalance:** Take a few moments to reflect on the areas of your life where you may feel out of balance. This could be a work-life imbalance, emotional stress, or neglecting self-care in favor of external demands. Write down what you wish to bring into balance.

3. **Set Your Intention for Balance:** Once you've reflected, hold the small scale or balancing objects in your hands. Visualize these objects coming into perfect balance, representing the balance you wish to achieve in your own life. Say:

"By the light of the equinox bright,
I seek balance in both day and night.
As the Earth turns and seasons flow,
In perfect harmony, my life will grow."

1. **Use the Water for Emotional Balance:** Dip your fingers into the bowl of water and sprinkle a few drops over your heart. As you do this, visualize your emotions becoming calm and balanced. Say:

"Water pure, balance my soul,
Help me feel calm, centered, and whole."

1. **Charge the Crystal:** Hold the crystal or stone in your hands, focusing on its energy of balance. As you hold it, imagine it amplifying your intention to restore balance in your life. Place the stone in the center of your altar, between the two candles, as a symbol of your aligned energy.

2. **Close the Ritual:** Allow the candles to burn for a few minutes longer as you focus on the feeling of balance within yourself. When you're ready, extinguish the candles and carry the crystal with you or place it somewhere you'll see it often to remind you of the balance you've cultivated.

This Equinox Balance Ritual helps you restore equilibrium in all areas of your life, aligning your personal energy with the natural balance of the season.

2. Harvest Reflection Spell

The Autumn Equinox is a time of reflection, marking the culmination of the harvest season. This spell is designed to help you reflect on the "harvest" of your own life—your accomplishments, growth, and the lessons you've learned over the past months.

Ingredients:

- A gold or yellow candle (for abundance and reflection)
- A small bowl of autumn leaves, corn, or grains (for the harvest)
- A piece of paper and pen
- A clear quartz or citrine crystal (for clarity and abundance)

Instructions:

1. **Light the Candle:** Light the gold or yellow candle to represent the energy of the harvest and abundance. As the flame flickers, focus on the blessings, accomplishments, and growth you've experienced over the past year.
2. **Reflect on Your Harvest:** Spend a few moments reflecting on what you've "harvested" in your own life. This could include personal achievements, spiritual growth, relationships, or even challenges you've overcome. Write down at least three things you're proud of or grateful for.
3. **Place the Harvest Items:** Place the bowl of autumn leaves, corn, or grains in front of the candle, symbolizing the abundance and growth in your life. As you place the items, say:

"With this harvest, I reflect,
On the blessings I collect.

Abundance flows from what I've sown,
The seeds of life that I have grown."

1. **Set Future Intentions:** After reflecting on your accomplishments, consider what you still want to cultivate or bring to fruition. Write down one or two intentions for the coming months—goals, dreams, or areas of growth you wish to focus on as the year draws to a close.

2. **Charge the Crystal:** Hold the clear quartz or citrine crystal in your hands, focusing on the energy of clarity and abundance. Visualize the crystal amplifying your reflection and helping you manifest your future intentions. Place the crystal on your altar or carry it with you as a reminder of the abundance you've created.

3. **Close the Spell:** Allow the candle to burn for a few minutes while you reflect on your "harvest" and your future intentions. When you're ready, extinguish the candle and place the reflection and intention paper in a safe place, where you can revisit it in the future.

This Harvest Reflection Spell helps you honor your accomplishments, express gratitude for the blessings you've received, and set clear intentions for continued growth.

3. Equinox Gratitude Meditation and Ritual

Gratitude is a key theme of the Autumn Equinox, as it marks the completion of the harvest and the opportunity to give thanks for the abundance you've received. This meditation and ritual focuses on cultivating gratitude and using it to align your energy with the flow of the earth.

Ingredients:

- A white candle (for purity and clarity)
- A small offering of food or drink (such as apples, bread, wine, or tea)

- A comfortable space for meditation
- A journal or piece of paper and pen

Instructions:

1. **Light the Candle:** Begin by lighting the white candle to symbolize clarity and gratitude. As the flame burns, focus on the feeling of gratitude filling your heart and mind. Imagine the light of the candle representing the abundance you've received.
2. **Gratitude Meditation:** Sit comfortably in front of the candle and close your eyes. Take several deep breaths, allowing your body to relax. As you breathe in, think of something you're grateful for—a person, a moment, an achievement. With each breath, allow the feeling of gratitude to grow stronger.

Visualize yourself standing in the middle of a golden field, surrounded by the fruits of your harvest. Each item represents a blessing in your life. Spend a few moments walking through the field in your mind, touching the fruits of your labor and giving thanks for each one.

As you exhale, send a silent "thank you" out into the universe, acknowledging the gifts you've received.

1. **Offer Your Gratitude:** Once you feel the energy of gratitude flowing, take the small offering of food or drink and place it on your altar or outside in nature as a symbol of your thanks. As you make the offering, say:

"With this offering, I give my thanks,
For all the blessings in my ranks.
Abundance flows, and gratitude grows,
As I honor the harvest that life bestows."

1. **Write in Your Journal:** After the meditation, take a few moments to write down what you are most grateful for. Focus on the specific blessings in your life and how they have contributed to your growth and well-being.
2. **Close the Ritual:** Allow the candle to burn for a few more minutes as you sit in quiet reflection. When you're ready, extinguish the candle and carry the feeling of gratitude with you throughout the day.

This Gratitude Meditation and Ritual helps you align with the energy of the Autumn Equinox by focusing on thankfulness and appreciation for the abundance in your life.

4. Equinox Release and Renewal Ritual

The equinox is not only a time for reflection and gratitude but also a time for releasing what no longer serves you. This ritual focuses on letting go of old patterns, habits, or negative energy and welcoming a sense of renewal as you prepare for the final months of the year.

Ingredients:

- A black or gray candle (for release and transformation)
- A small piece of paper and pen
- A bowl of water or fireproof dish (for burning the paper)
- A lavender or sage bundle (for cleansing)
- A clear quartz crystal (for clarity and renewal)

Instructions:

1. **Light the Candle:** Light the black or gray candle to represent the energy of release and transformation. As the candle burns, visualize the flame burning away any negative or stagnant energy in your life. Say:

"By this flame, I release and clear,
All that I no longer hold dear.
What once was heavy, now takes flight,
Into the darkness, I send it tonight."

1. **Reflect on What Needs to Be Released:** Take a few moments to reflect on anything in your life that feels heavy, unhelpful, or stagnant. This could be old habits, limiting beliefs, toxic relationships, or anything else that is holding you back. Write down what you wish to release on the piece of paper.

2. **Burn or Submerge the Paper:** Once you've written what you wish to release, carefully burn the paper in the fireproof dish or submerge it in the bowl of water to symbolize the release of that energy. As the paper dissolves or burns, say:

"With this flame (or water), I release and let go,
All that hinders my life's flow.
Renewal comes with the moon's light,
I move forward, my path is bright."

1. **Cleansing with Sage or Lavender:** Light the sage or lavender bundle and use the smoke to cleanse yourself and your space, removing any lingering negativity. As you cleanse, say:

"With air and smoke, I now release,
All that blocks my inner peace.
Renewal comes, I am reborn,
As the day fades into morn."

1. **Charge the Crystal:** Hold the clear quartz crystal in your hands and focus on its energy of clarity and renewal. Visualize it amplifying your intention to release the old and embrace the new. Place

the crystal on your altar or carry it with you as a symbol of your fresh start.

2. **Close the Ritual:** Allow the candle to burn for a few more minutes while you focus on the feeling of release and renewal. When you're ready, extinguish the candle and take a few moments to breathe deeply, acknowledging the sense of freedom and lightness that comes from letting go.

This Release and Renewal Ritual helps you release old patterns and negative energy, clearing the way for new growth and opportunities as the year progresses.

Conclusion

The Autumn Equinox is a powerful time for reflection, balance, and renewal. By aligning your energy with the natural rhythms of the Earth, you can use this moment of equilibrium to seek harmony in your life, express gratitude for the blessings you've received, and set clear intentions for the months ahead.

Whether you are performing rituals for balance, reflection, gratitude, or release, the energy of the Autumn Equinox supports your journey of growth and transformation. By embracing the themes of balance, abundance, and renewal, you invite peace and harmony into your life as you prepare for the quiet, introspective months of winter.

Through these reflective rituals and spells, you take a powerful step toward aligning your intentions with the natural flow of the earth, creating a life that is in balance with the cycles of nature and filled with abundance and gratitude.

Chapter 26: Children's Thanksgiving Magic

Thanksgiving is a special time for families to come together and reflect on the blessings in their lives, and it's a wonderful opportunity to introduce children to the concepts of gratitude, love, and giving thanks in a fun and magical way. By involving children in simple spells, activities, and rituals designed specifically for them, you can help them cultivate a deep sense of appreciation and connection to the world around them. These practices encourage children to express gratitude, share love with others, and recognize the magic that exists in everyday life.

This chapter focuses on easy-to-understand, child-friendly magical activities that children can participate in during the Thanksgiving season. The goal is to make gratitude fun and engaging while introducing the little ones to the concept of using their intentions, creativity, and hearts to bring more love, kindness, and appreciation into the world.

The Importance of Teaching Children Gratitude

Gratitude is one of the most important life lessons that children can learn, as it helps them develop empathy, emotional intelligence, and a positive outlook on life. Teaching children to be grateful encourages them to focus on the good in their lives and fosters a deeper connection to their family, friends, and the environment. Gratitude also helps children understand the importance of giving and receiving love, creating strong relationships based on appreciation and kindness.

By introducing children to simple magical practices that incorporate gratitude, you're not only fostering their emotional development but also introducing them to the idea that their thoughts and actions have power. When children learn to express their gratitude through activities and spells, they become active participants in creating a more loving, compassionate world.

Preparing Children for Magical Activities

Before engaging children in magical activities, it's important to create a supportive and nurturing environment where they feel safe to express themselves. You can prepare the space for these activities by incorporating fun elements such as candles, crystals, or nature items, and by explaining the importance of setting intentions in a way that's easy for them to understand.

How to Prepare Children for Magical Activities:

1. **Explain the Concept of Magic Simply:** Tell children that magic is about focusing their thoughts and feelings on something special, like being thankful or wishing for happiness. Explain that when they do these activities, they are helping to create more love and kindness in the world.

2. **Create a Comfortable and Fun Space:** Make sure the area where you'll be working is comfortable and inviting for the children. Include items that they find interesting or comforting, such as soft blankets, cushions, colorful candles, or flowers.

3. **Encourage Creativity and Imagination:** Let children know that they can use their imagination to make these activities more magical. Encourage them to think of the colors, symbols, or words that make them feel happy and thankful.

4. **Be Patient and Open:** Allow children to express themselves freely and remind them that there are no wrong answers. The goal is to have fun and practice gratitude together.

Once the children are excited and ready, you can begin these fun and simple activities designed for them to express their gratitude and share love with others.

Simple Spells and Activities for Children's Thanksgiving Magic

The following spells and activities are easy for children to understand and perform, while still carrying the powerful energy of gratitude, love, and connection. These activities can be done with adult guidance or adapted for children to perform on their own, depending on their age and comfort level.

1. Gratitude Stones

This activity helps children express gratitude in a tangible way by turning simple stones into magical objects that carry their thankful thoughts.

Materials Needed:

- Small, smooth stones (one for each child)
- Paint or markers (for decorating)
- A special box or pouch (to hold the stones)

Instructions:

1. **Explain the Purpose of Gratitude Stones:** Tell the children that these stones are special because they will hold their thankful thoughts. Whenever they hold their stone, they'll remember all the good things in their lives.
2. **Decorate the Stones:** Give each child a smooth stone and allow them to decorate it using paint or markers. Encourage them to draw symbols or images that remind them of things they are thankful for, such as hearts, stars, or favorite animals.
3. **Set the Gratitude Intention:** Once the stones are decorated, gather the children in a circle and ask them to think of one thing they are really grateful for. This could be a person, a favorite toy, a fun activity, or even a pet. Have them hold their stone close and say aloud or silently:

"I'm thankful for [name what they are grateful for],
And with this stone, I hold my thanks inside,
Whenever I feel it, I remember my joy,
And my heart is filled with love and pride."

1. **Place the Stones in the Special Box or Pouch:** Once the children have infused their stones with gratitude, place the stones in a special box or pouch where they can be kept safe. Let them know they can take the stones out whenever they need a reminder of the things they are thankful for.

This Gratitude Stones activity helps children create a physical reminder of their gratitude, which they can carry with them or keep in a special place.

2. Thank You Tree

The Thank You Tree is a fun and interactive way for children to express what they are grateful for by adding colorful "leaves" of thankfulness to a tree throughout the Thanksgiving season.

Materials Needed:

- A small tree branch (or create a tree shape from paper or cardboard)
- Colored paper (cut into leaf shapes)
- String or tape (to attach the leaves)
- Markers or crayons

Instructions:

1. **Create the Thank You Tree:** Begin by finding a small tree branch and placing it in a vase or pot, or create a tree shape from cardboard or paper and stick it to a wall. Explain to the children that this tree will hold all of their thankful thoughts.

2. **Make the Leaves:** Cut out leaf shapes from colored paper and give one to each child. Ask them to think of something they are grateful for, then write or draw it on the leaf. For younger children, you can write their answers for them while they decorate the leaves.

3. **Attach the Leaves:** Once the leaves are decorated, help the children attach them to the tree using string, tape, or glue. As they place each leaf on the tree, have them say:

"Thank you for [what they are grateful for],
I'm thankful and I share,
My love and joy grow on this tree,
To show how much I care."

1. **Add New Leaves Throughout the Season:** Encourage the children to add new leaves to the Thank You Tree throughout the Thanksgiving season as they think of more things they are grateful for.

This activity teaches children to continuously practice gratitude and reflect on their blessings while creating a beautiful tree filled with love and thanks.

3. Love Sharing Jar

The Love Sharing Jar is a fun way for children to express love and kindness by filling a jar with good wishes and loving thoughts that can be shared with family or friends.

Materials Needed:

- A large glass jar (or a decorated box)
- Small pieces of paper (in different colors)
- Crayons, markers, or pencils
- Stickers or decorations for the jar

Instructions:

1. **Decorate the Jar:** Start by allowing the children to decorate the jar with stickers, markers, or other craft materials. Tell them that this jar will hold magical notes of love and kindness that can be shared with others.

2. **Create Love Notes:** Give each child several small pieces of paper and ask them to write or draw something loving or kind that they want to share with someone else. It could be a compliment, a happy thought, or a wish for someone to feel loved. Younger children can draw pictures, while older children can write short messages such as "I love you" or "You are special to me."

3. **Place the Notes in the Jar:** Once the notes are ready, fold them up and place them inside the jar. As each note goes into the jar, have the children say:

"With this note, I share my love,
Sending joy like stars above.
May kindness grow and hearts feel bright,
As we share our love and light."

1. **Share the Notes:** At the Thanksgiving table or throughout the holiday, encourage the children to pull notes from the jar and give them to family members or friends as an act of love and kindness.

The Love Sharing Jar activity helps children learn about giving love to others and spreading happiness in simple but meaningful ways.

4. Gratitude Bracelet

This fun craft allows children to make a magical bracelet that represents the things they are grateful for. Each bead added to the bracelet carries a thankful thought, creating a wearable reminder of the love and joy in their lives.

Materials Needed:

- Elastic string or yarn (to make the bracelet)
- Colorful beads (one for each thing the child is thankful for)
- Small charms (optional, for decoration)

Instructions:

1. **Explain the Meaning of the Bracelet:** Tell the children that this bracelet will be their "Thank You Bracelet," and each bead will represent something they are thankful for.
2. **Choose the Beads:** Let the children choose a bead for each thing they are grateful for. As they pick each bead, ask them to think of one thing they are thankful for, such as "I'm thankful for my family" or "I'm thankful for my pet."
3. **String the Beads:** Help the children string the beads onto the elastic string or yarn, saying aloud each thankful thought as they add a bead. For example:

"This bead is for my family,
Who love me every day.
This bead is for my friends,
Who make me laugh and play."

1. **Tie the Bracelet:** Once all the beads are added, tie the ends of the string together to form a bracelet. Let the children wear their

Gratitude Bracelets as a reminder of all the good things in their lives.

This Gratitude Bracelet activity is a fun, creative way for children to express thanks while making something they can keep or share with others.

5. Gratitude Circle

This activity involves gathering in a circle to express what each child is thankful for. It encourages children to share their feelings of gratitude in a supportive group setting.

Materials Needed:

- A small token (such as a crystal, a smooth stone, or a small stuffed animal)
- A comfortable space where everyone can sit in a circle

Instructions:

1. **Explain the Activity:** Tell the children that they will sit in a circle and take turns holding a special "Thank You Token." When they hold the token, it's their turn to say something they are grateful for.
2. **Pass the Token:** Begin by passing the token around the circle. When each child holds the token, they say something they are thankful for. For example, "I'm thankful for my mom" or "I'm thankful for my favorite book."
3. **Encourage Sharing:** Encourage the children to think of something different each time they receive the token. You can go around the circle multiple times, allowing them to share as many thankful thoughts as they like.
4. **End with a Group Affirmation:** After everyone has had a chance to share, close the activity with a group affirmation, such as:

"We are thankful, we are blessed,
For love, for joy, and for happiness.
With thankful hearts, we stand as one,
Sharing love with everyone."

This Gratitude Circle encourages children to express their feelings openly and to listen to the gratitude of others, fostering a sense of community and connection.

Conclusion

Introducing children to simple spells and activities that focus on gratitude, love, and kindness helps them understand the power of positive thinking and the magic of giving thanks. These activities not only make the concept of gratitude fun and engaging but also encourage children to practice thankfulness in their daily lives, building emotional resilience, empathy, and joy.

Whether they're creating Gratitude Stones, filling a Thank You Tree with love, or sharing kind words from a Love Sharing Jar, children can begin to recognize the importance of being grateful and spreading love to those around them. These magical practices provide a foundation for cultivating a lifetime of appreciation, connection, and positivity, making Thanksgiving a truly magical and meaningful experience for all.

Chapter 27: Banishing Negativity

Negativity can accumulate in our lives and environments over time, often without us even realizing it. Whether it comes from stress, conflict, negative thoughts, or external sources, this energy can weigh us down, cloud our emotions, and block the flow of positivity and gratitude. To make room for gratitude, peace, and abundance—especially during the Thanksgiving season—it's important to clear away negative energy and create a space for positive energy to flourish.

In this chapter, we will explore various spells and rituals designed to banish negativity, cleanse your environment, and invite in positive energy. By performing these spells, you can clear away any emotional, mental, or physical blockages that may be holding you back, allowing gratitude and positivity to flow more freely into your life.

The Importance of Banishing Negativity

Negativity can take many forms. It may manifest as stress, anger, anxiety, frustration, or self-doubt. Sometimes, it can come from external sources such as toxic relationships, difficult environments, or even negative energy left behind by others. Left unchecked, this negativity can grow, making it difficult to maintain a positive, grateful mindset.

Banishing negativity is not just about removing bad energy; it's also about clearing space for positive energy to thrive. By releasing negativity, you open yourself up to greater peace, clarity, and abundance. These spells will help you cleanse your mind, body, and surroundings, making it easier to focus on gratitude and the positive aspects of life.

Key benefits of banishing negativity include:

- **Emotional clarity:** Releasing negative thoughts and emotions allows you to see situations more clearly and respond from a place of calm.
- **Inner peace:** Banishing negativity creates a sense of inner calm and balance, reducing stress and anxiety.
- **Enhanced gratitude:** With negative energy cleared away, you can more easily focus on the blessings in your life and cultivate a sense of gratitude.
- **Positive energy flow:** Clearing negativity makes room for positive energy to enter your life, promoting happiness, abundance, and personal growth.

Preparing for a Banishing Ritual

Before performing any banishing spell or ritual, it's important to prepare yourself and your environment to ensure that you are fully aligned with your intention to clear away negativity. Cleansing your space, grounding yourself, and focusing on your goal will help create the right conditions for the spell to work effectively.

Step-by-Step Guide to Preparing for Banishing Negativity Rituals:

1. **Cleanse Your Space:** Begin by physically cleaning your space, removing clutter, dust, and anything that feels out of place. Physical cleanliness sets the stage for energetic cleansing, ensuring that your environment feels fresh and ready for the ritual.

2. **Gather Your Tools:** You'll need a few key tools to perform a banishing ritual, depending on the spell you choose. Common tools include:
    - **Sage or palo santo:** For smudging and cleansing negative energy.
    - **A black candle:** To symbolize protection and the removal of negativity.
    - **Salt or a bowl of water:** For grounding and purification.
    - **Crystals:** Such as black tourmaline, obsidian, or smoky quartz, which absorb and dispel negative energy.
    - **Incense or essential oils:** Use scents like frankincense, lavender, or rosemary to promote peace and protection.

3. **Ground Yourself:** Before starting the ritual, take a few moments to ground yourself. Sit comfortably with your feet on the floor and visualize roots growing from your feet into the earth. Feel yourself connecting to the earth's stable, grounding energy. This

will help center you and protect you during the banishing process.

4. **Set Your Intention:** Clearly state your intention to banish negativity. Be specific about what you are releasing—whether it's negative thoughts, emotions, or external influences. Your intention will guide the energy of the spell. For example: "I release all negative energy from my space and mind, making room for peace and positivity."

Once you've prepared your space, gathered your tools, grounded yourself, and set your intention, you are ready to begin the banishing rituals.

Banishing Spells to Clear Negativity and Invite Positive Energy

The following spells are designed to banish negative energy from your mind, body, and surroundings, creating space for peace, gratitude, and positive energy to flow. You can perform these spells individually or combine them for a more comprehensive banishing ritual.

1. Sage Smudging Ritual

Sage smudging is one of the most powerful and effective ways to clear negative energy from your space. This ritual uses the smoke from burning sage to cleanse away negativity and purify the environment, leaving your space feeling fresh and balanced.

Ingredients:

- A bundle of dried sage (or palo santo)
- A fireproof dish (to catch ashes)
- A black candle (for protection)

Instructions:

1. **Light the Candle:** Begin by lighting the black candle to symbolize protection and the removal of negativity. As the candle burns, visualize a protective barrier forming around you and your space.
2. **Light the Sage:** Carefully light the tip of the sage bundle until it begins to smolder and produce smoke. Hold the sage over a fireproof dish to catch any ashes that fall.
3. **Walk Through Your Space:** Starting at the entrance of your home or room, walk slowly through each area, allowing the sage smoke to drift into every corner. Pay special attention to areas where you feel negative energy may be concentrated, such as corners, closets, or high-traffic spaces. As you move, say:

"By smoke and sage, I cleanse and clear,
All negativity, disappear.

Only peace and love shall stay,
All dark energy, I send away."

1. **Smudge Yourself:** After you've smudged your space, smudge yourself by gently waving the sage smoke around your body, starting at your feet and moving upward. This will help remove any lingering negativity attached to your energy field.
2. **Close the Ritual:** Once you feel your space is fully cleansed, extinguish the sage in the fireproof dish and allow the candle to burn for a few more minutes. Focus on the feeling of peace and lightness that now fills the space.

This Sage Smudging Ritual is a powerful way to cleanse your home and yourself of negativity, creating a fresh, positive environment.

2. Black Salt Protection Spell

Black salt is often used in protection and banishing spells to ward off negative energy and prevent it from entering your space. This simple but effective spell uses black salt to create a protective barrier around your home.

Ingredients:

- Black salt (you can make this by mixing regular salt with ashes from a protective herb like rosemary or sage)
- A black candle (for protection)
- A small dish or container to hold the salt

Instructions:

1. **Light the Candle:** Begin by lighting the black candle to invoke protective energy. As the flame burns, visualize your home being surrounded by a protective shield that keeps all negativity out.
2. **Charge the Black Salt:** Hold the container of black salt in your hands and focus on your intention to banish negativity and protect your home. Say:

"Black salt strong, protect this place,
Shield my home from harm and trace.
No ill shall pass, no dark shall stay,
All negativity I send away."

1. **Sprinkle the Salt:** Walk around the perimeter of your home, sprinkling the black salt near doors, windows, and any other entry points. As you do this, visualize the salt creating an impenetrable barrier that blocks all negative energy from entering. Say:

"With this salt, I create a shield,
Protect this home, all harm is healed.
No darkness shall enter, no fear shall stay,
This home is blessed, night and day."

1. **Close the Spell:** Once you've sprinkled the black salt around your home, return to the candle and spend a few moments focusing on the protective energy that now surrounds your space. When you're ready, extinguish the candle.

This Black Salt Protection Spell creates a powerful barrier that prevents negative energy from entering your home, ensuring that your space remains safe and peaceful.

3. Negative Thought Banishing Ritual

This ritual focuses on clearing away negative thoughts, self-doubt, and limiting beliefs that may be holding you back from embracing gratitude and positivity. By writing down and releasing these negative thoughts, you can make room for more positive, empowering energy.

Ingredients:

- A black or gray candle (for release and transformation)
- A piece of paper and pen
- A fireproof dish (for burning the paper)
- A small bowl of water or salt (for cleansing)

Instructions:

1. **Light the Candle:** Light the black or gray candle to represent the energy of release and transformation. As the flame burns, visualize it burning away any negative thoughts or beliefs that have been weighing you down.
2. **Write Down Negative Thoughts:** On the piece of paper, write down any negative thoughts, fears, or self-doubts that you've been carrying. Be honest and specific. These could include thoughts like "I'm not good enough" or "I'll never succeed." As you write, focus on your intention to release these thoughts.
3. **Burn the Paper:** Once you've written down your negative thoughts, carefully burn the paper in the fireproof dish, visualizing the flames transforming the negativity into light. As the paper burns, say:

"With this flame, I release and clear,
All negative thoughts, all doubt and fear.
I banish these shadows, they fade away,
In their place, peace will stay."

1. **Cleanse with Water or Salt:** Once the paper has burned, dip your fingers in the bowl of water or salt and sprinkle a few drops over your head and heart. This will help cleanse your energy and replace the negative thoughts with positive energy. As you do this, say:

"Water pure, cleanse my mind,
Peace and clarity I now find.
All negativity I release,
I welcome love, I welcome peace."

1. **Close the Ritual:** Allow the candle to burn for a few more minutes as you focus on the feeling of peace and positivity filling your mind. When you're ready, extinguish the candle.

This Negative Thought Banishing Ritual helps clear away mental blocks and negative beliefs, allowing you to embrace a more positive, empowered mindset.

4. Protective Crystal Grid for the Home

This spell uses crystals to create a protective grid around your home, ensuring that negative energy is repelled and only positive, peaceful energy can flow freely. Crystals such as black tourmaline and smoky quartz are excellent for absorbing and dispelling negativity.

Ingredients:

- Four black tourmaline or smoky quartz crystals (for protection)
- One clear quartz crystal (for amplification)
- A small dish of salt (for purification)
- A white candle (for peace and clarity)

Instructions:

1. **Light the Candle:** Begin by lighting the white candle to symbolize peace and clarity. As the flame burns, focus on your intention to protect your home from negativity and create a peaceful environment.
2. **Set the Crystals:** Place the four black tourmaline or smoky quartz crystals at the four corners of your home, either inside or outside. These crystals will act as a protective barrier, absorbing any negative energy that tries to enter. As you place each crystal, say:

"Crystal strong, absorb all harm,
Protect this home, keep it warm.

No ill shall pass, no dark shall stay,
Only peace shall find its way."

1. **Place the Clear Quartz:** Place the clear quartz crystal in the center of your home, or in the room where your family gathers most often. This crystal will amplify the protective energy of the grid and invite positive energy to flow through the space. As you place it, say:

"Crystal clear, amplify light,
Bring peace and love, shining bright.
No harm shall come, no fear shall stay,
Only joy will fill this day."

1. **Charge the Grid with Salt:** Sprinkle a small amount of salt in the center of the grid, near the clear quartz crystal, to further purify and protect the space. As you do this, visualize the grid being activated, creating a shield of light around your home.
2. **Close the Ritual:** Allow the candle to burn for a few more minutes while you focus on the feeling of protection and peace surrounding your home. When you're ready, extinguish the candle and leave the crystal grid in place to continue protecting your space.

This Protective Crystal Grid helps shield your home from negative energy, creating a peaceful and harmonious environment for you and your family.

Conclusion

Banishing negativity is an essential part of creating a space where gratitude, peace, and positive energy can thrive. By performing these banishing rituals and spells, you can clear away negative energy from your mind, body, and surroundings, allowing you to focus more fully on the positive aspects of your life.

Whether you're using sage to cleanse your home, black salt to create a protective barrier, or crystals to build a grid of protection, these rituals empower you to take control of your environment and your mindset. With negativity cleared away, you can embrace the energy of gratitude, abundance, and personal growth, creating a life filled with light, love, and positivity.

Through these spells, you create a sacred space for yourself and your loved ones, free from negativity and open to the flow of positive energy during the Thanksgiving season and beyond.

Chapter 28: Fortune Talisman Creation

Talismans and amulets have been used for centuries to attract fortune, abundance, and protection. These small, symbolic objects are charged with intention and infused with magical energy to bring prosperity and good luck to the person who wears or carries them. During the Thanksgiving season, as we celebrate abundance and express gratitude, creating fortune talismans can be a powerful way to align with the energy of prosperity and invite more wealth and good fortune into your life.

In this chapter, we will explore how to craft and charge your own fortune talismans, using materials such as herbs, crystals, metals, and symbols traditionally associated with abundance. Whether you wear these talismans as jewelry, carry them in your pocket, or place them in your home, they will serve as constant reminders of your intentions and as magical tools to help attract prosperity into your life.

The Power of Fortune Talismans

Fortune talismans work by combining specific materials, symbols, and intentions to create a physical object that channels and focuses energy. When you carry or wear a talisman, it acts as a magnet for positive energy, helping to draw fortune, success, and abundance to you. These charms not only act as spiritual magnets for wealth but also as psychological reminders of your goals and desires, keeping you focused on achieving success.

Creating a talisman is a highly personal and intentional process. Each material and symbol used in the talisman carries its own unique energy and purpose, which, when combined, amplifies the energy of fortune and abundance.

Key benefits of fortune talismans include:

- **Attracting financial prosperity:** Talismans can be specifically crafted to attract wealth, success, and opportunities for financial gain.

- **Enhancing personal growth:** By focusing your intentions on abundance, you also attract opportunities for growth, success, and self-improvement.
- **Manifesting abundance in all areas of life:** Fortune doesn't only refer to material wealth—it also includes love, health, creativity, and personal fulfillment. Talismans can be crafted to attract any form of abundance you desire.
- **Providing protection from negative influences:** Many fortune talismans also offer protection against bad luck, negativity, or obstacles that may hinder your success.

Materials for Fortune Talismans

Before creating a talisman, it's important to gather materials that are traditionally associated with fortune, abundance, and protection. Each material carries its own magical properties and contributes to the overall energy of the talisman. Below are some common materials and their meanings in fortune talisman creation:

Crystals and Gemstones:

- **Citrine:** Known as the "merchant's stone," citrine is associated with wealth, abundance, and success in business. It helps manifest financial prosperity and good luck.
- **Green Aventurine:** This stone is often called the "stone of opportunity" and is known for attracting luck, especially in financial matters.
- **Pyrite:** Sometimes called "fool's gold," pyrite is a powerful stone for attracting wealth, abundance, and protection. It enhances willpower and helps manifest success.
- **Tiger's Eye:** A protective stone that also promotes good fortune and success in endeavors, especially in career and business.
- **Jade:** Jade is associated with luck, harmony, and long-term success, especially in health and relationships. It is a powerful stone for attracting overall abundance.

Herbs and Plants:

- **Basil:** A powerful herb for attracting wealth and financial success. It can be used in sachets, oils, or as part of a talisman.
- **Cinnamon:** Known for its ability to speed up manifestation, cinnamon attracts wealth, success, and abundance.
- **Bay Leaves:** Traditionally used for wishes and manifestations, bay leaves can help bring about financial success and good fortune.
- **Mint:** An herb associated with money and prosperity, mint can be used in talismans to attract financial gain.
- **Patchouli:** This earthy herb is known for drawing in abundance, both material and spiritual. It is often used in money-drawing spells and talismans.

Metals:

- **Gold:** A powerful metal associated with wealth, success, and the energy of the sun. Gold is often used in talismans to amplify prosperity.
- **Silver:** Associated with the moon and intuition, silver is a metal of abundance that also offers protection from negative influences.
- **Copper:** A metal associated with energy flow, copper helps attract wealth, love, and harmony.

Symbols:

- **Coins:** Using a coin in your talisman symbolizes wealth and prosperity. Old coins or coins from different countries can add extra energy to your talisman.
- **The Pentacle:** The five-pointed star in a circle is a symbol of protection, balance, and manifestation, making it a powerful addition to any talisman.

- **The Infinity Symbol (∞):** This symbol represents limitless abundance and the continuous flow of energy. It can be used to attract endless wealth and success.
- **The Rune Fehu (◇):** Fehu is a rune symbolizing wealth, prosperity, and abundance. It is often used in fortune talismans to attract financial success.
- **The Dollar Sign ($):** A simple yet powerful symbol of money and wealth, incorporating this symbol into your talisman helps focus the energy of financial abundance.

Step-by-Step Guide to Crafting a Fortune Talisman

Creating a fortune talisman involves selecting the right materials, setting clear intentions, and charging the talisman with your energy. Follow the steps below to craft a powerful fortune talisman designed to attract wealth and abundance.

Step 1: Set Your Intention

Before gathering your materials, take time to set a clear and specific intention for your talisman. What kind of fortune are you hoping to attract? Is it financial wealth, success in a business venture, or abundance in relationships and health? The clearer your intention, the more powerful your talisman will be.

Write down your intention in positive, present-tense language. For example:

- "I attract financial abundance into my life effortlessly."
- "Success and prosperity flow to me in all my endeavors."
- "I am surrounded by opportunities for wealth and growth."

Step 2: Gather Your Materials

Once you've set your intention, gather the materials you'll use to craft your talisman. Choose a combination of crystals, herbs, metals, and symbols that resonate with your intention. Here's an example of materials for a fortune talisman:

- **Citrine or Green Aventurine (for wealth and success)**
- **Cinnamon or Basil (to attract financial gain)**
- **A gold or silver coin (as a symbol of abundance)**
- **A small piece of gold or copper wire (to enhance the flow of energy)**
- **A pentacle charm (for protection and manifestation)**

You can place these items in a small cloth pouch, wrap them in fabric, or use them to create a wearable charm, such as a necklace or bracelet.

Step 3: Cleanse and Purify Your Materials

Before assembling your talisman, cleanse and purify each material to remove any unwanted or lingering energy. You can do this by:

- Smudging the materials with sage, palo santo, or incense.
- Holding the materials under running water (for water-safe items).
- Placing the materials in sunlight or moonlight for a few hours.

As you cleanse each item, visualize it being purified and charged with your intention.

Step 4: Assemble the Talisman

After cleansing your materials, it's time to assemble your talisman. Place each item together with care, focusing on your intention with each step. If you're using a cloth pouch or charm bag, fill it with your chosen crystals, herbs, metals, and symbols.

As you add each item, say aloud or silently what each piece represents:

- "With this citrine, I attract financial success."
- "With this basil, I draw in abundance and opportunity."
- "With this coin, I call in wealth and prosperity."

If you're creating a wearable talisman, such as a necklace, bracelet, or keychain, use a piece of cord or chain to tie everything together, infusing your energy and intention into the process.

Step 5: Charge the Talisman

Once your talisman is assembled, it's time to charge it with your energy and intention. Sit in a quiet, comfortable space, holding the talisman in your hands. Close your eyes and visualize a bright, golden light surrounding the talisman, filling it with your intention for fortune and abundance.

As you hold the talisman, repeat your intention aloud or in your mind, such as:

- "I charge this talisman with the power to attract wealth, success, and prosperity. Abundance flows to me easily and effortlessly."

You can also call upon any deities, spirits, or energies that resonate with you to bless and empower your talisman. Allow the talisman to rest in your hands or on your altar as you feel its energy growing.

Step 6: Use and Wear the Talisman

After charging the talisman, it's ready to be used. You can wear it as jewelry, carry it in your pocket, or keep it in a special place in your home where you see it often. The talisman will continue to work as long as you hold the intention of attracting fortune and abundance.

Each time you interact with the talisman, take a moment to reconnect with your original intention. You can also recharge the talisman during full moons or other auspicious times to keep its energy strong and active.

Fortune Talisman Creation Ideas

Here are a few specific ideas for creating fortune talismans based on different forms of abundance you may want to attract:

1. Money Magnet Talisman

This talisman is designed specifically to attract financial wealth and opportunities for monetary gain.

Materials:

- **Green aventurine** (for luck and financial success)
- **Cinnamon stick** (for prosperity and speed in manifesting money)
- **A coin** (to represent wealth and material gain)
- **A bay leaf** (for success and good fortune)

Instructions:

1. Place the green aventurine, cinnamon stick, coin, and bay leaf in a small green or gold pouch.
2. As you add each item, say aloud: "I attract financial abundance and prosperity into my life."
3. Charge the talisman by holding it and visualizing yourself surrounded by wealth and success. Carry the pouch with you to attract money and opportunities.

2. Business Success Talisman

This talisman is crafted to support success in business ventures, new projects, or career advancement.

Materials:

- **Citrine** (for success, business growth, and wealth)
- **Basil leaves** (for attracting customers and opportunities)
- **Gold coin or charm** (for prosperity and long-term success)
- **Copper wire** (to enhance the flow of energy and business success)

Instructions:

1. Wrap the citrine, basil leaves, and gold coin together with the copper wire, forming a small bundle.
2. Hold the bundle in your hands and set the intention for business success and growth, saying: "My business flourishes and grows, bringing wealth and success."
3. Keep the talisman near your workspace or place it in your office to attract new opportunities and financial gain.

3. Love and Abundance Talisman

This talisman focuses on attracting abundance in relationships, love, and emotional fulfillment, as well as material wealth.

Materials:

- **Rose quartz** (for love and emotional abundance)
- **Green aventurine** (for luck and prosperity in love and relationships)
- **A pink or red ribbon** (for love and harmony)
- **A silver charm or coin** (to represent abundance in all forms)

Instructions:

1. Tie the rose quartz and green aventurine together with the pink or red ribbon, adding the silver charm.
2. Hold the talisman and focus on attracting love and abundance into your life, saying: "I attract love, joy, and abundance in all areas of my life."
3. Carry the talisman with you or place it on your altar to invite love and positive relationships.

Conclusion

Fortune talismans are powerful tools that allow you to channel your intentions and the energy of prosperity into a physical object that you can carry with you or keep in your home. Whether you're seeking financial abundance, business success, or emotional fulfillment, crafting a talisman designed to attract fortune helps you focus on your desires and manifest them into reality.

By selecting the right materials, setting clear intentions, and charging your talisman with focused energy, you create a magical object that works continuously to draw wealth, success, and abundance into your life. With your fortune talisman in hand, you carry the power to manifest your dreams, aligning yourself with the flow of prosperity and creating a life of abundance and gratitude.

Chapter 29: Thanksgiving Night Wishes

Thanksgiving is a time to gather with loved ones and reflect on the blessings of the past year, but it is also an opportunity to set powerful intentions for the future. The night of Thanksgiving, often filled with warmth, joy, and gratitude, creates the perfect atmosphere for wish-making and spellwork under the stars. By tapping into the quiet, peaceful energy of the night sky, you can align your dreams and desires with the cosmic forces at play, setting the stage for manifestation in the coming year.

In this chapter, we will explore magical rituals and spells designed to help you connect with the energy of the stars and the universe, focusing on your deepest dreams and desires. These Thanksgiving night spells are intended to harness the quiet power of the night, encouraging you to dream big, set clear intentions, and align your personal wishes with the natural flow of the cosmos.

The Magic of Thanksgiving Night

Thanksgiving night is a powerful time to reflect on the past year while looking forward to what you wish to manifest in the coming months. The energy of gratitude, combined with the tranquility of the night sky, creates an ideal space for wish-making. The stars have long been seen as guides for navigation, both physically and spiritually, and by performing your spells under the stars, you can tap into their ancient wisdom and cosmic power.

Key themes for Thanksgiving Night Wishes include:

- **Reflection:** Taking time to reflect on the blessings you've received and using those reflections to fuel your dreams for the future.
- **Wish-Making:** Setting intentions and making wishes that align with your true desires for the coming year.
- **Cosmic Alignment:** Connecting with the stars and the universe to amplify the power of your dreams and desires.
- **Gratitude and Abundance:** Focusing on gratitude to attract more abundance into your life, using the night as a time to appreciate all that you have and set the stage for what's to come.

Thanksgiving night wishes are particularly potent because they combine the energy of gratitude with the magic of setting new intentions, allowing you to close one chapter and begin the next with clarity and purpose.

Preparing for Thanksgiving Night Spells

Before you perform any spellwork on Thanksgiving night, it's important to prepare yourself and your environment. Whether you'll be performing your ritual outdoors under the stars or from the comfort of your home, taking the time to set the right atmosphere will enhance the effectiveness of your spells.

Step-by-Step Guide to Preparing for Thanksgiving Night Spells:

1. **Choose Your Space:** If possible, perform your Thanksgiving night spellwork outdoors under the stars. Being in direct connection with the night sky helps amplify the power of your intentions. If the weather doesn't permit this, set up a space near a window where you can see the stars or bring representations of the night sky into your indoor space, such as star-themed candles, crystals, or decor.

2. **Cleanse and Ground Yourself:** Take a moment to ground yourself before beginning your ritual. You can do this through a brief meditation, walking barefoot on the earth, or simply sitting in silence while focusing on your breath. This grounding process helps you connect with the earth's energy and prepare for the work ahead.

3. **Gather Your Tools:** You'll need a few key tools to perform your Thanksgiving night spells, depending on the specific ritual you choose. Common tools include:
   - **Candles:** White, silver, or blue candles to represent the stars and the energy of the night.
   - **Crystals:** Clear quartz (for clarity), moonstone (for intuition), or lapis lazuli (for cosmic connection) are ideal for working under the stars.
   - **Paper and pen:** For writing down your wishes and intentions.

- ◦ **A small bowl of water or a mirror:** To reflect the night sky and connect with the energy of the stars.
- ◦ **Incense or essential oils:** Scents like lavender, frankincense, or sandalwood to create a peaceful, starry atmosphere.

4. **Set Your Intention:** Take time to reflect on what you truly desire for the coming year. Your intention is the heart of your spell, so be specific and clear about what you're wishing for. Whether you seek abundance, love, success, or personal growth, your intention should reflect your deepest dreams.

Once your space is prepared, your tools are gathered, and your intention is clear, you are ready to begin your Thanksgiving night spellwork.

Thanksgiving Night Spells for Wishes and Intentions

The following spells and rituals are designed to help you focus on your dreams, set intentions for the coming year, and harness the power of the night sky to amplify your wishes. These spells are best performed on Thanksgiving night, when the energy of gratitude and reflection is at its peak.

1. Starry Night Wish Spell

This simple yet powerful spell helps you make a wish under the stars, aligning your desires with the cosmic forces of the universe. By focusing on the energy of the stars, you can amplify your intention and set the wheels of manifestation in motion.

Ingredients:

- A white or silver candle (for star energy)
- A small piece of paper and pen (for writing your wish)
- A clear quartz crystal (to amplify your wish)
- A bowl of water or a small mirror (to reflect the night sky)

Instructions:

1. **Light the Candle:** Begin by lighting the white or silver candle to represent the energy of the stars. Place the candle in a central location in your space, such as an altar or outdoor area.

2. **Write Your Wish:** On the piece of paper, write down your wish or intention for the coming year. Be as specific as possible, focusing on what you truly desire. As you write, imagine your wish being carried up to the stars, where it will be magnified and brought to life.

3. **Charge the Wish with the Stars:** Hold the piece of paper with your wish in one hand and the clear quartz crystal in the other. Close your eyes and visualize the night sky filled with stars. See each star twinkling with cosmic energy, ready to carry your wish out into the universe. Say:

"Stars above, so pure and bright,
I send my wish into the night.
With your power, it will grow,
Bringing fortune, love, and flow."

1. **Reflect the Night Sky:** Place the bowl of water or the mirror where it can reflect the stars (or imagine the stars if you're indoors). Gently place the piece of paper with your wish near the water or mirror, symbolizing your connection to the stars. Allow the candle to burn while you focus on the image of the stars magnifying your wish.

2. **Close the Spell:** After spending a few moments in quiet reflection, fold the piece of paper and keep it in a special place, such as your altar or a journal. You can also choose to burn the paper in the candle's flame to release your wish to the universe. As you close the spell, say:

"By the stars' light, my wish takes flight,
Manifesting now, pure and bright."

This Starry Night Wish Spell helps you send your deepest desires into the cosmos, allowing the energy of the stars to amplify and manifest your dreams.

2. Moon and Stars Dream Manifestation Ritual

This ritual is designed to help you focus on long-term dreams and desires, using the energy of the moon and stars to set intentions for the coming year. It's ideal for those who wish to manifest big goals, whether in career, relationships, or personal growth.

Ingredients:

- A blue or silver candle (to represent the moon and stars)
- A moonstone or lapis lazuli crystal (for cosmic alignment and intuition)
- A small journal or notebook (to record your dreams and intentions)
- Lavender or sandalwood incense (for peaceful, dreamy energy)

Instructions:

1. **Light the Candle and Incense:** Begin by lighting the blue or silver candle to represent the energy of the moon and stars. Light the lavender or sandalwood incense to create a calming, meditative atmosphere. As the candle and incense burn, take a few deep breaths to ground yourself and connect with the energy of the night.

2. **Meditate on Your Dreams:** Sit comfortably and hold the moonstone or lapis lazuli crystal in your hands. Close your eyes and focus on the night sky, visualizing the stars twinkling above you. Think about your biggest dreams and desires—those that will take time to manifest but are deeply important to you. Let your mind wander to these dreams, allowing your intuition to guide you.

3. **Write Down Your Intentions:** Open your journal or notebook and write down your long-term intentions and dreams for the coming year. These could be goals for your career, relationships, personal growth, or spiritual development. As you write, focus

on how these dreams make you feel, and allow yourself to fully imagine what it would be like to achieve them. Say:

"Moon and stars, hear my plea,
Bring my dreams to life for me.
By your light, I set my aim,
With your power, I stake my claim."

1. **Charge the Crystal:** Once you've written down your dreams, hold the moonstone or lapis lazuli crystal over the candle flame (safely) and visualize the energy of the moon and stars being absorbed into the crystal. This crystal will now serve as a reminder and amplifier of your dreams. Place the crystal on top of your journal to charge both with the energy of the night.
2. **Close the Ritual:** Allow the candle and incense to burn for a few more minutes while you reflect on your dreams and desires. When you're ready, extinguish the candle and keep the crystal and journal in a special place where you can revisit them throughout the year.

This Moon and Stars Dream Manifestation Ritual helps you focus on long-term goals and set powerful intentions for manifesting your biggest dreams.

3. Thanksgiving Night Gratitude and Wish Spell

This spell combines the energy of gratitude with wish-making, allowing you to reflect on what you've already received while setting intentions for the future. By focusing on both gratitude and desire, you create a balanced and powerful energy that enhances manifestation.

Ingredients:

- A gold or white candle (for gratitude and light)
- A piece of paper and pen (for writing wishes and gratitude)
- A small pouch or jar (to store your wishes)
- Rose quartz or citrine (to attract abundance and love)
- Frankincense or rosemary incense (to purify and enhance the spell)

Instructions:

1. **Light the Candle and Incense:** Begin by lighting the gold or white candle to represent the light of gratitude and the energy of your wishes. Light the frankincense or rosemary incense to purify the space and create a magical atmosphere.

2. **Write Your Gratitude List:** On one side of the paper, write down at least three things you are deeply grateful for this year. These could be blessings you've received, lessons you've learned, or experiences that have enriched your life. As you write, focus on the feeling of gratitude filling your heart.

3. **Write Your Wishes:** On the other side of the paper, write down your wishes and intentions for the coming year. These could be desires for abundance, love, success, or personal growth. Be clear and specific about what you want to manifest.

4. **Charge the Paper:** Hold the piece of paper in your hands and visualize it glowing with golden light. Imagine the energy of your

gratitude and wishes merging, creating a powerful force for manifestation. As you hold the paper, say:

"Gratitude and wishes blend,
Bringing blessings that never end.
By this light, I call to me,
All I desire, so mote it be."

1. **Store the Wishes:** Fold the paper and place it in a small pouch or jar, along with the rose quartz or citrine. This pouch or jar will hold the energy of your gratitude and wishes, amplifying their power over time. Keep it in a special place where you can revisit it throughout the year.
2. **Close the Spell:** Allow the candle and incense to burn for a few more minutes while you focus on the feeling of gratitude and anticipation for your wishes. When you're ready, extinguish the candle and thank the universe for the blessings you've received and the wishes that are on their way.

This Thanksgiving Night Gratitude and Wish Spell helps you combine the energy of thankfulness with the power of intention, creating a balanced and potent force for manifestation.

4. Night Sky Reflection Ritual

This ritual is designed for deep reflection and connection with the stars. It helps you tap into the wisdom of the night sky, allowing you to receive guidance for the year ahead while setting powerful intentions.

Ingredients:

- A blue or silver candle (for cosmic connection)
- A journal or notebook (for reflections and intentions)
- A small mirror or bowl of water (to reflect the stars)
- A clear quartz or amethyst crystal (for clarity and intuition)

Instructions:

1. **Light the Candle:** Begin by lighting the blue or silver candle, symbolizing your connection to the cosmos. Place the mirror or bowl of water in front of the candle to reflect the stars and create a space for deep reflection.

2. **Meditate on the Stars:** Sit comfortably and gaze into the mirror or bowl of water, imagining the stars reflecting back at you. Allow your mind to quiet as you focus on the vastness of the night sky. Ask the universe for guidance on your path for the coming year, and remain open to any insights or messages you receive.

3. **Write Down Your Reflections:** Open your journal and write down any thoughts, feelings, or insights that come to you during the meditation. These reflections may help you clarify your intentions and dreams for the future.

4. **Set Your Intention:** Once you've reflected, write down a clear and specific intention for the coming year. Focus on what you truly desire and how you wish to grow. As you write, say:

"By the stars and moon so bright,
I set my path in this quiet night.

With wisdom clear and heart so true,
I call my dreams to come through."

1. **Charge the Crystal:** Hold the clear quartz or amethyst crystal over the mirror or bowl of water, allowing it to absorb the energy of the stars. This crystal will now hold the wisdom and guidance of the night sky. Keep it with you or place it on your altar to continue receiving insights.

2. **Close the Ritual:** Allow the candle to burn for a few more minutes while you reflect on the insights you've gained. When you're ready, extinguish the candle and thank the stars for their guidance.

This Night Sky Reflection Ritual helps you connect deeply with the cosmos, gaining clarity and guidance for the year ahead while setting powerful intentions for your dreams.

Conclusion

Thanksgiving night offers a unique and magical opportunity to reflect on the blessings of the past year while setting intentions for the future. By performing spells under the stars, you align your wishes with the cosmic forces at play, amplifying the power of your dreams and desires.

Whether you're making a simple wish under the stars, reflecting on long-term goals, or combining gratitude with wish-making, these Thanksgiving night spells help you tap into the energy of the universe and manifest your deepest desires. With the stars as your guide, you can dream big and set powerful intentions for the coming year, knowing that the universe is working in harmony with your wishes.

Chapter 30: Manifesting the Future Harvest

The concept of planting seeds—both literal and metaphorical—is a powerful symbol in magical practice, representing the process of setting intentions and nurturing them over time to eventually reap the rewards. Manifesting future abundance, or the "future harvest," requires not only the clear intention of what you wish to achieve but also the dedication and care needed to ensure its growth. Like a farmer tending to crops, you must focus on nurturing your goals, protecting them from harm, and allowing time for them to grow and flourish.

In this chapter, we will explore spells and rituals specifically designed to manifest long-term abundance and prosperity. These spells focus on setting strong intentions for the future, planting the seeds of your desires, and nurturing them to ensure that they bear fruit. By working with these powerful spells, you can cultivate future prosperity in all areas of your life, including wealth, career, relationships, and personal growth.

The Power of Planting Seeds for Future Abundance

Manifesting long-term abundance requires patience, vision, and trust in the process of growth. Like the cycles of nature, your intentions take time to develop, and they require the right conditions to thrive. By planting the seeds of your desires now, you are aligning yourself with the natural flow of the universe, trusting that your efforts will eventually lead to a bountiful harvest.

Key themes of future harvest manifestation include:

- **Intention-Setting:** Clarifying what you wish to manifest and planting the "seeds" of those desires.
- **Nurturing Growth:** Cultivating your goals through regular action, care, and focus, ensuring that they have the resources needed to thrive.
- **Patience and Trust:** Allowing time for your intentions to develop, trusting that they will come to fruition in the right moment.
- **Gratitude and Appreciation:** Recognizing that abundance is a cycle, and giving thanks for the blessings you've already received as you prepare for future success.

By focusing on long-term manifestation, you create a steady, sustainable flow of prosperity that continues to grow over time, just like a well-tended garden.

Preparing for Future Harvest Manifestation Rituals

Before performing any spell to manifest long-term abundance, it's important to take time to reflect on what you truly wish to achieve in the future. Whether you are focusing on financial success, personal fulfillment, or growth in relationships, setting clear intentions and gathering the right tools will help ensure that your goals are aligned with the natural flow of the universe.

Step-by-Step Guide to Preparing for Future Harvest Manifestation:

1. **Clarify Your Intentions:** Take time to reflect on what areas of your life you wish to cultivate abundance in. Are you focused on financial prosperity, personal growth, career success, or abundance in relationships? Be as specific as possible about your goals and what future harvest you wish to manifest.

2. **Visualize the Growth Process:** As part of clarifying your intention, visualize the process of growth from seed to harvest. Imagine your goals as tiny seeds that need to be planted, watered, nurtured, and protected. Consider the steps you will take in the coming months or years to help those seeds grow into their fullest potential.

3. **Gather Your Tools:** The following tools are commonly used in future harvest manifestation rituals. Choose the ones that resonate with your intention and energy:

     ◦ **Seeds or plant-based symbols:** Actual seeds, leaves, or acorns can represent the planting of your goals. You can also use herbs associated with growth, such as basil or rosemary.

- ◦ **Crystals:** Green aventurine (for growth and opportunity), citrine (for abundance), and clear quartz (for amplifying intentions).
- ◦ **Candles:** Green candles for prosperity and growth, gold candles for abundance, or white candles for clarity and purity.
- ◦ **A small pot of soil:** To represent the fertile ground where your intentions will grow.
- ◦ **Incense or essential oils:** Scents like sandalwood, patchouli, or cedarwood, which are often associated with abundance and grounding.

4. **Ground and Center Yourself:** Before beginning your ritual, spend a few moments grounding and centering yourself. You can do this by sitting quietly, taking deep breaths, or meditating on the feeling of the earth beneath you. This will help you connect with the earth's energy, which is essential for manifesting future harvests.

Once you've clarified your intentions, gathered your tools, and grounded yourself, you're ready to begin the process of planting your seeds of abundance.

Spells and Rituals for Manifesting the Future Harvest

The following spells focus on planting the seeds of your desires and nurturing them over time to ensure long-term success. Each spell is designed to help you set powerful intentions, align your energy with the natural cycles of growth, and trust in the process of manifesting future abundance.

1. Seed of Prosperity Planting Spell

This spell focuses on planting the seeds of financial abundance and prosperity for the future. By physically planting a seed in the earth, you symbolically plant your intention, allowing it to grow and flourish over time.

Ingredients:

- A small pot of soil or a patch of earth
- A seed (such as sunflower, basil, or mint) to represent your intention
- A green or gold candle (for abundance)
- A piece of paper and pen (for writing your intention)
- A crystal (green aventurine or citrine) to amplify your intention

Instructions:

1. **Light the Candle:** Begin by lighting the green or gold candle to represent the energy of abundance and growth. As the flame burns, visualize the light filling your space with prosperity and opportunity.

2. **Write Your Intention:** On the piece of paper, write down your intention for financial abundance. Be clear and specific about what kind of prosperity you wish to manifest. For example: "I plant the seed of wealth, and financial abundance grows steadily

in my life." As you write, imagine this intention becoming a seed that will grow over time.

3. **Plant the Seed:** Take the seed in your hand and hold it over the candle flame (at a safe distance). Visualize the seed absorbing the energy of your intention. Say:

"This seed I plant with care and might,
Grows prosperity day and night.
As it blooms, my wealth will rise,
Bringing fortune before my eyes."

1. **Bury the Seed:** Place the seed in the pot of soil or in the earth, covering it gently with dirt. As you bury the seed, imagine your intention being planted deep in the earth, where it will grow and manifest in the months to come. Place the crystal near the seed or bury it alongside it to amplify the energy of growth.

2. **Water the Seed:** Gently water the seed, symbolizing the nurturing and care you will give to your intention. As you water the seed, say:

"As this seed grows strong and tall,
So too does abundance come to call.
I nurture my goals with love and light,
And prosperity blooms in clear sight."

1. **Close the Spell:** Allow the candle to burn for a few more minutes while you focus on the feeling of prosperity growing in your life. When you're ready, extinguish the candle and place the pot or plant in a sunny spot where it can grow. Tend to the plant regularly, just as you would tend to your goals.

This Seed of Prosperity Planting Spell helps you align your intentions with the natural cycles of growth, allowing financial abundance to bloom in your life.

2. Future Abundance Candle Ritual

This candle ritual focuses on setting long-term intentions for abundance in all areas of life—whether financial, emotional, or spiritual. By charging a candle with your intention and allowing it to burn over time, you create a powerful symbol of steady growth and future prosperity.

Ingredients:

- A green, white, or gold candle (for abundance and growth)
- A small piece of paper and pen (for writing your intention)
- Cinnamon or patchouli incense (for abundance and manifestation)
- A crystal (citrine or green aventurine) to amplify your intention

Instructions:

1. **Light the Incense:** Begin by lighting the cinnamon or patchouli incense to create a magical atmosphere that enhances abundance. As the smoke rises, visualize the energy of wealth, growth, and opportunity filling your space.
2. **Write Your Intention:** On the piece of paper, write down your specific intention for future abundance. Whether you're focusing on financial success, personal growth, or abundance in relationships, be clear and specific about what you wish to manifest. For example: "I manifest long-term prosperity and joy in all areas of my life."
3. **Charge the Candle:** Hold the candle in your hands and focus on your intention. Visualize the candle as a beacon of light, radiating your desires into the universe. Say:

"Candle bright, flame of light,
Bring abundance day and night.
As you burn, my goals take form,
Prosperity grows and keeps me warm."

1. **Place the Paper Under the Candle:** Fold the piece of paper with your intention and place it under the candle. As you light the candle, imagine the flame igniting the energy of your intention and sending it out into the universe to manifest. Place the crystal near the candle to amplify the energy.

2. **Burn the Candle Over Time:** Allow the candle to burn for a short period each day, focusing on your intention as you watch the flame. Each time you light the candle, visualize your goals growing stronger and closer to realization. Say:

"As this flame burns, my harvest grows,
Abundance in my life now flows.
Prosperity, success, and joy I see,
My future harvest comes to me."

1. **Close the Ritual:** Once the candle has burned down, place the paper with your intention and the crystal in a special place, such as your altar or a box, where you can revisit them as a reminder of your long-term goals.

This Future Abundance Candle Ritual helps you set strong intentions for long-term success and prosperity, allowing your goals to grow steadily over time.

3. Harvest Moon Manifestation Spell

The energy of the harvest moon, typically occurring in the fall, is perfect for planting long-term intentions and manifesting abundance. This spell aligns with the cycles of the moon, using its energy to enhance the growth of your desires and ensure future prosperity.

Ingredients:

- A silver or white candle (to represent the moon's energy)
- A small bowl of water (to represent the moon's reflection)
- A moonstone or clear quartz crystal (for clarity and amplification)
- A small seed or plant (to symbolize growth)
- Lavender or sandalwood incense (for peace and intuition)

Instructions:

1. **Light the Incense:** Begin by lighting the lavender or sandalwood incense to create a peaceful, meditative atmosphere. As the smoke rises, connect with the energy of the moon, visualizing its soft glow illuminating your intentions.
2. **Write Down Your Intention:** Take a moment to reflect on what you wish to manifest in the coming months. Write down your intention on a small piece of paper, focusing on long-term goals related to abundance, growth, and prosperity. For example: "I plant the seed of success and allow it to grow into full abundance."
3. **Charge the Water with Moonlight:** Place the small bowl of water where it can reflect the moon or candlelight. Hold the moonstone or clear quartz crystal over the water and visualize the energy of the moon amplifying your intention. Say:

"Moon so bright, guide my way,
Help my dreams grow day by day.
As your light reflects and glows,
My future harvest steadily grows."

1. **Plant the Seed:** Take the small seed or plant and hold it in your hands. Visualize your intention taking root and growing into a bountiful harvest. Plant the seed in the soil, saying:

"With this seed, my dreams take root,
Growing strong and bearing fruit.
Under moon and starry sky,
My future harvest will multiply."

1. **Close the Spell:** Once the seed is planted, allow the candle and incense to burn for a few more minutes while you focus on the feeling of abundance growing in your life. When you're ready, extinguish the candle and place the crystal near the plant to continue nurturing its energy.

This Harvest Moon Manifestation Spell uses the energy of the moon to plant the seeds of future abundance, allowing your goals to grow in alignment with the lunar cycle.

4. Future Prosperity Crystal Grid

This spell focuses on using crystals to create a grid that attracts long-term abundance and prosperity. By arranging crystals in a specific pattern, you amplify their energy, allowing your intention to grow steadily over time.

Ingredients:

- A green aventurine or citrine crystal (for abundance and growth)
- A clear quartz crystal (to amplify your intention)
- Small crystals such as jade, pyrite, or tiger's eye (for attracting wealth and success)
- A piece of paper with your intention written on it

Instructions:

1. **Write Your Intention:** Begin by writing down your intention for future prosperity on a small piece of paper. Be clear and specific about what you wish to manifest in the long term.
2. **Create the Grid:** Place the green aventurine or citrine crystal in the center of your space, representing the heart of your intention. Surround it with the smaller crystals, arranging them in a circular or geometric pattern. As you place each crystal, visualize it amplifying the energy of abundance.
3. **Charge the Grid:** Hold the clear quartz crystal in your hand and move it in a clockwise motion around the grid, visualizing the energy flowing through the crystals and amplifying your intention. As you do this, say:

"Crystals bright, amplify light,
Bring abundance, pure and bright.
As this grid grows strong and true,
My future harvest will come through."

1. **Place Your Intention:** Fold the piece of paper with your intention and place it beneath the central crystal. This will anchor your intention to the grid, allowing it to grow and manifest over time.
2. **Maintain the Grid:** Keep the crystal grid in place for as long as you wish to work on manifesting your future harvest. You can revisit it daily, focusing on your intention and visualizing it growing into full prosperity.

This Future Prosperity Crystal Grid allows you to focus on long-term abundance by using the energy of crystals to amplify and sustain your intentions.

Conclusion

Manifesting the future harvest is about setting clear intentions for long-term abundance and nurturing those goals with patience, care, and trust in the natural flow of the universe. By performing these spells and rituals, you plant the seeds of prosperity, allowing them to grow steadily over time and eventually bear fruit.

Whether you're planting seeds of financial success, personal growth, or abundance in relationships, the process of setting intentions, nurturing them, and trusting in their growth helps you align with the cycles of nature. Through these powerful spells, you cultivate a life of abundance and joy, knowing that the future harvest will come when the time is right. By planting these seeds now, you set the stage for future prosperity and fulfillment, allowing your dreams to flourish in the months and years to come.

Appendix

Appendix A: Glossary of Spell Terms

In this glossary, you will find definitions of key magical terms and concepts used throughout the book. Whether you are new to spellwork or an experienced practitioner, this guide provides clear explanations of the terms related to spellcasting, rituals, and magical tools. Understanding these concepts will deepen your knowledge and enhance your practice as you work with the spells and rituals presented in this book.

Abundance:

The state of having more than enough of something, often referring to wealth, prosperity, or resources. In spellwork, abundance can also refer to emotional, spiritual, or relational fulfillment. Spells for abundance aim to attract this overflowing energy into the caster's life.

Altar:

A sacred space where magical work is performed. An altar may include candles, crystals, herbs, and other magical tools that represent the elements, deities, or intentions of the spellcaster. It is often used as the focal point for rituals and spellcasting.

Amulet:

An object worn or carried for protection or to bring good luck. Amulets are often inscribed with symbols or charged with magical energy. Unlike a talisman, which is used to attract a specific outcome, an amulet's primary purpose is to guard against harm or negative influences.

Astrological Alignment:

The positioning of celestial bodies—such as the moon, planets, and stars—at a specific time. Many spellcasters choose to perform certain rituals during favorable astrological alignments, such as new moons or planetary conjunctions, to enhance the power of their spells.

Banishing:

The act of removing or driving away negative energy, harmful entities, or unwanted influences. Banishing rituals are often performed before setting intentions to clear space for new energy to flow in. Sage smudging, salt, and protective symbols are commonly used in banishing spells.

Blessing:

A spell or ritual performed to invoke positive energy or divine favor. Blessings are often used to consecrate objects, protect loved ones, or attract positive outcomes such as peace, health, and prosperity.

Candles in Spellwork:

Candles are a key tool in spellcasting, symbolizing energy, light, and transformation. The color of the candle is important, as different colors correspond to different intentions (e.g., green for prosperity, white for purity, red for passion). Lighting a candle during a spell amplifies the energy of the spell and helps focus the caster's intention.

Charging:

The process of infusing an object—such as a crystal, talisman, or candle—with magical energy. This can be done through visualization, chanting, or using elements such as moonlight, sunlight, or crystals. Charging an object enhances its power and aligns it with the caster's intention.

Circle:

A protective, sacred space cast by a spellcaster before performing a ritual or spell. The circle acts as a boundary that keeps out negative energy while containing the magical energy raised during the ritual. It is often drawn or imagined as a circle of light, sometimes physically marked with salt or stones.

Correspondences:

The magical associations of specific materials, colors, herbs, and objects with particular energies or outcomes. For example, rosemary is often associated with protection, love, and memory, while citrine is linked to abundance and manifestation. Spellcasters use correspondences to select the right ingredients for their spells.

Crystals:

Minerals that carry specific energetic vibrations. Different crystals are used in spellwork to enhance certain types of energy, such as love, healing, protection, or abundance. For example, rose quartz is used for love spells, while amethyst is known for its spiritual and healing properties.

Divination:

The practice of seeking insight or guidance from spiritual or magical sources through tools such as tarot cards, runes, scrying, or pendulums. Divination is often used before spellwork to understand the potential outcomes or to gain clarity about a situation.

Elemental Magic:

A form of spellwork that involves invoking the power of the four classical elements: Earth, Air, Fire, and Water. Each element represents different aspects of life and is called upon to bring balance or focus during rituals. Earth symbolizes stability, Air represents intellect, Fire embodies passion and transformation, and Water signifies emotion and intuition.

Empowerment:

The act of infusing oneself or a magical tool with personal power and confidence. Empowerment in magic often involves visualization, affirmations, or rituals that help the practitioner feel strong and capable of manifesting their intentions.

Energy Work:

The practice of manipulating energy—whether personal, elemental, or cosmic—during spellwork. Spellcasters often use techniques like visualization, breathing exercises, and gestures to direct energy toward their desired outcome.

Full Moon:

A phase of the moon when it is fully illuminated. The full moon is a powerful time for performing spells related to manifestation, abundance, and completion. Many spellcasters believe that the energy of the full moon amplifies the potency of their magic.

Grounding:

A technique used to connect oneself with the earth's energy, often performed before or after spellwork to balance and stabilize the practitioner's energy. Grounding helps release excess energy and ensures that the spellcaster remains focused and centered.

Herbs in Spellwork:

Herbs are often used in spells for their magical properties. For example, basil is known for its prosperity and protection qualities, while lavender is associated with peace and love. Herbs can be burned, carried, or placed in sachets and spell jars.

Incantation:

A series of words or phrases spoken during spellwork to focus the caster's intention and direct magical energy. Incantations often rhyme and are spoken with strong emotion to amplify their power.

Intent/Intention:

The clear, focused goal or desire behind a spell. Intention is the driving force of any spell, and spellcasters must be specific and clear about their desires to direct the flow of energy. A well-defined intention ensures that the spell will have the desired effect.

Lunar Magic:

Magic that is specifically aligned with the phases of the moon. Each phase has its own energy: the New Moon is for setting intentions, the Waxing Moon is for growth, the Full Moon is for manifestation, and the Waning Moon is for banishing or releasing.

Manifestation:

The process of bringing something into reality through focused intention, belief, and action. In spellwork, manifestation refers to the outcome of a spell or ritual, where the desired result comes to fruition in the practitioner's life.

Meditation:

A practice of quieting the mind, focusing inward, and connecting with spiritual or magical energy. Meditation is often used before or during spellwork to enhance focus, raise energy, or receive intuitive guidance.

New Moon:

A phase of the moon when it is not visible in the sky. The new moon represents new beginnings and is an ideal time for setting intentions, starting projects, or planting the "seeds" of future manifestations.

Pentacle:

A five-pointed star enclosed within a circle, symbolizing protection, balance, and the five elements (Earth, Air, Fire, Water, and Spirit). The pentacle is often used in protection spells and as a symbol of the witch's craft.

Protection Spell:

A spell or ritual performed to shield the spellcaster or their loved ones from harm, negative energy, or unwanted influences. Protection spells often involve creating boundaries, invoking guardian spirits, or using tools like protective stones (e.g., black tourmaline) and herbs (e.g., rosemary or sage).

Ritual:

A series of structured, symbolic actions performed with intent to create change or raise energy. Rituals often involve candles, incense, crystals, herbs, and sacred objects, and are used to mark significant events, honor deities, or manifest specific outcomes.

Sacred Space:

A physically or energetically cleansed area where spellwork or rituals are performed. Sacred spaces are often created by casting a circle or placing objects that represent the elements, deities, or ancestors. This space is meant to be free of distractions and negative energy.

Sigil:

A symbol created by the spellcaster to represent a specific desire or intention. Sigils are typically made by combining letters or symbols into a design and then charging it with energy through visualization or ritual. Once charged, the sigil serves as a magical tool to manifest the intention it represents.

Smudging:

The practice of burning sacred herbs—such as sage, palo santo, or sweetgrass—to cleanse a space, object, or person of negative energy. Smudging is commonly used at the beginning of rituals to purify the environment and create a sacred space for spellwork.

Spell:

A deliberate act of magic performed with the intention of creating a specific outcome. Spells typically involve a combination of visualization, spoken words (incantations), and magical tools such as candles, crystals, and herbs. The effectiveness of a spell depends on the clarity of the intention, the energy raised, and the focus of the practitioner.

Talisman:

An object created and charged with the intention of attracting a specific outcome, such as wealth, love, or protection. Talismans are often inscribed with symbols, words, or sigils and are worn or carried by the practitioner to continually draw the desired energy.

Visualization:

A technique used in spellwork where the practitioner imagines their desired outcome as if it has already happened. Visualization helps focus the mind and direct energy toward manifesting the intention. It is a key component in many forms of magic.

Waning Moon:

The phase of the moon after the full moon, when the moon appears to shrink. The waning moon is a powerful time for spells related to banishing, releasing, and letting go of unwanted energies, habits, or influences.

Waxing Moon:

The phase of the moon when it is growing in light, leading up to the full moon. The waxing moon is an ideal time for spells that involve growth, attraction, and manifestation, as the increasing light symbolizes the growing energy of the spell's intention.

Wheel of the Year:

The cycle of seasonal festivals observed in many pagan traditions, marking the changing phases of the natural world. The eight sabbats of the Wheel of the Year—Samhain, Yule, Imbolc, Ostara, Beltane, Litha, Lammas, and Mabon—are times of celebration, reflection, and ritual, each with its own associated energies and themes.

Conclusion

This glossary provides a foundation for understanding the magical terms and concepts used throughout the book. Each term is an essential part of spellwork and helps to create a deeper connection between the spellcaster and their intentions. Whether you are working with crystals, casting a circle, or performing a ritual under the full moon, knowing the meaning and purpose behind each term enhances your practice and helps you manifest your desires with greater clarity and power.

Appendix B: Herbal Correspondences

Herbs have been used for centuries in magical practices for their potent energetic properties. Each herb carries its own unique vibration and can be used to align with specific intentions. In this appendix, we focus on herbs that are particularly useful for spells related to gratitude, love, and prosperity. Whether you're working with these herbs in the form of dried plants, oils, or incense, their magical properties can enhance your spells, rituals, and daily practices.

This extensive guide provides you with an understanding of each herb's magical qualities, allowing you to incorporate them into your work to manifest gratitude, attract love, and invite prosperity into your life.

Herbs for Gratitude

These herbs help cultivate a sense of thankfulness, appreciation, and inner peace. They are ideal for spells and rituals aimed at expressing gratitude or increasing awareness of the blessings in one's life.

Basil (Ocimum basilicum):

- **Magical Properties:** Gratitude, protection, abundance
- **Uses:** Basil is a powerful herb for cultivating gratitude and recognizing the blessings in life. It can be used in gratitude spells, added to ritual baths, or carried as a charm to help maintain a thankful mindset. It also brings prosperity and protection, making it a versatile herb for multiple intentions.
- **Methods:** Burn basil as incense, add fresh leaves to an altar, or sprinkle dried basil in a gratitude jar.

Sage (Salvia officinalis):

- **Magical Properties:** Cleansing, wisdom, clarity, gratitude
- **Uses:** Sage is commonly used for cleansing rituals, clearing negative energy to make space for feelings of gratitude. It's ideal for creating a clean, purified space where you can reflect on your blessings. Its association with wisdom also helps bring clarity to what you should be thankful for.
- **Methods:** Smudge with sage to cleanse spaces, or brew sage tea while focusing on your blessings.

Rosemary (Rosmarinus officinalis):

- **Magical Properties:** Memory, gratitude, protection, clarity
- **Uses:** Rosemary's association with memory makes it an excellent herb for reflecting on and honoring past blessings. It helps bring clarity to your mind, allowing you to focus on gratitude and appreciate the abundance around you. It also offers protection, ensuring that negative energies do not interfere with your sense of peace.
- **Methods:** Place rosemary on your altar, use in cooking as a way to "cook with gratitude," or burn rosemary in rituals to remember and honor blessings.

Chamomile (Matricaria chamomilla):

- **Magical Properties:** Peace, relaxation, gratitude, purification
- **Uses:** Chamomile is often used in spells for peace and relaxation, making it a great herb for cultivating gratitude by promoting a calm and reflective state of mind. Its soothing energy encourages self-love and appreciation of life's simple joys.
- **Methods:** Use in tea or ritual baths to promote a peaceful environment for reflection, or add dried chamomile to gratitude sachets.

Lavender (Lavandula angustifolia):

- **Magical Properties:** Peace, gratitude, emotional healing, clarity
- **Uses:** Lavender is renowned for its calming properties, helping to create a peaceful space for reflection and meditation on the blessings in your life. It's an ideal herb to use in gratitude spells or rituals, as it promotes a sense of inner calm and clarity.
- **Methods:** Use lavender oil in aromatherapy, place lavender on your altar, or make a gratitude charm filled with lavender to keep with you.

Herbs for Love

These herbs are associated with attracting and fostering love, enhancing relationships, and promoting self-love. They are used in spells and rituals to strengthen bonds, draw romantic energy, or deepen emotional connections.

Rose (Rosa spp.):

- **Magical Properties:** Love, romance, beauty, peace
- **Uses:** Rose petals are one of the most powerful symbols of love in magic. Whether you're working to attract a romantic partner or deepen an existing relationship, roses promote love, beauty, and emotional connection. Roses also help with self-love and inner peace, allowing you to appreciate your own worth.
- **Methods:** Use dried rose petals in love sachets, add fresh roses to your altar, or create rose water for anointing in love rituals.

Cinnamon (Cinnamomum verum):

- **Magical Properties:** Passion, attraction, love, success
- **Uses:** Cinnamon's fiery energy makes it an excellent herb for enhancing passion and attraction in love spells. It stimulates both romantic and sexual energy, making it perfect for spells that focus on new relationships or reigniting the spark in existing ones. Cinnamon also brings warmth, comfort, and a sense of joy to relationships.
- **Methods:** Add cinnamon to love potions, burn it as incense during love spells, or sprinkle it around candles when performing rituals for attraction and passion.

Jasmine (Jasminum spp.):

- **Magical Properties:** Love, sensuality, spiritual connection
- **Uses:** Jasmine is known for its association with love, sensuality, and spiritual bonding. It's often used in spells to deepen emotional and physical connections between partners, as well as to attract a soulmate. Its ethereal energy promotes not only romantic love but also deep spiritual connection.
- **Methods:** Use jasmine oil in love spells, place jasmine flowers near your bed to enhance romantic dreams, or add jasmine to bath rituals for love and attraction.

Hibiscus (Hibiscus sabdariffa):

- **Magical Properties:** Passion, love, fertility, beauty
- **Uses:** Hibiscus is a vibrant herb used to promote passion, love, and attraction. It is often used in spells that call for intense romance, physical connection, and desire. It also encourages emotional openness and receptivity in relationships.
- **Methods:** Brew hibiscus tea for a love-enhancing ritual, or create a charm with dried hibiscus petals to attract romantic partners.

Vanilla (Vanilla planifolia):

- **Magical Properties:** Love, sensuality, warmth, comfort
- **Uses:** Vanilla's warm and comforting energy is often used in love spells that focus on deepening emotional connections and bringing comfort and security to relationships. It's also linked to sensuality and can be used to create a romantic, intimate atmosphere.
- **Methods:** Use vanilla-scented candles or oil in love rituals, or add vanilla to baked goods and share them with a partner as a gesture of affection.

Yarrow (Achillea millefolium):

- **Magical Properties:** Love, courage, healing, harmony
- **Uses:** Yarrow is a versatile herb that promotes love, healing, and harmony in relationships. It is often used in spells to heal rifts between partners or to bring courage to express love and affection. Yarrow also has protective qualities, guarding relationships against negativity.
- **Methods:** Add yarrow to sachets for relationship protection, use it in healing love spells, or place dried yarrow on your altar to promote harmony.

Herbs for Prosperity

These herbs are traditionally used in spells and rituals aimed at attracting wealth, financial success, and overall abundance. They can be incorporated into your magical practice to enhance prosperity and ensure that abundance flows freely into your life.

Mint (Mentha spp.):

- **Magical Properties:** Prosperity, abundance, success, money
- **Uses:** Mint is strongly associated with money and prosperity spells. Its fresh, vibrant energy is ideal for attracting new financial opportunities, business success, and abundance. Mint is often used in money-drawing sachets or sprinkled in wallets to ensure financial growth.
- **Methods:** Carry fresh mint leaves in a sachet for attracting money, use mint oil to anoint candles in prosperity rituals, or place mint in your home to draw in wealth.

Bay Leaf (Laurus nobilis):

- **Magical Properties:** Success, prosperity, protection, manifestation
- **Uses:** Bay leaves are powerful for manifesting desires, particularly in the realm of prosperity and abundance. Often used to write wishes or intentions on, bay leaves can be burned to release your desires to the universe. They are also protective, ensuring that prosperity is not hindered by negativity.
- **Methods:** Write financial goals on bay leaves and burn them in a prosperity ritual, or add bay leaves to a money-drawing charm or jar spell.

Clover (Trifolium spp.):

- **Magical Properties:** Luck, prosperity, protection, fortune
- **Uses:** Clover, especially the rare four-leaf variety, is a symbol of luck and prosperity. It's used to bring good fortune in business, financial ventures, and personal wealth. Clover is also protective, ensuring that the prosperity it brings is long-lasting.
- **Methods:** Carry a dried clover leaf in your wallet or place it in a charm bag for financial luck, or use clover in spell jars for attracting wealth and success.

Patchouli (Pogostemon cablin):

- **Magical Properties:** Wealth, prosperity, growth, grounding
- **Uses:** Patchouli is one of the most well-known herbs for wealth and prosperity. Its earthy energy attracts long-term financial growth and stability. It is also used in business success spells, as it promotes steady, reliable results in financial matters.
- **Methods:** Burn patchouli incense during money-drawing rituals, anoint money or financial documents with patchouli oil, or use dried patchouli leaves in charm bags or spell jars for prosperity.

Basil (Ocimum basilicum):

- **Magical Properties:** Prosperity, luck, wealth, success
- **Uses:** In addition to being a gratitude herb, basil is commonly used in spells for financial prosperity and business success. Its bright, expansive energy helps attract wealth and opportunities, and it's often included in money-drawing spells or charm bags.
- **Methods:** Add fresh basil to your wallet for financial luck, brew basil tea in abundance rituals, or anoint candles with basil oil for prosperity spells.

Cinnamon (Cinnamomum verum):

- **Magical Properties:** Prosperity, success, abundance, protection
- **Uses:** Cinnamon is a powerful money-drawing herb. Its fiery energy speeds up the manifestation of wealth and success, making it a popular ingredient in prosperity spells. Cinnamon also provides protection, ensuring that financial gains are maintained.
- **Methods:** Sprinkle cinnamon powder on candles for money spells, use cinnamon oil to anoint financial documents, or carry cinnamon sticks in your purse or wallet for good fortune.

Ginger (Zingiber officinale):

- **Magical Properties:** Success, prosperity, confidence, energy
- **Uses:** Ginger is often used in spells that need a quick boost of energy and power, particularly when trying to manifest financial success. Its stimulating properties can help jumpstart business ventures or other projects related to wealth and abundance.
- **Methods:** Add ginger to money-drawing spells, use ginger oil in prosperity anointing rituals, or include dried ginger in sachets for financial growth.

Conclusion

This appendix provides you with a detailed list of herbs and their magical correspondences related to gratitude, love, and prosperity. Whether you are using these herbs in rituals, spells, or daily magical practices, their natural energies can help you focus your intentions and align with the desired outcomes. By incorporating these powerful plants into your work, you deepen your connection to the earth's abundance and enhance your ability to manifest gratitude, love, and prosperity in your life.

Appendix C: Crystal Correspondences

Crystals have long been revered for their unique energetic properties and their ability to amplify, balance, and manifest specific intentions. In this appendix, we will explore the crystals that align with the themes of Thanksgiving—gratitude, love, family harmony, prosperity, and abundance. These crystals can be used in spells, rituals, meditations, or as talismans to enhance your connection with the energy of Thanksgiving and foster feelings of appreciation, unity, and wealth.

This comprehensive guide will help you understand the properties of each crystal, how it can be used, and the specific Thanksgiving-related themes it enhances. Whether you wear these crystals, place them on your altar, or use them in ritual work, they will help amplify your intentions during this special time of year.

Crystals for Gratitude

Gratitude is a central theme during Thanksgiving, as it encourages us to reflect on our blessings and give thanks for the abundance in our lives. The following crystals are ideal for fostering a sense of gratitude and appreciation, helping you connect more deeply with the energy of thankfulness.

Rose Quartz:

- **Properties:** Unconditional love, self-love, gratitude, emotional healing
- **Thanksgiving Theme:** Gratitude, love, emotional balance
- **Uses:** Rose quartz is the ultimate crystal for promoting feelings of love and gratitude. It helps open the heart chakra, allowing you to experience deeper emotional connections with others and yourself. It encourages you to recognize and appreciate the love and abundance already present in your life.
- **Methods:** Hold rose quartz in your hand while meditating on gratitude, place it on your altar as a symbol of thankfulness, or

wear it to encourage loving and appreciative energy throughout the day.

Citrine:

- **Properties:** Joy, abundance, manifestation, gratitude
- **Thanksgiving Theme:** Gratitude, joy, prosperity
- **Uses:** Citrine is known as the "merchant's stone" and is strongly associated with joy, abundance, and gratitude. It helps amplify positive energy and encourages a grateful mindset by promoting optimism and emotional balance. Citrine is particularly powerful for reflecting on the abundance in your life and setting intentions for future prosperity.
- **Methods:** Place citrine on your altar or in your workspace to enhance gratitude and abundance, or carry it with you to encourage feelings of thankfulness and joy throughout the day.

Green Aventurine:

- **Properties:** Growth, luck, prosperity, gratitude
- **Thanksgiving Theme:** Gratitude, growth, prosperity
- **Uses:** Green aventurine is associated with abundance, luck, and personal growth. It helps open your heart to gratitude and encourages you to appreciate the blessings in your life, both material and spiritual. It also enhances optimism, making it easier to focus on what you have rather than what you lack.
- **Methods:** Meditate with green aventurine to cultivate a grateful mindset, use it in abundance and prosperity rituals, or place it in your home to encourage feelings of gratitude and positivity.

Amethyst:

- **Properties:** Spirituality, clarity, peace, gratitude
- **Thanksgiving Theme:** Gratitude, spiritual reflection, peace
- **Uses:** Amethyst is a powerful stone for spiritual growth, inner peace, and clarity. It helps you see beyond the material world and focus on the deeper, more meaningful aspects of life. By connecting you to higher consciousness, amethyst encourages gratitude for both spiritual and physical blessings.
- **Methods:** Use amethyst in meditation to reflect on the blessings in your life, place it on your altar to encourage a peaceful, grateful atmosphere, or wear it to enhance spiritual connection and appreciation.

Selenite:

- **Properties:** Purity, clarity, peace, gratitude
- **Thanksgiving Theme:** Gratitude, peace, emotional clarity
- **Uses:** Selenite is known for its ability to cleanse and purify energy, making it an excellent crystal for clearing away negativity and creating a peaceful environment for gratitude rituals. It promotes mental clarity and helps you focus on the positive aspects of your life, cultivating a sense of appreciation and inner peace.
- **Methods:** Place selenite in your home or on your altar to promote peace and gratitude, or use it during meditation to clear away negative thoughts and enhance your focus on the blessings in your life.

Crystals for Love and Family Harmony

Thanksgiving is a time for gathering with loved ones, and the energy of love, unity, and family harmony is especially important during this season. The following crystals are ideal for enhancing familial bonds, fostering love, and promoting harmony within family gatherings.

Carnelian:

- **Properties:** Vitality, courage, warmth, family connection
- **Thanksgiving Theme:** Family harmony, love, joy
- **Uses:** Carnelian is a warm, energizing stone that promotes connection, warmth, and joy within families. It helps foster feelings of love, support, and understanding, making it an ideal crystal for family gatherings during Thanksgiving. Carnelian also encourages creativity, which can help smooth over tensions or disagreements.
- **Methods:** Place carnelian in the center of your Thanksgiving table to encourage harmony, or carry it with you to family gatherings to promote warmth, joy, and understanding.

Rhodonite:

- **Properties:** Emotional healing, love, forgiveness, family connection
- **Thanksgiving Theme:** Love, forgiveness, family harmony
- **Uses:** Rhodonite is known for its ability to heal emotional wounds and promote forgiveness and understanding. It's particularly helpful for family dynamics, where old conflicts or tensions may arise. Rhodonite encourages love and compassion, helping to smooth over past hurts and foster stronger bonds.
- **Methods:** Meditate with rhodonite before family gatherings to promote emotional healing, place it on your altar to encourage forgiveness and love within your family, or carry it with you to maintain harmony during gatherings.

Garnet:

- **Properties:** Love, commitment, passion, emotional warmth
- **Thanksgiving Theme:** Love, family harmony, commitment
- **Uses:** Garnet is a stone of love, commitment, and emotional warmth. It deepens emotional connections and strengthens family bonds, making it an excellent crystal for promoting love and unity during Thanksgiving. Garnet's energy is grounding, helping to create a stable and supportive environment for family gatherings.
- **Methods:** Wear garnet jewelry during family gatherings to enhance emotional warmth, place it in the center of your home to promote harmony, or use it in love spells focused on strengthening family relationships.

Moonstone:

- **Properties:** Emotional balance, intuition, harmony, peace
- **Thanksgiving Theme:** Family harmony, peace, emotional balance
- **Uses:** Moonstone is known for its calming and balancing properties, making it an ideal stone for promoting peace and harmony within family settings. It helps regulate emotions, ensuring that gatherings are filled with love and understanding rather than tension or conflict.
- **Methods:** Place moonstone in the center of your Thanksgiving altar or table to encourage emotional balance and harmony, or carry it with you to family gatherings to maintain a sense of peace and calm.

Lapis Lazuli:

- **Properties:** Wisdom, communication, truth, harmony
- **Thanksgiving Theme:** Family harmony, communication, love
- **Uses:** Lapis lazuli is associated with truth, wisdom, and clear communication, all of which are essential for maintaining harmony during family gatherings. It encourages open, honest conversations and helps resolve misunderstandings or conflicts in a loving and compassionate way.
- **Methods:** Use lapis lazuli in rituals aimed at improving family communication, place it in common areas of the home to promote harmony, or wear it to encourage clear, loving dialogue during family events.

Crystals for Prosperity and Abundance

Prosperity and abundance are central themes during Thanksgiving, when we reflect on the harvest and the blessings we have received throughout the year. These crystals help attract wealth, success, and material abundance while also promoting a sense of appreciation for what you already have.

Pyrite:

- **Properties:** Wealth, prosperity, success, protection
- **Thanksgiving Theme:** Prosperity, wealth, success
- **Uses:** Pyrite, often called "fool's gold," is a powerful stone for attracting financial prosperity and success. Its energy helps manifest wealth and abundance, making it an ideal crystal for rituals focused on attracting or maintaining material abundance. Pyrite also offers protection, ensuring that your gains are not lost.
- **Methods:** Place pyrite in your wallet or on your altar to attract wealth, or use it in spells aimed at manifesting financial success and abundance.

Tiger's Eye:

- **Properties:** Confidence, courage, prosperity, grounding
- **Thanksgiving Theme:** Prosperity, courage, manifestation
- **Uses:** Tiger's eye is a grounding stone that promotes courage and confidence, both of which are necessary for manifesting abundance and success. It helps you focus on your goals and take action to achieve prosperity. It is also protective, helping you stay grounded while pursuing wealth and success.
- **Methods:** Use tiger's eye in manifestation rituals, carry it with you to attract opportunities for success, or place it on your altar to promote confidence and prosperity.

Jade:

- **Properties:** Wealth, luck, harmony, health
- **Thanksgiving Theme:** Prosperity, abundance, harmony
- **Uses:** Jade is a stone of luck, prosperity, and long-term success. It is particularly powerful for ensuring financial stability and attracting good fortune in both personal and professional endeavors. Jade also promotes harmony, ensuring that your pursuit of abundance is balanced and peaceful.
- **Methods:** Place jade in your home or workspace to attract prosperity, use it in abundance spells, or carry it with you to attract good fortune and wealth.

Clear Quartz:

- **Properties:** Amplification, clarity, manifestation, abundance
- **Thanksgiving Theme:** Prosperity, manifestation, gratitude
- **Uses:** Clear quartz is known as the "master healer" and is one of the most versatile crystals in spellwork. It amplifies energy and can be programmed for any intention, including manifesting abundance and prosperity. It is also excellent for enhancing gratitude, helping you appreciate the abundance already present in your life.
- **Methods:** Use clear quartz in abundance grids, place it on your altar to amplify prosperity spells, or carry it with you to attract success and wealth.

Peridot:

- **Properties:** Wealth, growth, prosperity, joy
- **Thanksgiving Theme:** Prosperity, joy, gratitude
- **Uses:** Peridot is a bright, joyful stone that promotes prosperity and financial growth. Its energy helps clear blockages that may be preventing abundance from flowing into your life, ensuring that you are open to receiving wealth and success. Peridot also enhances feelings of joy and gratitude, making it ideal for Thanksgiving spells focused on abundance.
- **Methods:** Wear peridot jewelry to attract wealth, place it in your home to invite prosperity, or use it in spells focused on manifesting financial growth.

Crystals for General Thanksgiving Themes

In addition to gratitude, love, family harmony, and prosperity, Thanksgiving also represents themes of peace, unity, and reflection. The following crystals can be used in rituals or meditations that focus on these broader Thanksgiving themes, helping you align with the energy of the season.

Smoky Quartz:

- **Properties:** Grounding, protection, clarity, peace
- **Thanksgiving Theme:** Grounding, peace, emotional balance
- **Uses:** Smoky quartz is a grounding and protective stone, helping to stabilize emotions and create a sense of peace and clarity. It's excellent for family gatherings, as it helps dispel tension and promotes a calm, balanced atmosphere.
- **Methods:** Place smoky quartz in communal spaces to promote peace and balance, or carry it with you to family gatherings to stay grounded and centered.

Sunstone:

- **Properties:** Joy, vitality, abundance, positivity
- **Thanksgiving Theme:** Gratitude, joy, abundance
- **Uses:** Sunstone radiates warmth, joy, and positive energy. It is excellent for fostering feelings of happiness and gratitude, making it ideal for Thanksgiving rituals. Sunstone also helps manifest abundance and prosperity by encouraging a joyful and optimistic mindset.
- **Methods:** Wear sunstone during Thanksgiving celebrations to enhance feelings of gratitude and joy, or place it on your altar to promote abundance and happiness.

Bloodstone:

- **Properties:** Healing, strength, courage, protection
- **Thanksgiving Theme:** Family unity, protection, healing
- **Uses:** Bloodstone is known for its healing and protective properties. It is especially powerful in family settings, where it promotes unity, understanding, and emotional healing. Bloodstone also strengthens bonds and offers protection to loved ones.
- **Methods:** Use bloodstone in rituals focused on family healing and unity, or place it in your home to protect your family and promote strong, loving relationships.

Conclusion

Crystals are powerful tools for aligning with the energy of Thanksgiving, whether you are focusing on gratitude, love, family harmony, or prosperity. By incorporating these crystals into your spells, rituals, or daily practices, you can amplify your intentions and connect more deeply with the themes of Thanksgiving. Whether placed on your altar, carried as talismans, or used in meditations, these crystals will help you manifest a bountiful, joyful, and harmonious Thanksgiving season.

Appendix D: Moon Phase Guide: How Each Phase of the Moon Affects Spellwork

The moon's phases have a profound effect on spellwork, and each phase holds unique energy that can enhance specific types of magical work. By aligning your spells with the moon's cycles, you can tap into the lunar energy to amplify your intentions and increase the effectiveness of your rituals. This guide provides a detailed explanation of each moon phase and how it can be used in spellwork, helping you time your rituals for optimal results.

The moon goes through eight distinct phases during its 29.5-day cycle, with each phase influencing spellwork in different ways. These phases are categorized by their relationship to the moon's waxing (growing) and waning (shrinking) cycles, as well as key points like the new moon and full moon, which offer powerful energies for manifestation and release.

1. New Moon: New Beginnings, Intention Setting, and Manifestation

The new moon marks the beginning of the lunar cycle when the moon is not visible from Earth. This phase represents a fresh start and is a powerful time for setting new intentions, planting the seeds of your desires, and manifesting new opportunities.

Magical Focus:

- **New beginnings:** The new moon is ideal for spells related to new ventures, projects, and personal transformations.
- **Setting intentions:** Use this phase to clarify your goals and set specific intentions for the lunar cycle ahead.
- **Manifestation:** The energy of the new moon supports manifesting what you want to bring into your life, particularly if it is something new or requires growth.

Best for Spells Related To:

- New jobs, relationships, or projects
- Starting new habits or routines
- Personal growth and self-improvement
- Inviting new energy into your life

Spellwork Suggestions:

- **New Moon Intention Setting:** Write down your goals for the upcoming cycle on a piece of paper and meditate on them. Visualize the outcome you desire, and place the paper on your altar or under your pillow to hold your intentions close.
- **Manifestation Jar Spell:** Create a jar filled with herbs, crystals, and symbols that represent your goals. Seal it during the new moon and place it where you can see it daily as a reminder of your intentions.

2. Waxing Crescent Moon: Growth, Action, and Opportunity

The waxing crescent phase occurs after the new moon as a small sliver of the moon becomes visible. This phase is associated with growth, expansion, and taking action on the intentions set during the new moon.

Magical Focus:

- **Building momentum:** The waxing crescent moon is ideal for spells that require gradual growth, such as attracting new opportunities or gaining strength in an area of your life.
- **Taking action:** This is the time to start working toward your goals by taking practical steps and allowing your intentions to gain momentum.

Best for Spells Related To:

- Career growth and financial gain
- Expanding knowledge or skills
- Increasing love or friendship
- Strengthening health and vitality

Spellwork Suggestions:

- **Career Growth Candle Spell:** Light a green or gold candle while focusing on your professional or financial goals. Visualize opportunities flowing to you as the moon grows brighter.
- **Friendship Growth Charm:** Create a charm with symbols representing friendship or love and carry it with you to strengthen bonds and attract new connections.

3. First Quarter Moon: Overcoming Obstacles, Decision-Making, and Strength

The first quarter moon occurs when half of the moon is illuminated, signaling a time to face challenges and make important decisions. This phase is perfect for spells that focus on overcoming obstacles, building strength, and making choices that support your goals.

Magical Focus:

- **Overcoming challenges:** The first quarter moon helps you address obstacles and roadblocks in your path. It's a time to confront challenges head-on and focus on solutions.
- **Making decisions:** If you've been uncertain about a particular decision, this phase offers the clarity and strength needed to make confident choices.

Best for Spells Related To:

- Overcoming fears or personal challenges
- Strengthening resolve or willpower
- Making important decisions
- Problem-solving in relationships or career

Spellwork Suggestions:

- **Overcoming Obstacles Ritual:** Write down any obstacles you're facing and burn the paper in a fire-safe dish while visualizing yourself overcoming each challenge.
- **Decision-Making Meditation:** Light a white candle and meditate on the decision you need to make. Ask for clarity and guidance as you work through the pros and cons.

4. Waxing Gibbous Moon: Refinement, Focus, and Preparation

The waxing gibbous moon is the phase leading up to the full moon, where the moon is almost fully illuminated. This phase is ideal for refining your intentions, focusing on details, and making final preparations before manifesting your desires at the full moon.

Magical Focus:

- **Refinement:** Fine-tune your goals and intentions during this phase, paying attention to the details and ensuring everything is in place.
- **Focus:** Use this time to focus your energy and efforts on specific areas that need attention before the full moon.
- **Preparation:** Prepare for the full moon's powerful energy by organizing and finalizing your plans.

Best for Spells Related To:

- Completing projects
- Refining intentions or goals
- Increasing focus and clarity
- Preparing for major events or transitions

Spellwork Suggestions:

- **Refining Intentions Spell:** Take time to revisit the intentions you set during the new moon. Write down any adjustments or clarifications you want to make and visualize the refined outcome.
- **Focus and Clarity Spell:** Light a blue candle to represent mental clarity and focus. Meditate on the areas of your life that need more attention and ask for guidance to fine-tune your actions.

5. Full Moon: Power, Manifestation, and Completion

The full moon is one of the most powerful phases for spellwork. The moon is fully illuminated, symbolizing the completion of a cycle and the manifestation of intentions set during the new moon. This phase is a time for celebration, gratitude, and working with the heightened energy of the lunar cycle.

Magical Focus:

- **Manifestation:** The full moon's energy is perfect for spells that focus on bringing your intentions into full realization. Anything you've been working on will reach its peak during this phase.
- **Completion:** The full moon marks the culmination of your efforts, making it ideal for spells related to completing projects or reaching milestones.
- **Power:** This phase offers heightened magical energy, making it perfect for powerful rituals, spiritual work, and connection with the divine.

Best for Spells Related To:

- Manifesting long-term goals
- Celebrating achievements
- Enhancing psychic abilities and intuition
- Charging magical tools and crystals

Spellwork Suggestions:

- **Full Moon Manifestation Ritual:** Write down everything you want to manifest and place it under the full moonlight. Charge crystals and magical tools in the moonlight to amplify their energy.

- **Gratitude Ritual:** Reflect on everything you've accomplished since the new moon and give thanks for the abundance in your life. Light candles and celebrate your achievements.

6. Waning Gibbous Moon: Gratitude, Release, and Reflection

The waning gibbous moon follows the full moon and is a time of reflection, gratitude, and release. This phase encourages you to acknowledge the abundance and growth that has occurred while also letting go of what no longer serves you.

Magical Focus:

- **Gratitude:** Reflect on your accomplishments and express gratitude for the blessings in your life.
- **Release:** This phase is perfect for releasing negative energy, bad habits, or anything that has reached its end.
- **Reflection:** Take time to reflect on what has worked well and what needs to be released as the moon's energy begins to wane.

Best for Spells Related To:

- Letting go of unhealthy attachments
- Releasing bad habits or negative energy
- Giving thanks for growth and abundance
- Reflecting on lessons learned

Spellwork Suggestions:

- **Releasing Ritual:** Write down anything you want to release—such as bad habits, fears, or negative emotions—and burn the paper as you visualize yourself letting go.
- **Gratitude Meditation:** Meditate on everything you're grateful for, and light a candle to honor the abundance you've manifested.

7. Last Quarter Moon: Release, Reassessment, and Transition

The last quarter moon occurs when half of the moon is visible again, signaling a time to reassess and let go. This phase is about release, transition, and preparing for new beginnings during the next lunar cycle.

Magical Focus:

- **Reassessment:** Take stock of what has worked and what hasn't. This is a time to reassess your goals and let go of anything that didn't manifest as expected.
- **Release:** Use this phase to release anything that no longer serves you—whether it's physical clutter, emotional baggage, or outdated goals.
- **Transition:** Prepare for the next new moon by clearing space for new intentions and opportunities.

Best for Spells Related To:

- Releasing old goals or projects
- Clearing out emotional or physical clutter
- Preparing for new opportunities
- Transitioning from one phase to another

Spellwork Suggestions:

- **Decluttering Ritual:** Go through your home or workspace and clear out anything that no longer serves you. Use this as a metaphor for releasing emotional or mental clutter.
- **Letting Go Spell:** Light a black candle and meditate on the things you're ready to release. Visualize them fading away as the candle burns down.

8. Waning Crescent Moon: Rest, Healing, and Introspection

The waning crescent moon is the final phase before the new moon. It's a time for rest, healing, and introspection, where you can look inward and reflect on the lessons learned during the lunar cycle. This phase is about preparing yourself for the next new moon and replenishing your energy.

Magical Focus:

- **Rest and recovery:** After the work of the previous phases, the waning crescent moon is a time to rest and recharge your energy.
- **Healing:** This is a time for self-care, emotional healing, and spiritual reflection. Focus on nurturing yourself and healing any emotional wounds.
- **Introspection:** Use this phase for quiet reflection and meditation, preparing yourself for the new moon's fresh start.

Best for Spells Related To:

- Healing emotional or physical wounds
- Rest and relaxation
- Deep introspection and self-care
- Preparing for new beginnings

Spellwork Suggestions:

- **Healing Ritual:** Light a blue or green candle and focus on healing any emotional or physical wounds. Surround yourself with calming crystals like amethyst or rose quartz and take time for self-care.
- **Rest and Recharge Meditation:** Meditate with a black tourmaline or selenite crystal to cleanse your energy and replenish your strength in preparation for the new moon.

Conclusion

Understanding the influence of each moon phase can greatly enhance your spellwork and help you align your intentions with the natural cycles of the moon. Whether you're planting the seeds of new goals during the new moon, manifesting your desires at the full moon, or releasing old energy during the waning phases, working with the moon's energy allows you to harness the powerful forces of nature to achieve your desired outcomes.

By timing your spells to match the lunar phases, you can amplify your magical practice and work in harmony with the cycles of the universe. Each phase of the moon offers a unique opportunity to focus your energy and manifest your intentions, creating a deeper connection between your spellwork and the natural world.

Appendix E: Additional Resources

For those looking to deepen their understanding of Thanksgiving magic, spellwork, and the broader world of witchcraft, this appendix provides a curated list of books, websites, and online communities that offer further reading, research, and exploration. Whether you're new to magical practice or a seasoned practitioner, these resources will help you expand your knowledge, connect with like-minded individuals, and discover new approaches to Thanksgiving and gratitude-focused magic.

Books on Magic, Gratitude, and Thanksgiving Themes

1. *The Witch's Book of Self-Care* **by Arin Murphy-Hiscock**

- **Focus:** Self-care rituals, spells, and practices
- **Why It's Recommended:** This book offers practical rituals and spells for emotional, physical, and spiritual well-being, many of which focus on gratitude and self-nurturing. Its calming, introspective practices can be especially helpful during Thanksgiving, a time for reflection and appreciation.

2. *The Book of Crystal Spells: Magical Uses for Stones, Crystals, Minerals… and Even Sand* **by Ember Grant**

- **Focus:** Crystal magic
- **Why It's Recommended:** Crystals play a large role in Thanksgiving magic, especially for spells related to gratitude, abundance, and family harmony. This book explores the magical properties of crystals and includes practical guidance on how to incorporate them into your spellwork, including rituals for attracting abundance and fostering gratitude.

3. *The Green Witch: Your Complete Guide to the Natural Magic of Herbs, Flowers, Essential Oils, and More* **by Arin Murphy-Hiscock**

- **Focus:** Natural magic and earth-based spells
- **Why It's Recommended:** *The Green Witch* is an excellent resource for working with the earth's energy and using herbs, flowers, and natural elements in magic. This book's guidance on working with nature aligns perfectly with Thanksgiving themes of harvest, abundance, and connection to the earth.

4. *Encyclopedia of Magical Herbs* **by Scott Cunningham**

- **Focus:** Comprehensive guide to magical herbs and their uses
- **Why It's Recommended:** For those looking to explore herbal correspondences in more depth, this encyclopedia is a classic in the field of magic. It provides detailed information on hundreds of herbs, including their magical properties and uses in spells. This is a must-have resource for anyone interested in using herbs in Thanksgiving-related magic for gratitude, love, and prosperity.

5. *The Magical Household: Spells & Rituals for the Home* **by Scott Cunningham and David Harrington**

- **Focus:** Home and family-focused spells and rituals
- **Why It's Recommended:** Thanksgiving is often centered around the home and family gatherings. This book focuses on magical practices that create harmony, protection, and abundance in the home—perfect for preparing your space for Thanksgiving celebrations and fostering peace during family gatherings.

6. *Earth Power: Techniques of Natural Magic* by Scott Cunningham

- **Focus:** Natural magic, elemental magic
- **Why It's Recommended:** This book offers practical methods for working with natural elements, such as earth, air, fire, and water, in spellwork. Thanksgiving often focuses on the harvest and the natural world, making this a valuable resource for those looking to align their magic with the cycles of nature and seasons.

7. *The Element Encyclopedia of 5,000 Spells* by Judika Illes

- **Focus:** Comprehensive spell book
- **Why It's Recommended:** If you're looking for a wide range of spells, this massive tome covers everything from love and protection to abundance and gratitude. Many of the spells within can be adapted for use during Thanksgiving, particularly those focused on gratitude, love, prosperity, and family unity.

Websites for Thanksgiving Magic and Spellwork

1. *Learn Religions - Paganism and Wicca Section* (www.learn-religions.com/paganism-wicca-4685032)

- **Focus:** General information on paganism, Wicca, and witchcraft
- **Why It's Recommended:** Learn Religions offers a comprehensive section on Paganism and Wicca, covering a wide range of topics including sabbats, moon phases, ritual tools, and magical practices. It includes articles on seasonal celebrations like Thanksgiving and other harvest festivals, making it a great starting point for beginners.

2. *The Witch's Guide* (www.thewitchsguide.com)

- **Focus:** Witchcraft tools, spells, and education
- **Why It's Recommended:** This website offers spell kits, ritual tools, and a variety of educational blog posts on spellwork, herbs, and moon magic. The blog covers a wide range of topics, including gratitude rituals and spells for abundance, which are relevant for Thanksgiving magic.

3. *Witchvox* (www.witchvox.com)

- **Focus:** Online community for witches and pagans
- **Why It's Recommended:** Witchvox has long been a hub for witches, pagans, and magical practitioners. While the site itself contains educational resources, the real value is in its community boards, where you can connect with other practitioners to share ideas, spells, and rituals for specific themes like gratitude and prosperity.

4. *Patheos Pagan Channel* (www.patheos.com/pagan)

- **Focus:** Pagan perspectives, blogs, and articles
- **Why It's Recommended:** Patheos Pagan hosts a diverse collection of articles and blog posts written by pagan authors. Topics range from rituals, magic, and spirituality to practical advice for integrating magical practices into everyday life. Seasonal rituals, including those aligned with Thanksgiving and harvest themes, are frequently discussed.

5. *The Hoodwitch* (www.thehoodwitch.com)

- **Focus:** Modern witchcraft and magical tools
- **Why It's Recommended:** The Hoodwitch is a modern, accessible resource for witches of all levels, offering articles, guides, and products focused on spellwork, self-care, and magic. They frequently discuss topics like moon rituals, gratitude spells, and manifestation, making it an excellent resource for Thanksgiving magic.

Online Communities and Forums for Further Exploration

1. *Witchcraft Subreddit* **(www.reddit.com/r/witchcraft)**

- **Focus:** Online community for discussing witchcraft
- **Why It's Recommended:** The Witchcraft subreddit is a large, active community of witches from around the world. Users share spells, rituals, and personal experiences, making it a valuable resource for discussing Thanksgiving spells, rituals for gratitude, and general seasonal magic.

2. *Sacred Mists Online Coven* **(www.sacredmists.com)**

- **Focus:** Online coven and school of witchcraft
- **Why It's Recommended:** Sacred Mists is an online school and coven offering courses in witchcraft, magic, and herbalism. For those looking to dive deeper into their magical studies, the school provides structured lessons as well as a supportive community for sharing rituals and seasonal magic, including Thanksgiving-focused practices.

3. *The Witches Circle on The Cauldron* **(www.ecauldron.com/ forum.php)**

- **Focus:** Pagan and witchcraft discussion forums
- **Why It's Recommended:** The Cauldron is a longstanding online community where witches, pagans, and magical practitioners share ideas, ask questions, and discuss their spiritual practices. It's an excellent place to connect with others and explore ideas for Thanksgiving spells and rituals.

4. *Facebook Groups: Witches & Pagans* **(Search "Witches & Pagans" in Facebook groups)**

- **Focus:** Community groups for witches and pagans
- **Why It's Recommended:** There are numerous Facebook groups for witches, pagans, and magical practitioners that focus on spellwork, seasonal rituals, and general magical practices. These groups often have discussions around seasonal celebrations, gratitude, and family-centered rituals, which can be helpful for Thanksgiving magic.

5. *Instagram Hashtags: #WitchCommunity, #WitchesOfInstagram, #GratitudeMagic* **(www.instagram.com)**

- **Focus:** Social media community of modern witches
- **Why It's Recommended:** Instagram is home to a vibrant community of witches and magical practitioners who share their rituals, altar setups, spells, and seasonal practices. Searching through hashtags like #WitchCommunity and #WitchesOfInstagram can provide inspiration for Thanksgiving magic, gratitude spells, and family-focused rituals.

Additional Educational Resources

1. *The Modern Witch Podcast* **(www.modernwitch.com)**

- **Focus:** Interviews, discussions, and modern witchcraft
- **Why It's Recommended:** This podcast provides insights from experienced witches and magical practitioners, discussing modern witchcraft practices and seasonal magic. It's an excellent way to stay connected to the magical community and find inspiration for rituals and spells.

2. *The Hermetic Library* (**www.hermetic.com**)

- **Focus:** Esoteric and occult knowledge
- **Why It's Recommended:** This extensive digital library contains a wealth of resources on magic, astrology, occultism, and esoteric traditions. If you're interested in exploring the deeper magical philosophies and techniques behind spellwork, this library is an excellent starting point.

3. *Wicca Teachings YouTube Channel* (**www.youtube.com/ user/WiccaTeachings**)

- **Focus:** Educational videos on Wicca and witchcraft
- **Why It's Recommended:** This YouTube channel offers educational videos on Wiccan beliefs, practices, and rituals, as well as specific spells and seasonal celebrations. It's a helpful resource for those looking to learn more about magical practices aligned with the cycles of nature, including Thanksgiving.

4. *YouTube: Harmony Nice* (**www.youtube.com/c/HarmonyNice**)

- **Focus:** Modern witchcraft and personal practice
- **Why It's Recommended:** Harmony Nice is a popular YouTuber who shares her journey in modern witchcraft. She provides tutorials, spell guides, and insights into seasonal rituals, making it a valuable resource for those new to witchcraft or interested in Thanksgiving magic.

Conclusion

This appendix provides a wide array of resources for further exploring Thanksgiving magic, seasonal spells, and the themes of gratitude, love, family harmony, and abundance. Whether you're looking to deepen your understanding of spellwork, connect with other witches and pagans, or simply find inspiration for new rituals, these books, websites, and communities offer valuable knowledge and support.

By exploring these additional resources, you'll not only enhance your magical practice but also find new ways to align with the energy of the Thanksgiving season, creating a richer and more spiritually fulfilling experience. Whether through books, online communities, or practical tools, there are countless opportunities to continue your journey into Thanksgiving magic.

Appendix F: Index of Spells

This comprehensive index categorizes all the spells presented throughout the book, allowing you to quickly locate and reference specific spells for various intentions. Whether you're seeking spells for gratitude, love, prosperity, or seasonal magic, this index is organized by theme and purpose for easy navigation. Each category includes the spell name and a brief description to guide you in selecting the appropriate spell for your needs.

Gratitude Spells

1. Gratitude Charms (Chapter 1):

- **Description:** Simple daily rituals and charms that foster a sense of appreciation and thankfulness, helping to cultivate a mindset of gratitude throughout the day.

2. Thanksgiving Night Gratitude and Wish Spell (Chapter 29):

- **Description:** A spell performed under the stars that combines gratitude with wish-making to manifest new blessings while appreciating the ones you already have.

3. Waning Gibbous Gratitude Ritual (Chapter 7 - Moon Phases and Thanksgiving):

- **Description:** A ritual during the waning gibbous moon phase to give thanks for the abundance in your life and reflect on your accomplishments.

4. Gratitude Journaling Spell (Chapter 14):

- **Description:** A practice of using writing as a tool to express gratitude and manifest future blessings by combining magical intention with reflective journaling.

Love Spells

1. Family Harmony Spell (Chapter 3):

- **Description:** A spell designed to foster peace, understanding, and love within family gatherings, particularly during holiday celebrations like Thanksgiving.

2. Circle of Love Group Ritual (Chapter 18):

- **Description:** A group spell performed with family or friends to strengthen bonds, deepen emotional connections, and promote harmony in relationships.

3. Love and Friendship Talisman (Chapter 5):

- **Description:** A charm spell designed to strengthen bonds with loved ones and friends by enhancing emotional connections and fostering a sense of unity.

4. Heart-Opening Thanksgiving Ritual (Chapter 5 - Love and Friendship):

- **Description:** A ritual that uses herbs and candles to open your heart to love, encouraging stronger emotional connections during Thanksgiving gatherings.

Prosperity and Abundance Spells
1. Harvest Blessings Spell (Chapter 2):

- **Description:** A spell to bless the harvest, food, and abundance in all its forms, ensuring that prosperity flows freely in your life during the Thanksgiving season.

2. Fortune and Prosperity Ritual (Chapter 6):

- **Description:** Rituals aimed at attracting abundance, financial blessings, and good fortune during the Thanksgiving period, using herbs, candles, and magical symbols.

3. Manifesting the Future Harvest Spell (Chapter 30):

- **Description:** A long-term prosperity spell that focuses on planting the seeds of intention for future abundance and success, using symbolic actions to nurture those goals.

4. Business Success Talisman (Chapter 28):

- **Description:** A talisman spell crafted to support business success and financial growth, enhancing opportunities for prosperity in career ventures.

Family and Harmony Spells
1. Family Harmony Spell (Chapter 3):

• **Description:** A spell specifically designed to foster peace, love, and understanding during family gatherings, ensuring smooth interactions and harmonious relationships.

2. Thanksgiving Altar Magic (Chapter 15):

• **Description:** A ritual for setting up a Thanksgiving altar that promotes love, harmony, and abundance in family gatherings, creating a sacred space for spellwork and gratitude.

3. Circle of Love Group Ritual (Chapter 18):

• **Description:** A group spell for strengthening emotional bonds with family and friends, encouraging deeper connections and harmonious relationships during Thanksgiving.

4. Moonstone Family Harmony Spell (Chapter 3 - Family Harmony):

• **Description:** A spell that utilizes the energy of moonstone to promote peace and emotional balance in family relationships during the holiday season.

Seasonal and Thanksgiving-Themed Spells
1. Thanksgiving Night Wish Spell (Chapter 29):

- **Description:** A spell performed under the night sky during Thanksgiving, focusing on making wishes and setting intentions for the coming year, using the power of the stars.

2. Feasting Rituals (Chapter 12):

- **Description:** Spells and rituals to bless the Thanksgiving feast, ensuring that each dish is filled with love, abundance, and positive energy for the family.

3. Harvest Moon Ritual (Chapter 23):

- **Description:** A ritual that aligns with the energies of the autumn harvest moon, focusing on gratitude and manifestation for the blessings of the season.

4. Thanksgiving Weather Magic Spell (Chapter 21):

- **Description:** A spell that calls for favorable weather for outdoor Thanksgiving celebrations, invoking the elements to ensure pleasant conditions for gatherings.

Candle Magic Spells

1. Gratitude Candle Spell (Chapter 9 - Candle Magic for Thanksgiving):

- **Description:** A spell that uses candles to channel gratitude and appreciation, focusing on amplifying the energy of thankfulness and blessings in your life.

2. Love and Harmony Candle Spell (Chapter 9 - Candle Magic for Thanksgiving):

- **Description:** A candle spell that promotes love and harmony during Thanksgiving gatherings, helping to create a peaceful and loving atmosphere.

3. Prosperity Candle Ritual (Chapter 6):

- **Description:** A spell that utilizes green or gold candles to attract abundance, financial blessings, and success during the holiday season.

4. Full Moon Candle Spell (Chapter 7 - Moon Phases and Thanksgiving):

- **Description:** A powerful spell performed during the full moon to manifest intentions and bring desires to fruition, using candles to focus and direct energy.

Crystal Magic Spells

1. Thanksgiving Gratitude Grid (Chapter 10 - Crystal Enchantment):

- **Description:** A crystal grid spell that focuses on amplifying gratitude, using specific stones arranged in a geometric pattern to draw in energy for thanksgiving and blessings.

2. Love and Friendship Crystal Spell (Chapter 5 - Love and Friendship):

- **Description:** A spell that uses rose quartz and green aventurine to strengthen bonds with friends and loved ones, encouraging emotional connection and harmony.

3. Prosperity Crystal Grid (Chapter 30 - Manifesting the Future Harvest):

- **Description:** A crystal grid designed to attract long-term abundance and success, using stones like citrine, jade, and green aventurine to amplify the energy of prosperity.

4. Healing and Emotional Balance Spell (Chapter 10 - Crystal Enchantment):

- **Description:** A spell using amethyst and moonstone to promote healing, emotional balance, and peace within relationships, especially during family gatherings.

Herbal Magic Spells

1. Herbal Gratitude Spell (Chapter 8 - Herbal Gratitude):

- **Description:** A spell that incorporates gratitude herbs such as rosemary, basil, and chamomile, using their energies to foster a sense of appreciation and peace.

2. Prosperity Herb Sachet (Chapter 28 - Fortune Talisman Creation):

- **Description:** A spell that uses herbs like mint, cinnamon, and bay leaves to create a sachet for attracting wealth and financial success during the Thanksgiving season.

3. Herbal Teas and Potions for Gratitude (Chapter 22):

- **Description:** Recipes for teas and potions made with herbs that promote relaxation, gratitude, and bonding, perfect for Thanksgiving gatherings.

4. Love and Harmony Herb Spell (Chapter 5 - Love and Friendship):

- **Description:** A spell that uses herbs like rose petals and lavender to enhance love, harmony, and peace within friendships and family relationships.

Protection and Banishing Spells

1. Banishing Negativity Spell (Chapter 27):

- **Description:** A powerful spell designed to cleanse away negativity, ensuring that positive energy flows freely and that you can focus on gratitude and blessings during Thanksgiving.

2. Protection and Blessing Ritual for the Home (Chapter 24 - Blessing the Home):

- **Description:** A spell to cleanse and protect the home, ensuring peace, protection, and prosperity throughout the holiday season by using herbs, crystals, and candles.

3. Full Moon Banishing Ritual (Chapter 7 - Moon Phases and Thanksgiving):

- **Description:** A spell performed during the waning phase of the full moon to release negative energy, old patterns, or toxic influences that no longer serve you.

4. Cleansing and Protection Spell for Family Gatherings (Chapter 3 - Family Harmony):

- **Description:** A spell that uses protective herbs and crystals to cleanse the space before family gatherings, ensuring that only positive, loving energy remains.

Moon Phase Magic Spells

1. New Moon Intention Setting Spell (Chapter 7 - Moon Phases and Thanksgiving):

- **Description:** A spell for setting new intentions and planting the seeds of manifestation during the new moon phase, using the energy of new beginnings.

2. Waxing Crescent Manifestation Spell (Chapter 7 - Moon Phases and Thanksgiving):

- **Description:** A spell that focuses on building momentum and manifesting growth during the waxing crescent phase, perfect for attracting new opportunities and abundance.

3. Full Moon Gratitude Spell (Chapter 7 - Moon Phases and Thanksgiving):

- **Description:** A spell performed during the full moon to give thanks for the abundance and blessings in your life, enhancing the energy of gratitude and fulfillment.

4. Waning Crescent Healing Ritual (Chapter 7 - Moon Phases and Thanksgiving):

- **Description:** A ritual during the waning crescent phase that focuses on emotional healing, rest, and introspection, helping you prepare for new beginnings in the next lunar cycle.

Nature-Based Spells

1. Nature Offerings Spell (Chapter 11):

- **Description:** A spell that uses natural elements such as leaves, pinecones, and autumnal flowers to create offerings for the earth, fostering a sense of connection and gratitude for the natural world.

2. Harvest Moon Ritual (Chapter 23):

- **Description:** A spell that aligns with the autumn harvest moon to manifest abundance and reflect on the blessings of the earth, using natural elements and moon energy.

3. Seasonal Divination Spell (Chapter 19):

- **Description:** A divination spell using tools like tarot, runes, or crystals to gain insights and guidance during the Thanksgiving season, aligning with the natural cycles.

4. Thanksgiving Cornucopia Spell (Chapter 16):

- **Description:** A spell that involves creating a cornucopia filled with enchanted objects representing wishes, blessings, and abundance for the upcoming year.

Conclusion

This Index of Spells provides a comprehensive and categorized reference for all the magical workings presented in the book. Whether you are seeking spells for gratitude, love, prosperity, or protection, you can easily find the right spell by using this index. By organizing the spells into clear categories, this appendix allows you to navigate the content effortlessly and choose the perfect spell for your specific needs, enhancing your magical practice and helping you align with the powerful energies of the Thanksgiving season.

<u>Message from the Author:</u>

I hope you enjoyed this book, I love astrology and knew there was not a book such as this out on the shelf. I love metaphysical items as well. Please check out my other books:

-Life of Government Benefits

-My life of Hell

-My life with Hydrocephalus

-Red Sky

-World Domination:Woman's rule

-World Domination:Woman's Rule 2: The War

-Life and Banishment of Apophis: book 1

-The Kidney Friendly Diet

-The Ultimate Hemp Cookbook

-Creating a Dispensary(legally)

-Cleanliness throughout life: the importance of showering from childhood to adulthood.

-Strong Roots: The Risks of Overcoddling children

-Hemp Horoscopes: Cosmic Insights and Earthly Healing

- Celestial Hemp Navigating the Zodiac: Through the Green Cosmos

-Astrological Hemp: Aligning The Stars with Earth's Ancient Herb

-The Astrological Guide to Hemp: Stars, Signs, and Sacred Leaves

-Green Growth: Innovative Marketing Strategies for your Hemp Products and Dispensary

-Cosmic Cannabis

-Astrological Munchies

-Henry The Hemp

-Zodiacal Roots: The Astrological Soul Of Hemp

- Green Constellations: Intersection of Hemp and Zodiac

-Hemp in The Houses: An astrological Adventure Through The Cannabis Galaxy

-Galactic Ganja Guide

Heavenly Hemp
Zodiac Leaves
Doctor Who Astrology
Cannastrology
Stellar Satvias and Cosmic Indicas
Celestial Cannabis: A Zodiac Journey
AstroHerbology: The Sky and The Soil: Volume 1
AstroHerbology:Celestial Cannabis:Volume 2
Cosmic Cannabis Cultivation
The Starry Guide to Herbal Harmony: Volume 1
The Starry Guide to Herbal Harmony: Cannabis Universe: Volume 2

Yugioh Astrology: Astrological Guide to Deck, Duels and more
Nightmare Mansion: Echoes of The Abyss
Nightmare Mansion 2: Legacy of Shadows
Nightmare Mansion 3: Shadows of the Forgotten
Nightmare Mansion 4: Echoes of the Damned
The Life and Banishment of Apophis: Book 2
Nightmare Mansion: Halls of Despair
Healing with Herb: Cannabis and Hydrocephalus
Planetary Pot: Aligning with Astrological Herbs: Volume 1
Fast Track to Freedom: 30 Days to Financial Independence Using AI, Assets, and Agile Hustles
Cosmic Hemp Pathways
How to Become Financially Free in 30 Days: 10,000 Paths to Prosperity
Zodiacal Herbage: Astrological Insights: Volume 1
Nightmare Mansion: Whispers in the Walls
The Daleks Invade Atlantis
Henry the hemp and Hydrocephalus

10X The Kidney Friendly Diet
Cannabis Universe: Adult coloring book

Hemp Astrology: The Healing Power of the Stars
Zodiacal Herbage: Astrological Insights: Cannabis Universe: Volume 2
Planetary Pot: Aligning with Astrological Herbs: Cannabis Universes: Volume 2
Doctor Who Meets the Replicators and SG-1: The Ultimate Battle for Survival
Nightmare Mansion: Curse of the Blood Moon
The Celestial Stoner: A Guide to the Zodiac
Cosmic Pleasures: Sex Toy Astrology for Every Sign
Hydrocephalus Astrology: Navigating the Stars and Healing Waters
Lapis and the Mischievous Chocolate Bar

Celestial Positions: Sexual Astrology for Every Sign
Apophis's Shadow Work Journal: : A Journey of Self-Discovery and Healing
Kinky Cosmos: Sexual Kink Astrology for Every Sign
Digital Cosmos: The Astrological Digimon Compendium
Stellar Seeds: The Cosmic Guide to Growing with Astrology
Apophis's Daily Gratitude Journal

Cat Astrology: Feline Mysteries of the Cosmos
The Cosmic Kama Sutra: An Astrological Guide to Sexual Positions
Unleash Your Potential: A Guided Journal Powered by AI Insights
Whispers of the Enchanted Grove

Cosmic Pleasures: An Astrological Guide to Sexual Kinks
369, 12 Manifestation Journal
Whisper of the nocturne journal(blank journal for writing or drawing)

The Boogey Book
Locked In Reflection: A Chastity Journey Through Locktober
Generating Wealth Quickly:
How to Generate $100,000 in 24 Hours
Star Magic: Harness the Power of the Universe
The Flatulence Chronicles: A Fart Journal for Self-Discovery
The Doctor and The Death Moth
Seize the Day: A Personal Seizure Tracking Journal
The Ultimate Boogeyman Safari: A Journey into the Boogie World and Beyond

Whispers of Samhain: 1,000 Spells of Love, Luck, and Lunar Magic: Samhain Spell Book

Apophis's guides:

Witch's Spellbook Crafting Guide for Halloween

<u>Frost & Flame: The Enchanted Yule Grimoire of 1000 Winter Spells</u>

<u>The Ultimate Boogey Goo Guide & Spooky Activities for Halloween Fun</u>

Harmony of the Scales: A Libra's Spellcraft for Balance and Beauty
The Enchanted Advent: 36 Days of Christmas Wonders

Nightmare Mansion: The Labyrinth of Screams

If you want solar for your home go here: https://www.harborso-lar.live/apophisenterprises/

Get Some Tarot cards: https://www.makeplayingcards.com/sell/
apophis-occult-shop

Get some shirts: https://www.bonfire.com/store/apophis-shirt-emporium/

<u>Instagrams:</u>
@apophis_enterprises,
@apophisbookemporium,
@apophisscardshop
Twitter: @apophisenterpr1
Tiktok:@apophisenterprise
Youtube: @sg1fan23477, @FiresideRetreatKingdom

Podcast: Apophis Chat Zone: https://open.spotify.com/show/5zXbrCLEV2xzCp8ybrfHsk?si=fb4d4fdbdce44dec

Newsletter: https://apophiss-newsletter-27c897.beehiiv.com/